Perspectives on World War I Poetry

Perspectives on World War I Poetry

Robert C. Evans

B L O O M S B U R Y
LONDON • NEW DELHI • NEW YORK • SYDNEY

Bloomsbury Academic
An imprint of Bloomsbury Publishing Plc

50 Bedford Square
London
WC1B 3DP
UK

1385 Broadway
New York
NY 10018
USA

www.bloomsbury.com

Bloomsbury is a registered trade mark of Bloomsbury Publishing Plc

First published 2014

© Robert C. Evans, 2014

British Library Cataloguing-in-Publication Data
A catalogue record for this book is available from the British Library.

ISBN: HB: 978-1-4725-1021-1
PB: 978-1-4725-1310-6
ePDF: 978-1-4725-1041-9
ePub: 978-1-4725-0655-9

Library of Congress Cataloging-in-Publication Data
A catalog record for this book is available from the Library of Congress.

Typeset by Newgen Knowledge Works (P) Ltd., Chennai, India
Printed and bound in Great Britain

CONTENTS

PREFACE

This book

- is intended mainly for students and general readers seeking an introduction to various ways of looking at literature, especially the poetry of World War I;
- tries to give roughly equal weight to each of the literary theories discussed;
- tries to explain those theories in language that is clear and accessible;
- tries especially to show how each theory can be used and applied in practical ways to make sense of individual works of literature;
- is designed so that individual sections can be read in isolation but also so that each section builds on the one before it, with the most general discussions placed at the beginning of the book;
- is organized by dates of the poets' births, with the earlier poets preceding the later ones;
- includes poets from a range of English-speaking countries, including not only the United Kingdom but also the United States, Canada, Australia, South Africa, and others;
- includes a large proportion of women poets as well as gay poets and poets of color.

ACKNOWLEDGMENTS

I especially wish to thank David Avital of Bloomsbury Press for his enthusiastic support of this book and for his guidance in its preparation. I am also grateful to the various anonymous reviewers who endorsed the book and made very helpful suggestions about how to make it better.

My debts to my former teachers are too numerous and profound to list, but I would especially like to thank Alvin Kernan for his early support and encouragement and Robert L. Gale for his even earlier kindness. My debts to Robert and Marina Whitman are beyond measure.

My colleagues deserve many thanks, especially Eric Sterling and Alan Gribben. Over three decades I have had the pleasure to teach hundreds of students, especially in my Literary Criticism class, who have stimulated and challenged my own thinking. Christina M. Garner, who compiled Chapter 12, is one of the very best of these.

My deepest affection and thanks go, once more, to my wife, Ruth, who has given me more joy, laughter, and love than anyone could imagine. And I would be remiss if I did not thank three goofy dogs (Taylor, Martha, and Rafe) who make us smile and laugh many times every single day.

My debt to M. H. Abrams will be everywhere apparent in this text, and I hope I have adequately conveyed my admiration and respect for one of the most influential of modern literary theorists, who recently celebrated his hundredth birthday and is still going strong.

Introduction

Although literary theory is often considered highly abstract and intellectual and therefore remote from the concerns of "ordinary" people, any reader of a literary text inevitably uses a literary theory of some sort. Any reader, that is, inevitably makes assumptions about why and how a text should be interpreted, understood, or appreciated. Responding to a text inevitably involves applying these assumptions, whether or not we are consciously aware of doing so. One goal of literary theorists, then, is simply to encourage us to be more conscious of the assumptions we make and use when we read.

By being more conscious of these assumptions, we can not only use them more insightfully but can also consider their strengths and weaknesses, their relative advantages and disadvantages. We can consider whether and in what ways they seem valid; we can make sure that we better understand their larger implications; we can determine whether we are applying them consistently; and we can help ensure that the theory we use is a theory we have freely chosen rather than one we have merely taken for granted simply because it is practiced by others.

Studying literary theory, then, can not only introduce us to different ways of reading texts but can also encourage a fuller development of our minds by prompting us not only to think for ourselves but to make sure that we can explain why we have chosen to think and read as we do.

Studying literary theory, however, has become increasingly difficult as the number of such theories has itself increased, especially during the past century. So many theories now exist, and so many often seem so difficult to grasp, that it is little wonder that so many "ordinary" readers feel intimidated (or even repelled).

Trying to make sense of a given theory, and then trying to determine how that theory can be compared and contrasted with others, are genuinely daunting tasks. Different theorists seem not only to make fundamentally different assumptions but also, frequently, to speak fundamentally different languages—languages that often seem arcane and highly abstract. It is hardly surprising, then, that many readers, when confronted with the opportunity or need to expose themselves to theory, adopt the response of Melville's Bartleby and would simply "prefer not" to.

The Abrams scheme

Understanding the assumptions that lie within and beneath various literary theories becomes much easier when we heed the advice of M. H. Abrams, himself a highly influential theorist. Abrams suggested a scheme that is both firm enough and flexible enough to make sense of just about any theory one can imagine (see his famous book *The Mirror and the Lamp: Romantic Theory and the Critical Tradition* [Oxford: Oxford University Press, 1953], pp. 3–29). By applying this schematic approach to different theories, we can better understand both how they are similar and how they differ, and because the Abrams scheme encourages a systematic approach to various theories, it also makes it much easier to remember both their common and their distinctive features. Any schematic approach, of course, inevitably involves some simplification; in the final analysis, the best way to understand a particular theorist's ideas will be to examine them with individual care and attention. The Abrams scheme, however, provides a useful way to begin the study of literary theory and to organize both the tactics and the results of our thinking.

Briefly, Abrams argues that any literary theory that attempts to be complete will inevitably make certain fundamental assumptions about several basic aspects of literature. These aspects can be called the *writer*, the *text*, the *audience*, and "*reality.*" To these four categories we can add a fifth: the *critic*. Any theory of literature, in other words, will tend to make assumptions about the role of the writer, the features of the text, the traits of the audience, the nature of "reality," and the functions of the critic. Moreover, assumptions in one category will almost inevitably affect, or be consistent with, assumptions in another. Take an obvious example: if a theorist assumes that "reality" is fundamentally structured by inherent or imposed differences between the sexes, that assumption will in turn affect how the theorist imagines the role of the writer (male, female, sexist, liberationist, free, oppressed, etc.), the features of the text (progressive, conservative, experimental, traditional, flexible, rigid, etc.), the traits of the audience (men, women, repressed, tolerant, conservative, liberal, etc.), and the functions of the critic (a supporter of liberation; an advocate for previously ignored writers; a student of "male" and "female" habits of thinking and writing; etc.).

Or take another example: if a theorist assumes that a literary text is a work of careful craftsmanship, she will automatically assume that the writer will (or should) be a craftsman, that the audience will (or should) appreciate such craft, and that the critic will (or should) help call attention to the highly crafted intricacies of the text. The relationship between these other ideas and the theorist's assumptions about "reality" are not, in this instance, inescapably clear. Thus the theorist may (for instance) assume that "reality" itself is highly complex and highly coherent and that the complex, coherent text therefore reflects reality; or she may assume that "reality" is complex or incoherent and that the text therefore provides either a satisfying or an illusory alternative.

The category of "reality," in fact, is likely to be the most difficult category of the Abrams scheme to understand at first. For one thing, "reality" is likely to be defined differently by different theorists: some may emphasize individual psychological "reality"; some may stress social, economic, or political "reality"; some may focus on physical "reality"; some may even question the usefulness of the category (by suggesting, for instance, that an objective "reality" does not exist). Ironically, though, even theorists who doubt the existence of any independent "reality" will still need to use the concept. However, since "reality" can be defined so differently by so many different theorists, it seems best to highlight its debated, provisional status by placing the word in quotation marks or inverted commas. Most theorists can agree that literature involves texts, writers, audiences, and critics, but disputes about the nature of "reality" (or about how to understand it, if it can be understood) are often crucial to the differences between various theories. A Freudian critic makes different assumptions about "reality" than, say, a Jungian or Christian critic. Studying literary theory often involves studying different concepts of what is most fundamentally real.

The Abrams scheme provides us, then, with a simple but surprisingly adaptable method for making sense of nearly any theory we might confront or wish to use. It offers a means of appreciating both the comparisons and the contrasts between competing theories, and it even gives us a means of studying literature itself. (Abrams assumes, for instance, that every literary work will tend to embody a particular theory of literature. We might therefore analyze a story by asking what the story implies about the role of the writer, the features of the text, the traits of the audience, the nature of "reality," and the functions of the critic.) The scheme makes it easier to grasp and remember the distinctive features of different theories, and it also functions as a tool for understanding both the most ancient and the most recent theories of literature.

Literary theories: A brief overview

In a fortunate coincidence, four of the oldest but most important approaches to literature (approaches associated with Plato, Aristotle, Horace, and Longinus) happen to align nicely with each of the four basic emphases Abrams outlines—emphases on "reality," text, audience, and writer, respectively. Many later theories respond to or echo these first four, but every theory (according to Abrams) stresses one of the four components as its *key* component. In the following brief sketches, the key component of each theory is italicized. In each sketch, the word "reality" will be placed inside quotation remarks as a handy reminder that different theorists tend to define "reality" in different ways.

PLATONIC CRITICISM: Because Plato prizes an accurate, objective understanding of "*reality*," he sees "creative" writers and "literary" texts as potential distractions since they may lead the already-emotional audience to neglect proper pursuit of philosophical truth, which the critic should seek, explain, and defend by using logic and reason.

ARISTOTELIAN CRITICISM: Because Aristotle values the *text* as a highly crafted complex unity, he tends to see the author as a craftsman, the audience as capable of appreciating such craftsmanship, the text as a potentially valuable means of understanding the complexity of "reality," and the critic as a specialist conversant with all aspects of the poetic craft.

HORATIAN CRITICISM: Because Horace emphasizes the need to satisfy a diverse *audience*, he tends to see the author as attempting to please and/or teach them, the text as embodying principles of custom and moderation (so as to please the widest possible audience), "reality" as understood in traditional or conventional terms, and the critic as a fatherly advisor who tries to prevent the author from making a fool of himself.

LONGINIAN CRITICISM: Because "Longinus" (whose real identity is unknown) stresses the ideally lofty nature of the sublime (i.e. elevated) *author*, he tends to view the text as an expression of the author's power, the audience as desiring the ecstasy a great author can induce, social "reality" as rooted in a basic human nature that everywhere and always has a yearning for elevation, and the critic as (among other things) a moral and spiritual advisor who encourages the highest aspirations of readers and writers alike.

TRADITIONAL HISTORICAL CRITICISM: Because traditional historical critics tend to emphasize the ways social *"realities"* influence the writer, the writer's creation of a text, and the audience's reactions to it, they stress the critic's obligation to study the past as thoroughly and objectively as possible to determine how the text might have been understood by its original readers.

THEMATIC CRITICISM: Because thematic critics stress the importance of ideas in shaping social and psychological *"reality,"* they generally look for the ways those ideas are expressed by (and affect) the texts that writers create. They assume that audiences turn to texts for enlightenment as well as entertainment, and they often argue either that writers express the same basic ideas repeatedly or that the evolution of a writer's thinking can be traced in different works.

FORMALISM: Because formalists value the *text* as a complex unity in which all the parts contribute to a rich and resonant effect, they usually offer highly detailed ("close") readings intended to show how the work achieves a powerful, compelling artistic form. Formalist critics help audiences appreciate how a work's subtle nuances contribute to its total effect.

PSYCHOANALYTIC CRITICISM: Freudian or psychoanalytic critics emphasize the key role of the human mind in perceiving and shaping *"reality"* and believe that the minds of writers, audiences, and critics are highly complex and often highly conflicted (especially in sexual terms, and particularly in terms of the moralistic "superego," the rational ego, and the irrational "id"). They contend that such complexity inevitably affects the ways texts are written and read. The critic, therefore, should analyze how psychological patterns affect the ways texts are created and received.

ARCHETYPAL OR "MYTH" CRITICISM: Because archetypal critics believe that humans experience *"reality"* in terms of certain basic fears, desires, images (symbols), and stories (myths), they assume that writers will inevitably employ such patterns; that audiences will react to them forcefully and almost automatically; and that critics should therefore study the ways such patterns affect writers, texts, and readers.

MARXIST CRITICISM: Because Marxist critics assume that conflicts between economic classes inevitably shape social *"reality,"* they emphasize the ways these struggles affect writers, audiences, and texts. They assume that literature will either reflect, reinforce, or undermine (or some combination of these) the dominant ideologies (i.e. standard patterns of thought) that help structure social relations. Marxist critics study the complex relations between literature and society, ideally seeking to promote social progress.

STRUCTURALIST CRITICISM: Because structuralist critics assume that humans structure (or make sense of) *"reality"* by imposing patterns of meaning on it, and because they assume that these structures can only be interpreted in terms of the codes the structures embody, they believe that writers will inevitably rely on such codes to create meaning, that texts will inevitably embody such codes, and that audiences will inevitably use such codes to interpret texts. To understand a text, the critic must be familiar with the systematic codes that shape it; he must master the system(s) the text implies.

FEMINIST CRITICISM: Because feminist critics assume that our experience of "*reality*" is inevitably affected by categories of sex and gender (such as divisions between male and female, heterosexual and homosexual, etc.), and because they assume that (heterosexual) males have long enjoyed dominant social power, they believe that writers, texts, and audiences will all be affected (usually negatively) by "patriarchal" forces. The critic's job will be to study (and even attempt to counteract) the impact of patriarchy.

DECONSTRUCTION: Because deconstructive critics assume that "*reality*" cannot be experienced except through language, and because they believe that language is inevitably full of contradictions, gaps, and dead-ends, they believe that no writer, text, audience, or critic can ever escape from the irresolvable paradoxes language embodies. Deconstruction therefore undercuts the hierarchical assumptions of any other critical system (such as structuralism, formalism, Marxism, etc.) that claims to offer an "objective," "neutral," or "scientific" perspective on literature.

READER-RESPONSE CRITICISM: Because reader-response critics assume that literary texts are inevitably interpreted by individual members of the *audience* and that these individuals react to texts in ways that are sometimes shared, sometimes highly personal (and sometimes both at once), they believe that writers exert much less control over texts than we sometimes suppose, and that critics must never ignore the crucial role of audience response(s).

DIALOGICAL CRITICISM: Because dialogical critics assume that the (worthy) *text* almost inevitably embodies divergent points of view, they believe that elements within a text engage in a constant dialogue or give-and-take with other elements, both within and outside the text itself. The writer, too, is almost inevitably engaged in a complex dialogue, through the text, with his potential audience(s), and the sensitive critic must be alert to the multitude of voices a text expresses or implies.

NEW HISTORICISM: Because new historicist critics assume that our experience of "*reality*" is inevitably social, and because they emphasize the ways systems of power and domination both provoke and control social conflicts, they tend to see a culture not as a single coherent entity but as a site of struggle, negotiation, or the constant exchange of energy. New historicists contend that no text, audience, or critic can stand apart from contemporary (i.e. both past and present) dynamics of power.

MULTICULTURAL CRITICISM: Because multicultural critics emphasize the numerous differences that both shape and divide social *"reality,"* they tend to see all people (including writers, readers, and critics) as members of sometimes divergent, sometimes overlapping groups. These groups, whether relatively fluid or relatively stable, can include such categories as races, sexes, genders, ages, and classes, and the critic should explore how such differences affect the ways literature is both written and read.

POSTMODERNISM: Postmodernists are highly skeptical of large-scale claims that objective "truths" exist. They thus doubt the validity of "grand narratives" or all-encompassing explanations. They see such claims as attempts to impose order on a *"reality"* that is, almost by definition, too shifting or fluid to be pinned down. Postmodernists assume that if writers, readers, and audiences abandoned their yearning for such order, they would more easily accept end enjoy the inevitable paradoxes and contradictions of life and art. The postmodern critic will look for (and value) any indications of a text's instabilities or peculiarities.

ECOCRITICISM: Ecocritics stress the importance of nature, or physical *"reality"* and its impact on writers, readers, texts, and the functions of critics. Any human associated with the production or reception of literature necessarily has crucial relations, of one sort or another, with nature. Those relations can either be positive or negative, and humans in particular can have either good or bad impacts on their environments. Texts almost inevitably reflect, either explicitly or implicitly, a range of attitudes toward nature. Ideally, texts should help promote a healthy relationship between humans and the environment, and critics should examine precisely how that relationship is depicted or implied.

DARWINIAN CRITICISM: Darwinian critics assume that human beings and all other living things are the result of billions of years of the *"reality"* of physical evolution. Because human beings share a common evolutionary history, they share many ways of thinking, feeling, and behaving that are hardwired into their genes. Literature is therefore influenced (in the ways it is created, structured, and received) by the numerous psychological traits humans share. Critics should explore the ways literature is shaped by these traits and also the ways literature can help contribute to or detract from evolutionary "fitness."

Applying the theories: Carl Sandburg's "Grass"

Carl Sandburg (1878–1967) is a much-anthologized poet who was also one of the most popular American writers of the twentieth century. His brief poem "Grass," published during World War I, alludes to two of the most famous battles of that conflict (the battles at Ypres and Verdun). It also alludes to noted battles of the Napoleonic wars (at Austerlitz and Waterloo) and also to the most important battle of the American Civil War (at Gettysburg). Sandburg's poem is brief and highly accessible, and for both reasons it provides a good test case for suggesting, very quickly, how the various literary theories can be used to interpret a single work.

GRASS

Pile the bodies high at Austerlitz and Waterloo.
Shovel them under and let me work—
                 I am the grass; I cover all.

And pile them high at Gettysburg
And pile them high at Ypres and Verdun.   [5]
Shovel them under and let me work.
Two years, ten years, and passengers ask the conductor:
                 What place is this?
                 Where are we now?

                 I am the grass.   [10]
                 Let me work.

Readers influenced by PLATO, who distrusted appeals to mere emotion, might be suspicious of this poem and indeed of most literature, especially if they felt that the emotions "Grass" evokes were ignoble or selfish. Is the poem antipatriotic? Is it an implied protest against all war, implying that all wars are wasteful, that no war is worthwhile, and that no wars are ever fought on behalf of good and righteous causes? If so, then the poem would probably provoke Plato's disdain, since he believed that wars fought on behalf of justice and truth were worthy conflicts. A poem like this one might promote indiscriminate, irrational pacifism, resulting more from weakness and fear than from commitment to justice. On the other hand, the poem can be read as indicting the fickleness of human emotions. It can be read as mocking how quickly people forget heroism and self-sacrifice. Read in this way, it can be seen not as an antiwar poem per se but as a poem satirizing shallow emotionalism. It can be read as mocking the "passengers" (who symbolize most people) who are ignorant of the sacrifices others have made in their behalf. Of course, the fact that this message is not spelled out explicitly, and that the poem can be interpreted in various and even contradictory ways, might lead Plato to condemn this work (and poetry in general) for lacking the precision, clarity, and commitment to truth exhibited, in contrast, by philosophy.

ARISTOTLE, who valued literature in ways and to a degree that Plato did not, might admire "Grass" for various reasons. He would almost certainly appreciate anything that indicated Sandburg's literary craftsmanship, the poem's complex artistic unity, and the seriousness of the work's meaning—the kind of knowledge it contains and conveys. He would probably value, for instance, the craftsmanship displayed by the poem's heavy use of anaphora (the repetition of words or phrases at the beginnings of lines), as in the repetition here of "Pile," "And pile," "And pile," "Shovel," and "Shovel," and so on. Such phrasing implies the poet's concern with order and structure, and it displays his ability to use language to achieve powerful rhetorical effects. Aristotle would also be interested in the ways the poem is structured, as in its movement from the distant past to the closer past to the historical present. He would also value the ways the poem achieves symmetry when lines 10–11 echo lines 2–3. This is a serious poem on a serious subject. It conveys knowledge by using particular examples to imply a general philosophical lesson: that human beings tend to forget the worthy efforts and sacrifices made by people of the past.

HORACE, the great Roman poet and critic, argued that writers should first and foremost remember their obligations to satisfy their readers. They should use accessible, clear language, should achieve a kind of unity in their works that was not especially difficult to perceive, and should seek to teach, to please, or to do both at once. Sandburg's poem meets all these Horatian criteria. Therefore it should not surprise us that Sandburg was immensely popular. "Grass" might appeal simultaneously to pacifists or disillusioned veterans as well as to any veterans (and their families and friends) proud of their military service but who felt insufficiently appreciated. The poem avoids overt controversy (it is not passionately antiwar, for instance), and it thus risks offending few readers. Although it abandons conventional meter and rhyme schemes, its innovations are not especially radical. For all these reasons, Horace might well admire this poem.

LONGINUS, with his interest in lofty, elevated values and sublime emotions, might respond to this poem in varied ways, depending upon how he interpreted its basic meaning. He might read the poem, for instance, as an implied summons to appreciate the selflessness of men who died fighting for causes greater than themselves, especially the cause of freedom. He might also read the poem as an implied satire on the small-minded forgetfulness of those who fail to value the altruism of soldiers, past and present. Perhaps such forgetfulness results from our selfish preoccupations with narrow self-interests, particularly materialistic interests. In that case, Longinus would definitely admire the poem for reminding us of life's highest, truest, most spiritual values.

TRADITIONAL HISTORICAL critics try to establish the truth about a literary work's historical contexts and how they help determine the work's meanings. Such critics would provide information about the various battles the poem mentions, particularly about anything that made those battles symbolic or distinctive. The poem seems to imply, however, that ultimately all these battles have the same kind of historical significance: each symbolizes a moment in time that once seemed crucially important but that has now been forgotten or is being forgotten. A traditional historical critic would particularly want to relate "Grass" to its own era and to Sandburg's own life, including his political beliefs and the political beliefs of his contemporaries. An historical critic might also point to relevant historical data, such as the prevalence of train travel in the early twentieth century. Most first readers of "Grass" would have had personal experience in traveling by trains and would thus have been able to "relate" to the poem.

Many of Sandburg's contemporaries might also have known that numerous soldiers during World War I had literally been blown to bits and thus never received proper burials. Corpses were often quickly covered by mud, which was then eventually covered by grass that concealed the grim evidence of mass slaughter. Finally, a traditional historical critic might also want to situate this poem in literary history—particularly in the history of the kind of poetry that begins, in America, with Walt Whitman. Sandburg was, in his subjects, style, form, and public stance, one of Whitman's most deliberate followers.

THEMATIC critics, with their interest in the ideas implied or openly expressed in literary works, would obviously be interested in this poem. They might argue, for instance, that it explores such themes as the ideas (1) that war is a waste, (2) that people quickly forget fallen soldiers, and (3) that ultimately death and oblivion await us all. Thematic critics might suggest that such ideas help make the poem worth reading and help unify its various details and structure. They might contend that some of its themes are rather openly suggested, especially in lines 7–9, and that these lines are crucial precisely because they help give the poem its deeper significance. Removing those lines (thematic critics might argue) would make the poem much more ambiguous, much more open to interpretation, and much less meaningful than it now is.

FORMALIST critics use the method of "close reading" to examine literary works in great detail as works of art. Anything that contributed to the success of this poem as a work of *literature* (i.e. as a piece of language intriguing and effective *as* a piece of language) would interest a formalist, including this poem's use of anaphora, irony, personification, heavy metrical emphasis on key verbs, and use of free verse that nonetheless seems well structured and carefully crafted. A formalist might be interested in the poem's effectively matter-of-fact tone (not a single exclamation mark is used), which helps prevent the poem from sounding melodramatic or overwrought. Even the criticism of the train passengers—if that is what it is—is only implied rather than overt. Thus the poem is subtle in ways formalists prize, since being subtle implies more talent than being baldly propagandistic.

A formalist would begin analyzing this poem (or any poem) by starting with the first syllable and moving carefully forward. Here the first syllable is the strongly accented verb "Pile," which already suggests how energetic this poem about the dead will ironically seem. The opening word is a command, but at first we have no idea who is issuing this order. Later we discover that the energetic speaker is, paradoxically, "the grass" (3). Grass is rarely personified (as it is in this poem), and we usually imagine grass as passive and silent and hardly ever as the focus of thought. Immediately, then, the poem surprises us; it catches our attention and makes us want to read further.

Paradoxically, while the grass is personified, the dead humans are treated as mere material *things*—as "bodies" (1) shown no special dignity or respect (2). Yet the opening lines are effective not only because of their meaning but because of their sound effects, as in the use of assonance in the long *I* sounds of "Pile" and "high," the parallel rhythms of "*Austerlitz*" and "*Waterloo*," the strong metrical emphasis on numerous verbs, and the heavy metrical stress on "I." Grass, which we normally ignore, here demands our attention and asserts a surprising authority.

A formalist would move through the rest of the poem in similar ways, making several assumptions recently challenged by other kinds of critics: (1) that communication is possible; (2) that people can agree about interpretations; (3) that works can achieve some degree of coherence and unity; (4) and that the best works are those in which all the parts contribute to some complexly unified whole.

A PSYCHOANALYTIC critic might be interested in the ways "Grass" both reflects and appeals to the complexity of the human mind, including (potentially) the minds of the author, speaker, characters, and readers. Using terms associated with Sigmund Freud, the founder of modern psychoanalysis, a psychoanalytic critic might argue that war both results from and most deeply affects the "id," which is associated with our deepest emotions, including our deepest desires and fears. War results from the desire for power but leads, in many cases, to death, the fear of death, and grief about death. To the extent that war seems unjustified and immoral, it conflicts with conscience and justice, which are associated by Freud with the superego. "Grass" suggests that the living should be ashamed if they forget the dead or neglect to properly honor them. The fallen soldiers, presumably, died because of their selfless loyalty to causes greater than themselves (associated with the superego), while the people who forget or neglect them do so because they are preoccupied with their own selfish pleasures (associated with the id). The ego—the responsible, realistic, sensible self—seems represented primarily (and paradoxically) through the voice of the grass. Unlike the neglectful train passengers, the grass does its duty, gets about its work, and attends to the dead in its own reasonable way.

An ARCHETYPAL critic would also be interested in the ways this poem reflects desires and fears, but an archetypal critic would be much more interested than a psychoanalytic critic in *shared* fears and *shared* desires—the kinds of emotions that seem deeply implanted in all human beings rather than reflecting the particular psychology of individual persons. This poem, for instance, seems rooted in such common human fears as fear of death, fear of being forgotten, fear of being unappreciated, and fear of being swallowed up by the forces of nature. Whereas humans often think of their relations with nature in positive terms, and whereas grass in particular often symbolizes human control of nature and cooperation with it, here the standard symbolism of grass seems undercut and reversed. The grass in this poem is literally overwhelming; it is active, not passive; it is assertive, not compliant. It can be seen both as symbolizing oblivion and as symbolizing peace and healing. The poem exploits the almost universal fear of death, but it also perhaps appeals to the common human desire to finally be at peace, to be absorbed back into the earth from which we supposedly came, to become reunited with nature and remain so for eternity. Perhaps the poem also appeals to a deep-seated desire for justice—the belief that those who sacrifice themselves for others deserve to be remembered, respected, and honored.

A MARXIST critic, influenced by the critique of capitalism and ideals of communism associated with Karl Marx, would probably argue that wars serve the interests of the ruling economic classes and exploit the poor. Most of the "bodies" (2) the poem mentions would have been the bodies of the economically disadvantaged, whom wars kill in disproportionate numbers. Moreover, although the battles "Grass" mentions are usually considered great military victories, in fact they changed very little in any positive ways, at least from a Marxist point of view. Austerlitz enhanced the power of Napoleon, and Waterloo resulted in his final defeat, but neither battle fundamentally altered Europe's oppressive power structure. The poor remained poor; the rich remained rich; and although Napoleon lost leadership of France, his defeat did little to promote the interests of the working classes. Even Gettysburg, often seen as symbolizing the triumph of justice over slavery and racial oppression, ultimately did little to really improve the fortunes of African Americans. Likewise, Ypres and Verdun in World War I merely strengthened the wealthy and powerful.

Millions died in World War I for nothing; the war's main positive outcome was the collapse of the Russian monarchy and its replacement with a socialist, bolshevist state that would (or so it was hoped) someday lead the way to the international triumph of communism. In the meantime, "Grass" reminds us that for capitalism, people are mere bodies: they are used, used up, and then disposed of. The poem offers no religious consolations because religion is another instrument of the ruling classes; instead, the poem reminds us that ultimately we consist of matter and finally return to a purely material existence. In that sense and others, the poem is refreshingly unsentimental.

STRUCTURALIST critics are interested in ways humans make sense of reality by seeing it in terms of interrelated contrasts—so-called binary opposites. These interlock with and reinforce one another. Structuralists are also interested in the ways readers depend on cultural codes to help them interpret literary texts—codes embedded in the text because authors draw on them as well. It is partly by using and interpreting shared codes that we decipher any piece of writing. Thus, anyone reading and understanding the present sentence can do so by having mastered various relevant codes, including the rules of English spelling, grammar, punctuation, and sentence structure. These same codes are also relevant to interpreting Sandburg's poem or any other work of literature written in English. Even (or perhaps especially) when a writer challenges or violates an established code, his text derives part of its meaning from its relation *to* that code. Thus, Sandburg commits no real violations of English spelling, grammar, punctuation, or sentence structure in this poem (unless one considers the fragments in lines 4–5 violations). Partly for this reason, the poem seems relatively traditional despite its unconventional stanza structures and lack of rhyme. When the poem was first published, it would have struck many readers as somewhat daring because it *did* lack rhyme and consistent stanza structures, but it would also have struck some readers as participating in a different set of codes—codes first effectively championed in the United States by Walt Whitman.

In addition to being structured by the codes already mentioned, "Grass" can also be interpreted in terms of a number of interrelated "binary opposites," including past/present; life/death; humans/nature; soldiers/civilians; Europe/the United States; machines/nature; being remembered/being forgotten; importance/unimportance; action that is quick and violent/action that is slow and gradual; and so on. Part of a structuralist's "job" is to probe beneath a text's surface to discover the codes that help structure the work and thus give it meaning.

FEMINIST criticism deals with such matters as women writers, women readers, and women's issues. It also often deals with relations between the biological "sexes" (or between and among different societally constructed genders) and with the ways females are depicted, either explicitly or implicitly, in literary texts. Thus a feminist might begin analyzing "Grass" by noting that its author was a male who automatically benefited from being a man in a society almost entirely controlled by other men. Sandburg was thus more likely than a woman to be regarded as a "serious" writer by the literary establishment. He was also more likely to win attention, earn money, and achieve status and canonization. He benefited from a long tradition of previous male writers (such as Walt Whitman) who could serve as role models. And, as a male, he had extra credibility as a writer about topics normally seen as relevant to men, such as war. After all, the dead soldiers described in "Grass" were probably mostly men, while many of the ignorant train passengers would almost have to be women. Yet the poem fails to emphasize that men have been responsible for practically every war in human history, while women have often been victimized by war in numerous ways (partly by being wounded, raped, or killed themselves or by suffering losses as mothers, wives, sisters, or lovers of the soldiers who died). For a feminist critic, then, part of the interest of "Grass" would involve what it does *not* say—the kinds of meanings and people it omits.

DECONSTRUCTIVE critics might read Sandburg's "Grass" by breaking down the clear, simple "binary opposites" found or imposed by structuralist critics. Or, rather, deconstructors might argue that those neat distinctions have "always already" collapsed and that their instability simply needs to be revealed, not created. The poem seems to make a clear distinction, for instance, between the dead and the living, but in one sense the poem brings the dead back to life while implying that those presently alive will themselves be forgotten. Yet the clear distinction the poem implies between being remembered and forgotten is itself unstable. In the first place, practically all the battles the poem mentions are still very famous and were even more famous at the time Sandburg wrote. They had not been forgotten and still have not been forgotten; the mere fact that the speaker can mention them as examples contradicts any implication that most people do not remember them. The poem implicitly presents itself as a means of keeping the memory of such battles alive, yet the poem itself is far more likely to be forgotten than any of the battles it mentions. Nearly everyone has heard, for instance, of Waterloo and Gettysburg, but how many people have ever heard of Carl Sandburg's "Grass," famous though it may be among American teachers and students of literature? Thus the clear distinction the poem draws between what is remembered and what is forgotten collapses, as do many other clear distinctions when they are given a bit of thought. Grass, for instance, is normally associated with life but is here associated with death but is also still a symbol of life. Neither the world nor life nor literature are ever as neat and tidy and coherent (a deconstructor would argue) as formalists, structuralists, and most other theorists assume.

READER-RESPONSE critics might argue that the impact and even the meaning of Sandburg's poem might vary greatly from one reader, or kind of reader, to another. Soldiers, ex-soldiers, and their families and friends, for instance, might be disturbed and even angry that the sacrifices of people in the military can be forgotten as quickly and easily as this poem suggests. They might therefore admire the poem because it implicitly rebukes anyone who might fail to remember or honor the service of those who fought and died in behalf of others. Pacifists, however, might see the poem as implying the general wastefulness of war, which is tragic for anyone affected by war, whether they are soldiers or civilians. Some readers, in fact, might even argue that soldiers are far more likely to be remembered and honored than the completely innocent civilians (including many children) who die because of wars. Military monuments and cemeteries, after all, are not uncommon, but similar memorials to dead civilians are much more difficult to find. In short, for reader-response critics, possible reactions to "Grass" would depend greatly on who happened to be reading the poem, and varied responses should be not only expected but respected.

DIALOGICAL critics might be interested in the various kinds of "dialogues" Sandburg's poem implies, especially its explicit dialogue with its readers, the implied dialogue between the speaker of the poem and the people he describes, and the poem's dialogue with other works and other kinds of literature. "Grass," for instance, is obviously a response to the kind of poetry composed by Walt Whitman, yet it is actually tighter and more conventional in shape than much of Whitman's poetry. It is hard to read much of Sandburg's poetry, including this poem, without being reminded of Whitman's writing. In a sense, Whitman prepared the way for the kind of poetry Sandburg wrote. Whitman changed the ways many people thought about poetry and about what counted as an acceptable poem. He helped create a new kind of audience, and Sandburg's composition of "Grass" was affected by the existence of these new standards and new readers.

Yet "Grass" is also dialogical in a much more obvious sense: the grass speaks. It addresses readers, saying one thing openly ("Let me work") but implying something else: "do not be the kind of person who forgets the sacrifices of soldiers." But the grass is, of course, only the metaphorical voice of the poem's speaker, and the speaker is himself the creation of the poet, who probably agrees with the "message" this work conveys. That message itself is not likely to provoke much disagreement from readers, and so the poem itself is partly shaped by a culture that in fact respects soldiers far more than the poem implies. The poem, then, is in some ways more a reminder than a provocative challenge or criticism. "Grass" on one level seems satirical, but on another level it simply reinforces values that most of its readers would have taken for granted. The nature of the poem's readers thus affected what the poem could effectively "say" to them. Few if any of them would have disagreed with the points it seeks to make.

NEW HISTORICIST critics claim that their approach to history is more complex than that of traditional historical critics. New historicists pride themselves on being interested in a far wider range of historical contexts than was true of older historical approaches. They especially focus on persons, events, places, or topics that might seem "marginal" or that have been previously ignored. Ethnic, racial, and/or sexual minorities, for example, are far more likely to receive examination from new historicist critics than was true in the past. The same is true of the history of common people and everyday life. Whereas traditional historical critics tended to focus on "major" events and prominent political and religious figures, new historicists can potentially examine anything that might illuminate a culture and cultural products, including (but not necessarily limited to) literature. They are especially interested in power relations and the negotiations for power that occur in every aspect of a society.

New historicists might have much to say about Sandburg's "Grass." They might argue, for instance, that the poem is greatly concerned about the use and abuse of power, both in the past and in the present. The poem reminds us that war is less a matter of conflict between nations than between the nameless, numberless masses of men who fight, often die, and are then often quickly forgotten. These men are powerful in the sense that they are armed and are given the license to kill, but they also *lack* power because they must follow orders, face great danger, and often die in massive numbers. A new historicist might explore the connections between this poem and both militaristic and pacifist movements that existed at the time it was written. Even more significantly, they might argue that this poem actually contributed to political thinking of that era rather than being simply influenced by it. A new historicist might also note that "Grass" completely ignores the "major historical figures" of whom we often think when we think of wars—figures such as Napoleon, Wellington, Lincoln, Kaiser Wilhelm, Woodrow Wilson, and others. Instead, "Grass" emphasizes the importance of the forgotten common people who died and were buried in heaps. It expresses no interest in which sides won or lost the various conflicts it mentions; instead, it implies that dead enemy combatants on any or all sides finally had the same things in common: first death, and then oblivion. The poem can be read as having "subversive" political impact by implicitly condemning war and promoting pacifism, and in its own shape and language it can be seen as contributing to the steady democratization of poetry, while its message seems to imply a secular rather than religious response to death.

MULTICULTURAL critics argue that the writers, readers, speakers, and characters of literary works inevitably belong to particular kinds of groups. Sometimes these groups are fairly distinctive (e.g. men and women). Sometimes they overlap (e.g. black men and black women). Whereas archetypal critics emphasize traits people share, multicultural critics emphasize the traits that make different groups differ. Sandburg's "Grass," however, deliberately focuses on soldiers and civilians in general rather than on any particular *kinds* of soldiers and civilians. Admittedly, he mentions different battles associated with different nations and different historical eras. The poem's final effect, however, is to imply that ultimately all soldiers are essentially alike, and that most civilians are also the same. The grass does not distinguish a German soldier from a British soldier, nor does it distinguish a Union soldier from a Confederate soldier. Multicultural criticism, then, is not especially relevant to Sandburg's "Grass," but, by encouraging us to look for differences, it paradoxically helps illuminate their relative absence in this poem.

POSTMODERNIST critics are highly suspicious of commonly accepted "truths" that try to offer broad explanations of complicated situations or events. Sandburg's "Grass," for instance, can be read as a rejection of grand-scale patriotic narratives and the broad, all-or-nothing ideas they imply. Thus, rather than accepting or emphasizing simple, jingoistic accounts of the various battles it mentions, the poem instead suggests that the combatants were simply individual men who had much more in common than they had been led to believe. A dead Frenchman and a dead Englishman are still simply two dead men; the grand nationalistic narratives that made them think and act as enemies could never have flourished if those narratives had been subjected to skeptical scrutiny. Instead of suggesting that the battles it mentions were either completely good or bad or completely right or wrong, the poem allows us to draw our own conclusions. It pushes no simple political agenda. It cannot even be read as simply endorsing pacifism: it never suggests that all wars are wrong. In all these ways, then, the poem can seem postmodern in its refusal to offer grand assertions.

A reader interested in ECOCRITICISM might be particularly intrigued by Sandburg's "Grass." Ecocritics are especially interested in relations between humans and nature—an obvious theme of this work. Whereas many previous poets (especially Romantics) presented human speakers directly addressing nature, "Grass" presents nature explicitly, if only figuratively, speaking to humans. Grass is presented here as a part of nature that long outlives humans; it seems enduring, while individual persons seem merely temporary. In this sense, the poem implies that while the beauty of nature will exist forever, human lives are merely ephemeral. Yet, ecocritics might challenge this easy assumption, arguing that the destruction nature suffers from human warfare is now potentially just as devastating as the destruction people suffer. Indeed, an ecocritic might even argue that this poem, despite its emphasis on grass and nature, is still primarily androcentric—still primarily preoccupied with the fate of human beings, whom the poem treats as the most important creatures on the planet. The poem implicitly urges us not to take soldiers' sacrifices for granted, but in a sense this text can be accused of taking the existence and health of nature for granted. A more positive ecocritical reading of this work, however, might argue that "Grass" implies that ultimately human beings are absorbed back into the nature from which they emerged. In the final sense, humans are just as much a part of nature as grass is.

DARWINIAN critics, with their emphasis on the various ways in which evolution is relevant to literature, might find "Grass" interesting in a number of ways. They might argue, for instance, that war, throughout all recorded history, has helped determine which humans were most fit to survive in conflict with other humans. Efforts to be ready for war have often been seen as promoting such useful values as courage, physical fitness, altruism, and devotion to family and tribe. On the other hand, wars—especially in the modern period, and World War I in particular—have often exacted horrible genetic costs. Wars have frequently involved the wholesale destruction of some of the very best human beings, often before they were able to pass their genes on to the next generation by fathering children. The dead soldiers in Sandburg's poem are depicted as mere "bodies," but of course when they were living they were not only full of life but full of the potential of fostering new life. The poem may function, partly, to discourage this widespread genetic wastefulness. At the same time, since the tendency to make war seems probably "hardwired" into the minds of humans, the subject of this poem is unlikely ever to seem irrelevant or outmoded.

1

Thomas Hardy (1840–1928): "Channel firing"; "In time of 'the breaking of nations'"

CHANNEL FIRING

That night your great guns, unawares,
Shook all our coffins as we lay,
And broke the chancel window-squares,
We thought it was the Judgment-day

And sat upright. While drearisome   [5]
Arose the howl of wakened hounds:
The mouse let fall the altar-crumb,
The worms drew back into the mounds,

The glebe cow drooled. Till God called, "No;
It's gunnery practice out at sea   [10]
Just as before you went below;
The world is as it used to be:

"All nations striving strong to make
Red war yet redder. Mad as hatters
They do no more for Christés sake   [15]
Than you who are helpless in such matters.

"That this is not the judgment-hour
For some of them's a blessed thing,
For if it were they'd have to scour
Hell's floor for so much threatening. . . .   [20]

"Ha, ha. It will be warmer when
I blow the trumpet (if indeed
I ever do; for you are men,
And rest eternal sorely need)."

So down we lay again. "I wonder,   [25]
Will the world ever saner be,"
Said one, "than when He sent us under
In our indifferent century!"

And many a skeleton shook his head.
"Instead of preaching forty year,"   [30]
My neighbour Parson Thirdly said,
"I wish I had stuck to pipes and beer."

Again the guns disturbed the hour,
Roaring their readiness to avenge,
As far inland as Stourton Tower,   [35]
And Camelot, and starlit Stonehenge.

"Channel Firing" was published several months before the actual
start of World War I. Humorous and macabre, it imagines some
dead folk, buried in a country churchyard, who hear gunnery
practice in the English Channel and who assume from the booming
noise that the Final Judgment is at hand. The booms shake the
coffins of the dead (2), break windows near the altar of the nearby
church (3), and startle various kinds of nonhuman creatures. Dogs
howl (6), a mouse drops crumbs (perhaps from the consecrated
communion bread [7]), worms head underground (8), and a cow
drools as it stands on a small piece of land (a "glebe") owned by
the church.

Eventually, however, God himself reassures the corpses that the
sounds do not signal Judgment Day. Speaking in a surprisingly
colloquial tone, he tells them that the world is "just as it used to
be" (12) and that humans are still as warlike and as indifferent

to Christianity as before (13–16). For some of the living (God continues), it is best that Judgment Day has not yet come; otherwise they might suffer in hell for their belligerence (17–20). Judgment Day lies still in the future (if in fact it ever occurs, since humans need eternal rest [21–4]). Thus reassured, the corpses lie down, and one of them asks whether humans will ever be more rational than they were when the corpse himself died, during an apathetic era (25–8).

In response, many skeletons shake their heads, and a dead parson lying nearby wishes that he had spent his life enjoying sensual pleasures rather than preaching the gospel (29–32). As the poem ends, the guns boom again and can be heard inland at famous places associated with increasingly distant periods of English history (33–6).

Because LONGINUS admires humans who pursue lofty ideals and shun base materialism, he might value this poem's pervasive irony. Clearly the poem implicitly mocks the shallow values of most human beings, both past and present. People have long ignored elevated ideals, consumed instead by hatred, blood lust, and vengeance. Their guns may be "great" or huge (1), but they themselves are far from spiritual greatness. Instead, they actually destroy the very symbols (such as the chancel windows) associated with loftier values (3). Although we often consider animals inferior to humans in intellect and moral stature, the animals here behave sensibly. They have every reason to fear mankind (6–9). Yet the reference to the "worms" drawing back into "mounds" (perhaps graves?) implies that ultimately people become merely food for worms. In the long term, wars seem petty and unimportant.

Although God assures the poem's corpses that Judgment Day is still far off, the poem itself judges humans appropriately, at least from a Longinian point of view. Humans, according to Longinus, rarely live up to high spiritual standards. God, in this poem, symbolizes the spiritual loftiness Longinus prized (although God here speaks more colloquially than Longinus may have wished). The poem definitely shows how people fall short of lofty moral expectations and their real ethical potential. Those who fail to raise themselves spiritually while they live will (the poem implies) ultimately fall to the depths of hell. Longinus might therefore admire this poem for using irony to endorse, by implication, the worthy values the dead parson openly preached about for years (29–32). If open preaching does not work, perhaps sardonic irony can have some slight positive impact.

A TRADITIONAL HISTORICAL critic might try to determine such matters as the poem's time of composition, its date of initial publication (May 1, 1914 in the *Fortnightly Review* [Brooks, p. 10]), and especially the significance of its various historical allusions. Its allusions to the Bible would especially interest such a critic, and so would the rather cavalier tone of God's words. That tone suggests that God could seem less lofty, less exalted, more familiar in Hardy's time than he was typically imagined, for instance, when John Milton wrote *Paradise Lost*. Hardy's poem might interest a traditional historical critic, then, partly for what the poem suggests about the ways God, war, and human history itself could be imagined in 1914. A historical critic might also examine how the poem reflects details of Hardy's own life, including his loss of religious faith, his intimate familiarity with rural England, and his tendency to write as a specifically *English* poet. All these facets of Hardy's life arguably affected the poem's phrasing. Although situated, historically, in a particular time and place, the poem also implies that humans have not changed much over the centuries. Finally, a traditional historicist might also explore the poem's various revisions. In the earliest printing, for instance, God says "no, no" rather than "ha, ha" (21). In the later version, God sounds more mocking (and less reassuring) than in the original poem (Brooks, p. 10).

FORMALIST critics are concerned with the "close reading" of literature and with such matters as a work's beauty, its possible unity, and the potential relevance of even the slightest details of phrasing, meter, syntax, and structure. Therefore, literally every word and syllable of Hardy's poem would potentially interest a formalist, beginning with the opening phrase—"That night" (which implies precision and specificity)—as well as with the next phrase ("your great guns," with its strongly accented monosyllables and its emphatic alliteration). A formalist would also appreciate the surprise revealed by the second line, and also the symbolism of the third line's reference to a church damaged by preparations for war.

The abrupt transition from stanza one to stanza two—emphasized by "enjambment" (lack of punctuation at the end a line)—would also impress a formalist: Hardy's readers are caught by surprise just as the corpses have been. Effective assonance and alliteration appear in "howl," "hounds," and "mouse" and also in "let fall" and "altar" (6–7), and line 7 is effectively realistic, ironic, and irreverent. A formalist would also admire the appropriate stress on "in" in "into" in line 8, the effectively colloquial tone of "It's" in line 10, the clever use of euphemism ("went below") in line 11, and the implied references to blood and the double use of assonance in line 14. In line 15, "Christés" (rather than "Christ's") sounds evocatively medieval (and thus reminds us of Christianity's long history), while the shift in line 25 balances the similar shift in line 5. Cleanth Brooks, a leading American formalist, noted the somewhat comic tone of line 19 (describing skeletons shaking their heads), and indeed Brooks's explication of this poem is an exemplary formalist analysis (see "Works cited"). As Brooks shows, formalists are intrigued by effective writing down to the level of the smallest individual details.

DIALOGICAL critics are interested in the different "voices" works contain, as well as in the potential "dialogue" between a given work, its readers, and other texts. Thus Hardy's poem is "in dialogue" with the Christian Bible and Christian traditions. The Bible and those traditions present God much less colloquially than Hardy does. In "Channel Firing," God speaks in various tones, sounding sometimes dryly informative (10), sometimes sarcastic (14, 21), and sometimes compassionate (16). Hardy makes these voices interact. The entire poem itself is also in a kind of dialogue with the whole previous English poetic tradition, which had rarely presented God as irreverently in this work. "Channel Firing" is so effective partly because its tones are so different from what Hardy's readers did (and probably still do) expect.

Finally, MULTICULTURAL critics would also find much of interest in "Channel Firing." The poem reflects or alludes to various cultures, including Christian culture (3), rural culture (9), international culture (13), and medieval culture (15). It also implies differences between and even within cultures, since it suggests the possibility of war between different nations and within the supposedly common culture of Christendom. War, in fact, is a chief means by which one culture attempts to impose its will on other cultures, and during World War I Germans were often seen as explicitly fighting on behalf of a "Kultur" that their enemies rejected. Different kinds of culture are implied in the poem's final lines (35–6), each increasingly remote in time. Yet ultimately this poem, like much of Hardy's work, seems a clear reflection of specifically

English culture, partly because God speaks like a no-nonsense Englishman.

IN TIME OF "THE BREAKING OF NATIONS"

Only a man harrowing clods
In a slow silent walk
With an old horse that stumbles and nods
Half asleep as they stalk.

Only thin smoke without flame   [5]
From the heaps of couch-grass;
Yet this will go onward the same
Though Dynasties pass.

Yonder a maid and her wight
Come whispering by: [10]
War's annals will cloud into night
Ere their story die.

This poem, first published in 1916 (when the war was in its third year), alludes in its title to Jeremiah 51.20: "Thou art my battle axe and weapon of war: for with thee will I break in pieces the nations, and with thee I will destroy kingdoms." The poem offers three vignettes of rural life. Stanza one describes a man plowing a field with an old, half-asleep horse (1–4). Stanza two suggests that rural activities such as burning weeds in fields will endure much longer than the dynastic power of ruling families (5–8). Finally, stanza three points (in deliberately archaic language) to a young woman and her male suitor who converse quietly while walking. The poem ends by suggesting such courtship will endure long after any particular war has ended. In short, the poem suggests that wars are merely temporary and seem comparatively insignificant when contrasted with the basic, persistent activities of human life.

HORATIAN critics, influenced by or in sympathy with the ancient Roman poet Horace, value simplicity, unity, clarity, and moderation in literary works. They might therefore admire Hardy's lyric, which is unified partly because three different examples all illustrate the same basic point. The poem's diction is also exceptionally clear and plain. A regular rhyme scheme contributes further unity, and that rhyme scheme is itself highly conventional—another factor Horace would have prized because literary conventions, for him, merely codify custom. Conventions reflect the kind of writing that has appealed to past audiences, and the need to satisfy one's audience is the need Horace especially emphasizes. Hardy's poem was easy for its first audiences to appreciate, and the same is true today. Few readers might immediately know the meaning of "couch-grass," but despite this one very slight exception the poem possesses the kind of clarity Horace valued so highly.

ARCHETYPAL critics are especially interested in any traits most people share (including common desires and fears). They are also interested in anything enduring and fundamental to a shared "human nature." Hardy's poem would interest them because it emphasizes aspects of life (such as planting crops, harvesting crops, and romantic courtship) that seem to have existed everywhere and almost always. Indeed, the poem implies that such activities will endure long after the present war is merely a distant memory. Humans, the poem suggests, will always need to cultivate the land, and sexual attraction will endure as long as humans do. Hardy's poem (an archetypal critic might argue) emphasizes activities and feelings that are (and always will be) important, regardless of differences in such matters as race, religion, ethnicity, nationality, gender, class, and so on.

MARXIST critics are especially concerned with conflicts between economic classes, especially between classes with real economic power (such as the wealthy and the middle classes) and classes that are poor and oppressed (such as workers and peasant farmers). Certainly the farmer presented in Hardy's poem seems anything but wealthy: only one horse is mentioned, and the farmer must plow the fields himself rather than pay anyone else to do so. Presumably he also burns away weeds, while the conversing couple seem anything but wealthy, especially since they are described as "a maid and her wight" (9)—deliberately archaic phrasing suggesting that they are peasants. ("A lady and her love" would imply something entirely different.) The peasant, plowing the fields with his horse, might resemble the horse in the eyes of Marxists: both man and animal have to work hard, and, just as the horse has little control over his life, the same might be said of the peasant. It is people like this peasant who must fight the wars started by the wealthy and powerful—wars that benefit the wealthy and powerful. The lifestyle of peasants and workers may ultimately endure longer than the power of royal "Dynasties" (8), but royals in the meantime enjoy comforts and privileges that peasants can only imagine. Yet a Marxist might argue that English peasants and workers in Hardy's day were still far better off, economically, than peasants and workers in the colonies owned and exploited by the British empire. In various ways, this poem can therefore be read, from a Marxist point of view, as complicit in upholding the power structure of its day. It may in a sense celebrate the peasant class, but it does nothing to help improve their real material conditions.

NEW HISTORICIST critics, like Marxists, are often concerned with issues of social power and especially with groups who seem relatively powerless and marginalized. But new historicists are less likely than Marxists to advocate for any specific political and economic change. They are more likely to study social conditions of the past than to seek, explicitly, to alter social conditions of the present. New historicists often emphasize the ways powerful people may be less powerful than they seem, and also the ways powerless people may be more powerful than they at first appear. In these respects, Hardy's poem seems tailor-made for new historical analysis. The peasants it describes seem relatively powerless, yet their lifestyle (Hardy suggests) is more powerful and enduring than royal dynasties. In one sense the poem is arguably naïve: peasants in continental Europe during World War I (especially French peasants in northern France) knew just how destructive war could actually be—how much it could obliterate the landscape, kill noncombatants, and totally disrupt traditional rural life. Hardy's poem was written in 1915 and published in 1916, and by those dates the full deadly impact of the war on millions of European peasants was glaringly clear. A new historicist might argue that Hardy's poem, which so confidently implies the endurance of age-old traditions, may partly reflect wishful thinking. The poem is, however, relevant to the fall of at least two dynasties: both the German and Russian monarchies ultimately collapsed because of the war, and so the very war designed to protect and advance imperial power helped to destroy two major empires. New historicists, who emphasize the sheer complexity of historical events, would be intrigued by this kind of paradox.

DARWINIAN critics are influenced by ideas about human evolution, especially by ideas about traits, activities, and lifestyles that promote survival. Like archetypal critics, they might discuss

Hardy's poem by focusing on what it implies about behaviors common to most if not all successful human societies, such as tilling the land, domesticating animals, and, especially, perpetuating society through heterosexual reproduction. Hardy's poem implies the enduring importance of all these behaviors. Biology, in this poem and for many Darwinian critics, is ultimately more important than culture. Royal dynasties may come and go, and the annals of war may be compiled over the centuries, but the "story" (12) that is most crucial of all is the story of human reproduction and physical survival. Next to that narrative, all other stories pale in significance. A Darwinian critic might suggest, however, that Hardy's poem neglects to mention the baneful evolutionary consequences of war. Admittedly, some early twentieth-century advocates of warfare argued that war might ultimately benefit Europe by promoting military virtues such as discipline, physical health, and courage. Some even argued that war might help purge Europe of people who were weak or otherwise inferior. Yet, modern Darwinian critics might argue that Hardy's poem fails to emphasize that war often destroys the very bravest, healthiest, and fittest males, and that it often does so before those young men have a chance to reproduce and thereby benefit the gene pool.

A. E. Housman (1859–1936): *A Shropshire Lad* XXXV—"On the idle hill of summer"

ON THE IDLE HILL OF SUMMER

On the idle hill of summer,
    Sleepy with the flow of streams,
Far I hear the steady drummer
    Drumming like a noise in dreams.

Far and near and low and louder   [5]
    On the roads of earth go by,
Dear to friends and food for powder,
    Soldiers marching, all to die.

East and west on fields forgotten
    Bleach the bones of comrades slain,   [10]
Lovely lads and dead and rotten;
    None that go return again.

Far the calling bugles hollo,
    High the screaming fife replies,
Gay the files of scarlet follow: [15]
    Woman bore me, I will rise.

PLATONIC critics might find this poem variously interesting. They might particularly discuss its emphasis on music's power and its emphasis on reason versus emotion or passion. Plato believed that most humans are highly emotional and that music can have a particularly powerful emotional appeal. Because Plato also believed that humans should obey reason rather than follow passion, he distrusted anything that might undermine reason by inciting emotion. Anything that might appeal to emotion (such as music or poetry) should be banned or strictly controlled. Only poetry and music that encouraged virtue should be permitted in a well-governed republic.

How would Plato evaluate the music this poem describes? How would he react to the poem itself? Much would depend on his opinion of the war the poem implies. If the war were just and justifiable, then music encouraging soldiers could be justified as well. However, if the war were indeed just and justifiable, Plato would probably be troubled by the poem's emotional descriptions of it—descriptions that emphasize danger, death, and rotting bodies. Anything that might make soldiers (the defenders of the republic) afraid would bother Plato. Wars should promote justice and virtue, and soldiers should exhibit courage and be willing to suffer and die for the sake of the republic. However, a poem that emphasized suffering and death (such as this one), but that failed to emphasize the justness of the war, might seem highly suspicious to Plato. He might be particularly skeptical of the poem's extreme claims. Is it really true that in war *"All"* die (8) and that *"None . . . return"* (12; emphasis added)? Obviously not. Therefore, the poem may be guilty of irrational emotionalism and, for that very reason, subject to Plato's condemnation.

PSYCHOANALYTIC critics influenced by the ideas of Sigmund Freud might interpret this poem in light of Freud's emphasis on the so-called id. The id is the subconscious part of the mind; it is the part that is most emotional because it is the seat of our deepest individual desires, pleasures, fears, and psychological pain. The poem's first stanza not only emphasizes pleasure but alludes explicitly to the subconscious by mentioning "dreams" (4). Dreams, according to Freud, allow us access to our minds' deeper regions; they are therefore especially important subjects of psychoanalytical study. The first stanza's emphasis is almost entirely on pleasure and relaxation, but these qualities, in this instance, do not imply laziness or self-indulgence and thus would probably not embarrass the "ego" (the seat of reason, in Freud's view) or require censoring by the "superego" (associated with conscience and morality). The reference to the summertime "flow of streams" (2) suggests an innocent, natural pleasure, but the significantly different sound of drums may already imply something darker. The dream may turn into a nightmare. The opening stanza twice mentions drumming, as if linking it with dreaming and with intrusion into the speaker's consciousness. The poem appeals to our own subconscious minds through such subtle sound effects.

By the end of the second stanza, whatever pleasure the poem may have emphasized at first has been overtaken by allusions to fears and pain, especially the fear of death. The suffering and pain of war are not presented here as serving any higher, transcendent purpose. Nothing in these lines, in other words, associates war with the morality and higher ideals associated with the superego. Instead, stanza three continues to emphasize fears that arise from the id. In fact, the id may also be involved in the possibly homoerotic reference to "Lovely lads" (9). Housman, after all, was a closeted homosexual—a fact that would matter to some psychoanalytic critics.

The files of soldiers in scarlet uniforms may, subconsciously, remind the poem's speaker and/or readers of flowing blood (in contrast to the earlier "flow of streams" [2]). In any case, the speaker's final decision to "rise" and join others marching off to war may symbolize the id's submission to the ego (the reality principle) and the superego (the seat of conventional morality and public expectation). The poem moves, then, from emphasizing private pleasure to an emphasis on facing "reality" and doing one's duty. All three aspects of the Freudian paradigm—the id, ego, and superego—are arguably evident here. The speaker's closing allusion to his mother may, in fact, especially intrigue Freudians, since it may imply that he now does what his mother would expect, or since it may, if nothing else, imply that people generally do what is expected of them by society and/or their own consciences.

READER-RESPONSE critics usually believe that individuals or groups can and will react to the very same stimuli in various ways. Their reactions to this poem, for instance, would be guided less by the poem itself (which ultimately has no power to control responses) than by readers' own particular tendencies or values. Thus the poem's reference to "Lovely lads" (11) might evoke one response from, say, gay male readers and another from, say, mothers who had raised male children. Heterosexual women might regard the death of "Lovely lads" as particularly unfortunate, while homophobic readers might dislike the adjective "Lovely" to describe young men. Readers who considered World War I a justifiable conflict might dislike the poem's antiwar elements, while critics of that war—and/or of war in general—might appreciate this work for revealing war's ugliness and waste. Some readers might admire the speaker for ultimately "doing his duty," while others might view his final decision as weak. In short, for a reader-response critic, there would be almost as many potential responses to this poem as there are different kinds of potential readers.

DECONSTRUCTIVE critics look for ways any text is potentially open to readings that contradict or profoundly complicate the text's apparently "obvious" meaning. Deconstructors believe that no interpretation of any text can ever be finally plain. Any meanings "found" in a text are always open to question; multiple, contrasting interpretations are not only possible but inevitable. There is no end to possible interpretations, if only because any interpretation is itself open to multiple interpretations. Nothing controls or limits the nature or number of interpretations a text might receive.

One might argue, for instance, that this poem values pastoral peacefulness over destructive war. One might just as easily argue, however, that a nation devoted to pastoral peacefulness might be most vulnerable to attack. Thus pastoral peacefulness might paradoxically provoke war, just as war might help one appreciate pastoral peacefulness more than would such peacefulness itself, which can easily be taken for granted. One could argue (and some *did* argue) that the "idle" (1) behavior of the prewar English helped cause World War I. If the English had better prepared for war (so this argument went), war might never have occurred. Being "Sleepy" (2), in this sense, was likely to provoke conflict. Accordingly, peace and war are not clear, absolute opposites: peace can provoke war and war can provoke peace. Any supposedly hard-and-fast distinction can easily be deconstructed.

Similarly, one might argue that being awakened from the kind of idleness described in the opening stanza is not to be awakened at all in any simple and unambiguous sense. Being awakened from peace to war is, arguably, only to enter a different kind of sleep. If sleep means a loss of conscious, independent control over one's body and mind, what else is war but a kind of sleep? And yet war can also make a person more fully alert and conscious than almost any other state of existence. Once again, then, what seems a clear distinction (between being asleep and being awake) can be deconstructed. For deconstructors, seemingly hard-and-fast distinctions are never really hard and fast. Thus the speaker, at the end of the poem, seems to turn his back on his previous way of life, but, by speaking this very poem he suggests that he has not really turned away. He arguably shows courage by finally joining the army, but he arguably shows weakness, too. He arguably demonstrates his free will as the poem concludes, but perhaps he is merely succumbing to external pressures: any apparently clear distinction collapses, and the poem's final line is especially open to interpretation, with no obvious way of deciding which interpretation is "correct" and which is "incorrect." For a deconstructor, the very idea of a "correct interpretation" is literally a contradiction in terms.

ECOCRITICISM emphasizes humanity's relations with nature. At first, in Housman's poem, the speaker seems to be in utter harmony with his surroundings. In fact, it is not until line 3 that an "I" (presumably human) even appears. The poem's opening emphasis, then, is on natural beauty and natural pleasures by themselves. The word "Sleepy" (1) might even, at first, seem to describe the "hill" (2), as if even the ground were somehow alive. It is only when sounds created by humans enter the poem (3) that literal discord arises. The sound of the drum, in contrast to the sound of streams, is insistent, disruptive, and relentless. It thus arguably symbolizes the general impact humans have on nature—an impact that is often ruthlessly destructive.

In the second stanza, nature is mentioned only (and quite literally) in passing, as soldiers march down roads cut through the landscape (6). By stanza three, the initial harmony between humanity and nature has been thoroughly undercut, but the responsibility for this fact rests solely with humans. The fields that might have been (and probably once were) places for growing crops and sustaining life are now littered with corpses. The fields are "forgotten" (9), partly because their age-old agricultural functions have been forgotten; patches of land that once nurtured life now display grisly death. Many of the dead soldiers may have been farmers themselves, but now their formerly close cooperation with the land has been destroyed. By the very end of the poem, humanity's relationship with nature has been basically forgotten. All that matters to the speaker by the end of the work are his relations with other humans.

2

Alys Fane Trotter (1863–1961): "The hospital visitor"

THE HOSPITAL VISITOR

When yesterday I went to see friends—
(Watching their patient faces in a row
I want to give each boy a D.S.O.)
When yesterday I went to see my friends
With cigarettes and foolish odds and ends,   [5]
(Knowing they understand how well I know
That nothing I can do will make amends,
But that I must not grieve, or tell them so),
A pale-faced Iniskilling, just eighteen,
Who'd fought two years, with eyes a little dim   [10]
Smiled up and showed me, there behind the screen
On the humped bandage that replaced a limb,
How someone left him, where the leg had been
A tiny green glass pig to comfort him.

Here are men who've learned to laugh at pain.   [15]
And if their lips have quivered when they spoke,
They've said brave words, or tried to make a joke,
Said it's not worse than trenches in the rain,
Or pools of water on a chalky plain,
Or bitter cold from which you stiffly woke,   [20]

Or deep wet mud that left you hardly sane,
Or the tense wait for "Fritz's master stroke."
You seldom hear them talk of their "bad luck."
And suffering has not spoiled their ready wit,
And oh! You'd hardly doubt their fighting pluck   [25]
When each new generation shows their grit,
Who never brag of blows for England struck,
But only yearn to "get about a bit."

Trotter's poem "The Hospital Visitor" actually consists of two 14-line sonnets. In the first, the speaker describes visiting a hospital for men wounded in the war. She wishes she could give each of them "a D.S.O." (Distinguished Service Order), but instead she can only bring the cigarettes prized so much by soldiers during World War I. She realizes that nothing she brings can "make amends" for the wounds the suffering the soldiers have experienced. She sees one young man, a member of the Sixth (Iniskillings) Dragoon Regiment, an amputee who stoically shows her a small figurine he has been given as a gift. In the second sonnet, the speaker expresses admiration for the stoic attitudes of the hospitalized men, who say that their present conditions are no worse that their experiences in the battlefields, including the tension caused by anticipating an attack, by the Germans, intended to be decisive. The men are brave without seeming cocky, and they have quickly adapted to their new, reduced capacities.

ARISTOTLE, with his strong interest in literary genres, would probably be interested in the fact that Trotter's poem consists of two identically structured sonnets, each exhibiting the same unusual rhyme scheme (abba abab cdc dcd). The first eight lines of a Petrarchan sonnet would rhyme as follows: abba abba. In a Shakespearean, the first eight lines would rhyme abab cdcd. Trotter, then, uses the 14-line sonnet form, but she does not follow either of the most common rhyme schemes. She thus shows both a respect for literary tradition as well as a capacity to innovate—precisely the sort of attitude and skill that Aristotle (as well as Horace) admired. She demonstrates the craftsmanship an Aristotelian critic would appreciate.

Aristotle might also admire the work's length. It is neither too long nor too short; its length seems appropriate to its substance. Yet Trotter also shows her literary craftsmanship (always prized by Aristotle) by structuring the poem(s) so tightly and by making the structure seem unobtrusive. Everything, indeed, seems to "fit together" well in this work; the diction, in particular, seems perfectly appropriate to the subject matter: it is neither too lofty nor too plain. Anaphora (beginning a series of lines with the same word or words) is used especially effectively in the second sonnet (19–23) and is further evidence of Trotter's craftsmanship. For these reasons and many others, an Aristotelian critic would almost surely admire Trotter's artistic achievement.

THEMATIC critics emphasize the key ideas (or "themes") explored in literary works. Trotter's text explores various important ideas. These include patriotism, bravery, and stoicism, and especially the idea that soldiers' sacrifice should be respected. More generally, Trotter's poem exemplifies the very common theme of initiation, or the ways people (especially young people) move from one stage or style of life to another. This work also implies the importance of optimism when facing adversity, maintaining one's spirit and sense of humor despite pain, and the ideal resilience of the human spirit. Thematic critics, who value literature primarily for the meanings it conveys, would find much of interest in Trotter's poem.

FEMINIST critics might react to Trotter's text in various ways. Some feminists might even note, for instance, that nothing explicitly identifies the poem's speaker as female. Some readers might assume that the speaker is a woman simply because the author is a woman, and they might support this assumption by noting that the young man in the first poem shows his visitor a "tiny green glass pig" he has been given (14). Because of pressures to conform gender stereotypes, he might hesitate showing such a gift to another man but might willingly show it to a woman, especially an older, motherly woman. (Trotter herself was a little over fifty when the war began.) Nevertheless, surprisingly little phrasing confirms that the speaker is female.

How might feminists react to this poem? Almost inevitably, they would react variously, because there are different *kinds* of feminist critics, with different views and distinct purposes. One kind of feminist, for instance, might applaud a woman's poem about the war being studied at all. The main goal of one kind of feminist criticism is simply to recover forgotten, neglected texts by women, and this is one such text. Although it has begun to receive more attention lately, for decades and decades it was rarely discussed.

A feminist, then, might be pleased that it has recently become the focus of serious academic attention.

If we do assume that the speaker is a woman, feminists might again react variously. Some might argue that she conforms to a standard gender stereotype of women as caring and compassionate, especially in dealing with injured male soldiers. Women, of course, could simply not *be* soldiers during World War I, although many were nurses or worked in factories to help support the war effort. The speaker here, however, is presented as a hospital "visitor," not a nurse, and thus seems more distanced from the war effort than a nurse. She knows of the dangers and pain the men have faced on the battlefield, but she has not faced those hardships herself because, as a woman, she has not been *allowed* to face them.

Ironically, it is the poem's young men who have now, in a sense, been reduced to the status of stereotypical women of Trotter's day (at least the women of the middle and upper classes). Suddenly they are passive; their freedom is limited; they must be cared for by others; and, in a sense, they are no longer the vigorous, autonomous "men" they were when the war began. They are unlikely (if they are amputees) ever to serve in war again, and, if they are lucky, they will receive money from an outside source (a government pension)—money they do not earn by daily labor. In one more sense, then, they have symbolically come to resemble many women of their era.

READER-RESPONSE critics, interested in the ways individuals, groups, or eras respond to literature, might imagine a variety of possible responses to Trotter's poem. Readers particularly likely to be interested in this text might include veterans, wounded veterans, anyone seriously injured for any reason, and the families and friends of all the kinds of people already listed. Anyone who has ever visited a seriously ill person could "relate" to this poem, as could anyone who has ever admired the resilience of other people dealing with some severe challenge. Patriots of any kind might take a special interest in this poem—British patriots in particular. The speaker is also, in a sense, a surrogate for anyone lucky enough to have never faced a truly serious injury. This poem could also provoke widely varying but sometimes overlapping feelings in different kinds of persons. These feelings might include gratitude, regret, sympathy, shame, respect, and even anger (at the wastefulness of war). Reactions might vary according to one's gender, class, race, ethnicity, and stage in life, to mention just a few possibly relevant categories.

Someone reading this poem in 1918 might have responded to it differently than someone reading it in 2018. The text, in other words, could have different "meanings" to many different readers. Yet the poem does seem to imply an ideal reader: a patriot proud of British soldiers and respectful, in general, of human nature at its stoic, courageous best.

POSTMODERNIST readers tend to reject any hard-and-fast "rules" in responding to texts, such as the "rules" of literary genres. They usually admire texts that reject conventions and undermine expectations. Trotter's departure from the standard sonnet rhyme schemes is a small instance of such differentness, but a postmodernist might especially admire how she uses the sonnet form (with its very long and dignified history and frequent association with love poetry) to deal with such matters as war, wounds, amputations, and other unexpected subjects. A postmodernist might also argue that the poem is unstable in the views it implies about war: on the one hand it suggests, especially in the second sonnet, a real respect for British patriotism, but alternatively it forces us to contemplate the literally bloody, horrific personal consequences of war. Postmodernists question "grand narratives"—that is, any stories or value systems that purport to explain reality in simple, monolithic terms. (Conflicts between such simplistic ideologies are, in fact, often the root causes of wars.) Anyone who has read much poetry prompted by World War I will immediately see how greatly Trotter's work differs so much from other such verse. Many so-called war poems of the period seem hopelessly naïve, romantic, jingoistic, and superficial. Often such poems were produced by writers lacking firsthand experience with the war's grim realities. Yet hackneyed, conventional verse was also often written by actual soldiers. When reading such poems, one can usually safely predict what they will say. Trotter's sonnets are far less predictable and might therefore appeal to postmodernists, who tend to value anything new, distinctive, and disruptive.

Eva Dobell (1867–1973):
"In a soldier's hospital I: Pluck"; "In a soldier's hospital II: Gramophone tunes"

IN A SOLDIER'S HOSPITAL I: PLUCK

Crippled for life at seventeen,
    His great eyes seem to question why:
With both legs smashed it might have been
    Better in that grim trench to die
    Than drag maimed years out helplessly.   [5]

A child—so wasted and so white,
    He told a lie to get his way,
To march, a man with men, and fight
    While other boys are still at play.
    A gallant lie your heart will say.   [10]

So broke with pain, he shrinks in dread
    To see the "dresser" drawing near;
And winds the clothes about his head
    That none may see his heart-sick fear.
    His shaking, strangled sobs you hear.   [15]

But when the dreaded moment's there
    He'll face us all, a soldier yet,
Watch his bared wounds with unmoved air,
    (Though tell-tale lashes still are wet),
    And smoke his Woodbine cigarette.   [20]

HORACE, an important literary theorist who was also a practicing poet, emphasized that writers must first and foremost satisfy their audiences. Professional writers who failed to do so would fail to make a living. Even amateur writers who failed to satisfy audiences risked disdain and ridicule. Yet because Horace knew that audiences could be diverse, he recommended writing in ways that would appeal to diverse readers, including those who wanted literature to teach *and* those who wanted it to please. Works that did both, and that appealed to the widest range of readers, were most likely to succeed.

Horace might value Dobell's poem because it might potentially please numerous readers, including both young and old and both men and women. It emphasizes youthful valor; it reminds the aged of their own early vigor; it highlights male courage; and it features a (presumably female) speaker capable of appreciating such courage. The poem would appeal to practically anyone who valued bravery, including (for instance) both veterans and civilians. Veterans might appreciate the poem's emphasis on the dangers they faced, while civilians might appreciate its realistic glimpse of military life.

Horace prized works that were simple, unified, clear, accessible, and relatively conventional. Dobell's poem exhibits all these traits: its language is plain; its meter, stanza forms, and use of rhymes are traditional; and its diction and characterization fit its subject matter. It shows moderate innovation (the kind Horace prized), partly by dispensing with the sort of "artificial" rhetoric (including "thees," "thous," and classical allusions) that had come to seem shopworn and stale to many readers of Dobell's day. Nothing in this poem would provoke the laughter and ridicule Horace dreaded, and the poem would also satisfy Horace because its soldier behaves as we like to think the best soldiers do behave: he is brave, stoic, active, and spirited. Horace believed that various kinds of people conduct themselves in generally predictable ways: old men act differently than young boys, boys act differently than girls, and so on. The soldier in this poem thus implies a lesson about proper military conduct.

TRADITIONAL HISTORICAL critics believe that a literary work can only be most fully understood and appreciated if readers know what was happening, believed, and taken for granted when the work was written. Such critics might be interested, for instance, in the number and kinds of casualties during World War I, the nature and effectiveness of medical treatment soldiers received, and the kinds of weapons and warfare that might lead to "smashed" legs (3). Traditional historical critics might especially want to know how many soldiers served at age "seventeen" (1). What was the official age for enlistment? How could someone aged seventeen be so horrifically injured? Did many soldiers this young actually suffer this kind of injury? What kinds of futures could seriously injured veterans anticipate? These are just a few questions a traditional historical critic would want to answer after reading this poem. Any solid, relevant historical facts would interest this kind of critic.

PSYCHOANALYTIC critics, influenced by Sigmund Freud, might emphasize how this poem both reflects and affects the "id" (a subconscious part of the mind, preoccupied with pleasure and pain). The pain and suffering the poem depicts would arouse fear and revulsion in the injured soldier, the observant speaker, and the reader experiencing such suffering vicariously. This poem thus threatens the so-called pleasure principle associated with the id, and the poem seems especially tragic since the wounded soldier is only seventeen, an age often associated with the pleasure-seeking impulses of the id.

A Freudian might be especially interested in the *kind* of pain stressed here, which is not merely physical but mental. Reading the poem is only temporarily painful for the reader; having one's legs smashed and presumably amputated implies permanent psychological suffering for the young soldier. For a Freudian, his smashed legs might symbolize his damaged manhood and figurative loss of virility. Ironically, by going to war he was probably trying to prove himself a "man"; now, however, that very status has been threatened. Having moved (as Freud's disciple Jacques Lacan might put it) from the world of childhood (associated with mothers), he entered the world of fighting and manhood (associated with fathers). Now, however, he is being mothered again, and has, symbolically, become once more a "child" (6). His attempt to achieve psychological unity by performing the role of heroic man has led, ironically, to a kind of permanent fragmentation, both physically and psychologically. His effort to be a stereotypical adult male has led to symbolic castration. Ultimately he tries to retain and project his sense of himself as a stereotypically brave adult man—an effort implied by his silence, his pride in facing others while looking at his injured legs, and also his decision to smoke, in symbolically masculine fashion, one of the Woodbine cigarettes so favored by the troops.

ARCHETYPAL critics, influenced by Carl Jung, believe that most humans share certain fundamental psychological traits. These transcend differences of culture, race, nation, era, and so on. They often involve very fundamental needs, desires, and fears. Dobell's poem plays on nearly universal fears of pain and death and on equally universal desires for life and health. The poem's young soldier is the archetypal young warrior—strong, brave, resilient, and stoic. He is a hero who has emerged from a figurative grave (the trenches) and been reborn into a new (and new kind of) life. He has undergone, to an extreme degree, the kind of initiation usually involved in moving from boyhood to manhood, from being an adolescent to being an adult. Likewise, he has suffered, to an extreme degree, and very prematurely, the loss of youthful vigor and vitality. His injuries have doubly "Crippled [him] for life" (1): he will no longer be able to participate as fully in life as before, and for the rest of his life he will be physically handicapped. His noticeably "white" skin (6) symbolizes that he has been drained of the health and vitality most humans prize, and he experiences the "heart-sick fear" (14) most people feel—and have probably always felt—when facing severe pain. Yet he also shows the courage that we archetypically associate with the brave.

NEW HISTORICIST critics consider history far more complicated than is often assumed. They blame traditional historical critics for allegedly simplistic interpretations of the past. It would be difficult, for instance, to read Dobell's poem as either simply prowar or antiwar. Opponents of the war could read the poem as graphic evidence of the waste and tragic suffering caused by armed conflict. Defenders of the war, conversely, could point to the young wounded soldier as the kind of hero nations need. The poem's subtitle ("Pluck"—meaning courage or tenacity) suggests that Dobell herself may have favored the second interpretation. Yet Dobell (a new historicist might argue) was (and is) in no position to determine how others would interpret her poem. Opponents of the war could easily have read this text "against the grain": that is, in ways contradicting or contrasting with any apparently "intended" interpretation. The poem puts stark and disturbing images "into circulation" (a favorite new historicist term), and reading such poems might have undermined many readers' commitment to the war. Alternatively, this poem and similar texts may have helped prolong the war by extolling "pluck" and thus encouraging others to show comparable courage. From one point of view, the speaker deeply sympathizes with the soldier; from another, her praise of his "pluck" may encourage other youth to risk what he has risked and suffer as he has suffered. For new historicists, a work's meanings and its effects are likely to seem complex.

New historicists might also be interested in what this poem implies about shifting instabilities of power. The youth tried to assert and win power by joining the military, yet that effort has left him obviously weak. But his present physical weakness allows him to demonstrate both physical and psychological strength. This new power, however, is merely temporary: if he is lucky and survives, he will be permanently weakened. But he will have won, perhaps, new self-respect, and he may enjoy long-lasting respect from others. As this list of paradoxes suggest, new historicist explanations can often seem much more complex than the explanations often offered by traditional historical critics. History, for new historicists, is never simple, and interpreting its relevance to literature can never be simple either.

IN A SOLDIER'S HOSPITAL II: GRAMOPHONE TUNES

Through the long ward the gramophone
Grinds out its nasal melodies:
"Where did you get that girl?" it shrills.
The patients listen at their ease,
Through clouds of strong tobacco smoke: [5]
The gramophone can always please.

The Welsh boy has it by his bed,
(He's lame—one leg was blown away).
He'll lie propped up with pillows there,
And wind the handle half the day.   [10]
His neighbour, with the shattered arm,
Picks out the records he must play.

Jock with his crutches beats the time;
The gunner, with his head close-bound,
Listens with puzzled, patient smile: [15]
(Shell shocked—he cannot hear a sound).
The others join in from their beds,
And send the chorus rolling round.

Somehow for me these common tunes
Can never sound the same again: [20]
They've magic now to thrill my heart
And bring before me, clear and plain,
Man that is master of his flesh,
And has the laugh of death and pain.

Readers influenced by LONGINUS might react variously to this poem. Longinus especially valued lofty, elevated (or "sublime") writing that could overpower a reader, inducing a kind of ecstasy. Clearly Dobell's poem is not "sublime," thus illustrating how a theory can help us perceive a work's distinctive traits even when the work does not exemplify the criteria a theory emphasizes. Dobell's poem does not stress much that seems rousing or inspiring; instead, its focus is commonplace and quotidian. Nor does the poem seem the result of the almost divine "genius" Longinus so admired. To say this, however, is not to fault the poem. Instead, it is simply to observe that even when a theory seems irrelevant to a particular work, it can still help illuminate the work's features and nature.

Longinus might, however, admire this poem's emphasis on the importance to the human soul of art (in this case music), even if the art depicted here does not seem especially elevated or inspired (as lines 2–3 suggest). In a sense, this poem itself resembles the music it describes: it is simple, unsophisticated, and plain; it is not a work of "high art" but rather of "popular" culture. Yet both the tunes the poem describes and the poem itself help unite disparate persons in ways that Longinus, who admired art's power, might approve (see esp. 17–18). Music helps these men find joy in pain; it nurtures their spirits despite their shattered bodies. Longinus would especially admire the final two lines: "Man . . . is master of his flesh, / And has the laugh of [i.e. can laugh at] death and pain" (23–4). And Longinus might particularly value the idea that even popular art can have "magic" to "thrill" one's "heart" (21). This poem is less a celebration of art per se than of the spiritual and ethical loftiness true art can help inspire. The positive moral traits the poem praises reflect the speaker's appealing moral character. The poem may not ravish or transport us, but it does leave us feeling thoughtful and reflective in ways Longinus might definitely commend.

THEMATIC critics emphasize a work's central themes or ideas. Surely one main theme of this poem is music's power, but other, related ideas also seem either stated or implied. These include the mind's power over matter, the way music can promote fellowship, the importance of popular music to the health of individuals and cultures, the idea that even something apparently common can be noble, and the idea that the human spirit is indomitable. This poem resembles in some of its themes not only the other war poem by Dobell already discussed above but also many other war poems by numerous other authors. Thematic critics believe that poems can teach lessons, and one lesson this poem definitely teaches is stated quite explicitly in its final two lines. The poem's reasoning is inductive: the first part provides specific data from which the last part draws the appropriate argumentative conclusion.

MARXIST critics think most wars promote the power and interests of the ruling classes. Marxists definitely viewed World War I as such a conflict. To Marxists, it made little difference which side won. The war benefited capitalists and was one further means of exploiting workers. Literature written about the war might variously promote the interests of the upper classes, undermine those interests, or somehow do both to one degree or another.

Dobell's poem arguably promotes the interests of the powerful. It can be seen as functioning much as music does inside the poem: as a kind of opiate encouraging victims of war to accept their pain rather than opposing the exploitative economic system that promotes such suffering. For Marxists, World War I was a war among capitalists; it benefited capitalism and imperialism. Anything that sustained the war and discouraged workers from turning against their oppressors (as eventually happened in Russia) was a useful tool of the ruling class. Music functions this way in Dobell's poem, and so does the poem itself. The fact that the music described is "popular" music is all the more significant. Popular culture has here been appropriated by the powerful. It has been turned into a commodity produced by an industry. Rather than fostering an awareness of class conflict and encouraging the exploited to turn against the powerful, the music here focuses instead on mere individual romance ("Where did you get that girl?" [3]). Neither the poem nor the music it depicts promotes working-class interests. The community of hospitalized soldiers here is merely temporary. It will not last, and it will do nothing to help end the war or help prevent future wars. Indeed, a Marxist might read Dobell's poem as implied political propaganda: it helps justify the war and therefore helps promote future conflicts.

One can, of course, read the poem "against the grain" and see it as implicitly subversive, almost in spite of itself. Perhaps it undermines confidence in the war by bluntly depicting the soldiers' suffering. The poem's final lines, however, suggest that its speaker does not intend a meaning that is fundamentally radical or rebellious.

DIALOGICAL critics emphasize the interaction of different "voices," not only (1) within a text but also (2) among texts and (3) between a text and its readers. Dobell's poem illustrates all three kinds of dialogue. Just as the gramophone record asks an explicit question (a question each listener can answer differently), so the whole poem engages each reader in similar dialogue. It makes points and implicitly raises questions to which each reader will have a distinct response. When writing, Dobell had to consider the different possible reactions of different readers. Thus the poem was shaped partly by its potential readers even before it was created. If it sounded too naïve, it would have disappointed experienced soldiers. If it seemed too shocking and gruesome, it might have offended supporters of the war. If, on the other hand, it had been too jingoistic, it would have offended pacifists. By considering the different possible "voices" of different possible readers, Dobell was involved in a kind of dialogue even before the work was finished. Such dialogue may have promoted a moderate stance in the completed poem.

Dobell's poem was also inevitably involved in dialogue with other poems, especially other war poems. In addition, her poem implies a kind of dialogue (mostly silent) among the soldiers it depicts, and then it describes, in its reference to "the chorus rolling round" (18) a moment when all the various voices in the room join together, thus achieving—both literally and symbolically—a sort of harmony that the poem implicitly celebrates.

MULTICULTURAL critics are interested in the various subcultures that constitute any larger culture. Dobell's poem alludes to a number of these, especially the subcultures of (1) soldiers in general and (2) wounded soldiers in particular. Any distinct group might in this sense be considered a "subculture" and thus might prove interesting to multicultural critics. Dobell's poem provides snapshots of such distinct subcultures as hospital patients (4), tobacco smokers (5), Welsh soldiers (7), amputees (8), soldiers with other serious injuries (11), gunners and, by implication, other specific *kinds* of soldiers (14), and the shell shocked (16). The poem also suggests the power of popular music, which itself can promote (or even transcend) various subcultures. Finally, in fact, the speaker asserts a fundamental unity all humans share: the ability to use their minds and spirits to impose their wills upon their flesh (22–4). Ultimately the members of the various subcultures are united by a common love of popular music and by a common bravery when facing pain. The phrase "common tunes" suggests, on the one hand, the subcultures inspired and sustained by popular music. Yet these tunes are also "common" in a different sense: they promote unity among different persons and groups. Dobell's poem would particularly interest the subculture of multicultural critics concerned with "disability studies," a recent kind of multicultural criticism.

3

Charlotte Mew
(1869–1928): "May, 1915"

MAY, 1915

Let us remember Spring will come again
      To the scorched, blackened woods, where the
            wounded trees
Wait with their old wise patience for the heavenly rain,
Sure of the sky: sure of the sea to send its healing breeze,
      Sure of the sun. And even as to these   [5]
         Surely the Spring, when God shall please,
        Will come again like a divine surprise
To those who sit today with their great Dead, hands in their
    hands, eyes in their eyes,
At one with Love, at one with Grief: blind to the scattered
    things and changing skies.

Although the *Poetics*, by ARISTOTLE, focuses specifically on tragedy, many of its ideas also seem relevant to lyric poems. Mew's poem, for instance, satisfies many of Aristotle's poetic criteria. Its style is clear without being trivial. It uses current or popular words without restricting itself wholly to such language. Its structure, meter, and use of repetition help differentiate its phrasing from anything plain or ordinary (pp. 33–4). It is neither too long nor too short and is thus easy to remember (p. 24), and in this respect it differs from many ineffective war poems of the period, which often seem far too long and rambling. Its language is vivid (p. 33);

it lacks inconsistencies; and it achieves various kinds of unity and symmetry (pp. 29–30).

The poem opens by emphasizing "us" (1) and closes by emphasizing others (8). The beauty implied by the opening line is balanced by the ugliness depicted in the second, and the vivid imagery of line 2 balances the more general phrasing of line 1. The text's opening half emphasizes natural occurrences, while its second half emphasizes human emotions. The first half highlights damage to the landscape, while the second half stresses damage to humans and human feelings. Mew combines "scorched" and "blackened" for emphatic effect; she uses a metaphor when describing "wounded trees"; she employs alliteration effectively in lines 2 and 3; and she uses personification to good effect in the third line. Anaphora (repetition of the same or similar words at the beginnings of lines) is used skillfully in lines 4–6, and so on and so on. In short, Mew has produced the kind of carefully crafted, artistically unified text highly prized by Aristotle (and by many later formalist critics as well).

STRUCTURALIST critics look for the "binary opposites" humans use to impose structure or order on practically everything, including poems. Sometimes these binaries are explicit; sometimes they are largely implied; but it is by means of imposing binary structures that humans impose order on the universe. Mews' poem, for instance, is structured around a series of related binaries that include the following (with implied opposites inside square brackets):

memory/[forgetfulness]
spring/[winter]
healing/woundedness
[life]/death
vegetation/bareness
sureness/[uncertainty]
wisdom/[stupidity]
age/[youth]
rain/[drought]
sunlight/[darkness]
God/[the devil? godlessness?]

God/humans
God/nature
surprise/[monotony]
the living/the dead
love/[hate]
[joy]/grief
[sight]/blindness
change/[stasis]
us/[them]

Sometimes binaries are made explicit; usually, though, they are merely implied, as the square brackets indicate. The job of structuralists is to search for such binaries and determine precisely how, taken together, they help structure the text. In this instance, most of the terms on the left side of the list have positive connotations, while most on the right side have negative connotations. Taken all together, the binaries help organize and shape our comprehension of the poem.

DECONSTRUCTIVE critics, in contrast, look at how most attempts to impose clear and simple structures on reality inevitably fail. For deconstructors, hard-and-fast distinctions are difficult to make and sustain; obvious binaries break down the more one ponders them. Apparent opposites tend to bleed into one another; black and white merge into a kind of gray the more one considers their apparent differences. For deconstructors, neither life nor a text nor anything else is ever as neat and tidy as many of us (especially structuralists) might like to think.

Consider, for example, some of the binaries listed earlier. Mew's poem implies spring's superiority to winter, yet it was ironically in spring and summer that most deaths during World War I occurred. Fighting was especially difficult during winter. Thus the common binary (reflected in this poem) that associates spring with life and winter with death breaks down the more one considers it. Spring and summer were often the seasons of death during the war; winter was often the season of relative peace. But of course not even this distinction can be sustained because deaths occurred throughout the year to one degree or another.

Or, to take another example, Mew's poem implicitly privileges sureness over uncertainty. Here as elsewhere (a deconstructor world argue), binaries are not merely neutral and objective; one item in any binary is usually privileged over the other. Mew's poem celebrates sureness and certainty, as lines 4–6 clearly suggest. Yet the need to insist on something being "sure" inevitably implies that that thing is *not* sure; the certainty the poem asserts paradoxically implies that the speaker is not as certain as she seems. And, most significantly, the poem implies that God is all-powerful and all-good, although the poem also shows that he fails to use his power to promote good and prevent evil. Is God himself, then, partly evil for allowing carnage and suffering to continue? In theory, any clear distinction—such as the idea that God is the opposite of evil—is open to deconstruction.

ECOCRITICS are especially interested in relations between humans and nature, and Mew's poem is clearly relevant. Although the poem emphasizes that man wreaks havoc on nature, it also suggests that nature's renewal, which occurs each spring, can both symbolize and promote a similar, spiritual renewal in humans. The poem implies that in the process of destroying themselves, humans also often destroy nature, thereby in turn destroying an important aspect of their own lives. Destruction of nature can result in psychological self-destruction. In Mew's poem, nature is associated with an ancient, enduring wisdom, whereas humans are linked with a merely temporary—if persistent—foolishness. Yet the poem holds out the promise that a spiritual spring can come to grieving humans, just as the literal spring comes to an environment ravaged by war. God, the poem suggests, ultimately rules both man and nature and will provide for both—a view some ecocritics might consider fundamentally naïve and an example of wishful thinking. Some ecocritics might therefore read Mew's poem "against the grain," arguing that only humans can truly prevent natural destruction and human suffering.

DARWINIAN critics read literature in light of the causes and consequences of biological evolution. Some Darwinians argue, for instance, that humans thrive best as members of communities. This idea is relevant to Mew's opening reference to "us" (1), a word that both implies and promotes a community involving the poem's speaker and readers. The speaker presents herself as a source of wisdom, providing consolation and hope that can help encourage people to live when they face especially difficult circumstances, such as the deaths of loved ones. Just as the trees have faced danger but will survive, so (the speaker suggests) will grieving humans if they can just retain their sense of confidence and hope.

Some Darwinian theorists argue that human beings are naturally attracted to certain kinds of landscapes, especially involving grasslands and rivers—the kinds on which early humans evolved. Mew's poem, with its imagery of burnt and blackened trees, presents a landscape that is the precise opposite of this supposedly ideal environment. At the same time, the poem encourages readers to trust that all will eventually be well. Trust in the goodness of God (who may, in the final analysis, be merely a figment of the human imagination) can nevertheless have real "survival value." Some Darwinians argue that religion helps bind communities together and helps give both communities and their individual members an incentive to continue living, even in the face of enormous pain and destruction.

James Weldon Johnson
(1871–1938): "To America"

TO AMERICA

How would you have us, as we are?
Or sinking 'neath the load we bear?
Our eyes fixed forward on a star?
Or gazing empty at despair?

Rising or falling? Men or things?   [5]
With dragging pace or footsteps fleet?
Strong, willing sinews in your wings?
Or tightening chains about your feet?

LONGINUS, who emphasized that humans should be spiritually elevated, would probably admire Weldon's poem. Although not explicitly about the war, the poem was published when Weldon and other black Americans faced a painful paradox: the United States was officially committed to promoting democracy abroad while, at the same time, not all its citizens could participate fully in democracy at home. Weldon's text highlights this hypocrisy and implicitly encourages the United States to live up to its highest ideals—ideals of moral elevation that Longinus would have admired.

The poem's language, with its explicit contrasts between "Rising" and "falling" (5), is thoroughly Longinian. Human beings are not mere "things" (5); ideally their eyes *should* be "fixed forward on a star" (3). People who prevent others from achieving sublimity or elevation ultimately lower themselves, both spiritually and ethically, especially if their values are essentially selfish and materialistic. The poem avoids the bombastic diction Longinus despised; instead, its language is direct, brisk, and urgent, with a heavy use of anaphora that helps imply the speaker's moral passion and that seems designed to provoke such passion in readers, as well. The speaker projects dignity and self-respect, neither groveling nor displaying immoderate anger—two rhetorical approaches that Longinus explicitly condemned (p. 195). The speaker appeals to his readers' best instincts, implying that they can make themselves nobler by permitting blacks to display the noble natures they ideally possess as human beings.

THEMATIC critics are interested in the ideas literature expresses or implies, especially any (known as "central themes") that contribute to a work's structure or unity. One theme that obviously helps organize this poem is the contrast between lofty potential and unimpressive reality. This kind of contrast is expressed or implied throughout. The poem is literally argumentative and rhetorical: it seeks to provoke thought and change minds. It does not simply lyrically express personal emotions; it deals with ideas as well as feelings, including ideas of freedom and confinement and the contrast between self-interest and the interests of others. In fact, the poem tries to show that paradoxically, advancing the interests of black people is in the self-interest of America as a whole.

Johnson's poem is obviously relevant to READER-RESPONSE theory because it is quite clearly designed to *provoke* response. It is especially addressed to a particular group: American whites, particularly those with any political power. One can easily imagine a wide variety of possible responses to this work, including sympathy, hostility, and indifference (to mention just a few). Even blacks might respond (and/or might have responded) in different ways. Some might have agreed with the poem's sentiments; others might have considered the work a waste of time because of white racism; others might have seen the poem as too provocative; and still others might have considered it insufficiently angry and assertive. In short, the number and nature of responses would depend, according to reader-response critics, on readers' predispositions. Insofar as it appeals to its readers' better natures, it seems designed to provoke positive responses from the widest range of possible audiences.

DIALOGICAL critics might be interested in Johnson's poem because it is explicitly rhetorical. In other words, it is clearly *addressed* to specific readers and invites a kind of dialogue, as its heavy reliance on questions shows. It rejects an angry tone (which might have repelled some readers) and instead seems open and welcoming. Admittedly, the final line might seem menacing, but the poem implies that if whites ultimately find themselves tangled in metaphorical chains, they will have only themselves to blame. Dialogical critics might also be interested in this work's combination of different kinds of "voices." These include, for instance, voices using conventional or "standard" English, colloquial dialect (as in "'neath" [2]), impassioned speech (as in line 5, with its fragmentary questions), and "poetic" phrasing (as in "fleet" in line 6). Line 2, meanwhile, resembles phrasing from a "negro spiritual." The poem, a dialogical critic might argue, is both shaped by and seeks to shape the attitudes of the whites it addresses, just as it is also influenced by an awareness of potential black readers. In fact, the poem was probably initially read by many more African American readers than by whites, and thus the poem was probably "in dialogue" more with blacks than with any other audience of its time.

MULTICULTURAL critics would be interested in Johnson's poem partly because it explicitly deals with relations between the then-dominant white culture and the then-oppressed black culture in the United States. The need for such a poem would have struck many black readers as quite ironic, since it was published half a century after the American civil war. That war had been fought, ostensibly, to improve the lot of blacks in the United States. One way to read Johnson's poem is as an effort to promote the creation of a common culture that minimized the importance of racial differences. By writing basically in "standard," conventional English (rather than in the colloquial black dialect favored by some poets of his day), Johnson arguably tries to appeal across the lines of racial and cultural difference. This is especially true in line 7, where the speaker offers whites the chance to perceive blacks as "Strong, willing sinews in your wings." This metaphor implies that whites and blacks can ideally be parts of the very same strong body. But line 7 is immediately followed by a darker, more threatening line. That line suggests that if whites fail to act as they should, they may, ironically, find *themselves* enslaved, if only figuratively. The final line makes whites imagine themselves robbed of their freedoms, so that ultimately the poem appeals less to nobble ideals of brotherhood than to simple racial self-interest.

John McCrae (1872–1918): "In Flanders fields"

IN FLANDERS FIELDS

In Flanders fields the poppies blow
Between the crosses, row on row
That mark our place; and in the sky
The larks, still bravely singing, fly
Scarce heard amid the guns below.   [5]
We are the Dead. Short days ago
We lived, felt dawn, saw sunset glow,
Loved and were loved, and now we lie
In Flanders fields.
Take up our quarrel with the foe: [10]
To you from failing hands we throw
The torch; be yours to hold it high.
If ye break faith with us who die
We shall not sleep, though poppies grow
In Flanders fields.   [15]

McCrae's poem would probably have appealed variously to PLATO. Assuming that Plato would have supported the war against Germany as moral and just, it would be hard to ask for a better piece of propaganda. In fact, the poem was enormously popular during its day, and it remains one of the most famous of all poems in support of Britain and her allies. In Canada (McCrae's own country), the poem has achieved iconic status (it is even printed on currency). Although some critics dismiss it, their views would matter little to Plato, who judged literature politically, in terms of its usefulness to the republic. McCrae's poem would have seemed—and actually was—very useful to the Allied cause. It actually did help promote the war effort; it helped make the deaths of Allied soldiers seem purposeful and valuable, and it helped sustain the courage and spirit of the men who survived and the civilians whose support they needed. Supposedly it was written on the battlefield; McCrae was an experienced soldier. He thus would have genuinely known war and could thus (in Plato's view) speak with an authority. This is more the work of a soldier than of a mere poet. It is therefore immune from many of Plato's deepest objections to literature, especially the claim that poets usually speak without really understanding their subjects. Plato would probably also admire the speaker's courage and altruism. The poem is clear in phrasing and meaning, and it appeals to the audience's sense of morality and justice, not merely their emotions. For all these reasons, Plato would probably have valued this work as highly as the Allied governments did.

FORMALIST critics are especially interested in beauty and artistry and their possible absence. Many formalists embrace the standard opinion that McCrae's text is an unsuccessful poem, but others might try to argue that it succeeds. They might begin, for instance, by focusing on such matters as the use of alliteration in lines 1, 2, 4, 7, 8, 9, 11, 12, and 15. Some formalists might argue that the alliteration contributes to the poem's appealing "music" (although dissenters might find the alliteration excessive and intrusive). Defenders of this lyric might also admire its use of assonance in lines 2, 7, 8, 12, and 13, as well as the frequent combination of assonance *and* alliteration, as in lines 2, 8, and 13. Since formalists think memorable sound effects are often crucial to a poem's success, some might praise this work for the sounds it uses.

Formalists might also defend McCrae's poem for using vivid imagery, especially in its first stanza; for becoming employing abstract phrasing as it develops; and for referring to presumably red poppies, thus subtly implying bloody fields that are somehow also beautiful. The natural poppies surround man-made crosses, so that both nature and humans pay a silent tribute to the dead, but while the poppies blow freely, the crosses are rigid and erect. The poppies symbolize natural vitality (in contrast to the dead buried beneath them), while the crosses symbolize eternal spiritual life that transcends mere earthly death. Poppies, associated with narcotics, also symbolize a kind of sleep and rest, and while each season's crop of poppies will die and then be reborn, so, symbolically, have the men buried in the cross-covered graves died and been reborn. Both the crosses and the poppies, then, are paradoxically associated with both life *and* death, and paradoxes especially appeal to formalists, who tend to value complex meanings. Similar complexity appears in the fact that the fields (usually associated with openness, expansiveness, freedom, and vitality) are full of graves (associated with narrow confinement and death). The poppies grow freely; the crosses are arranged in neat, symmetrical rows. Formalists would admire how the poem not only uses images but uses them to contribute to the work's thematic unity.

A formalist analyzing McCrae's poem would ideally examine every single detail to determine how all of them contribute to the work's artistic effectiveness. Formalists might, for instance, particularly admire the irony that the speaker is somehow both alive and dead (another paradox); the surprising, abrupt brevity of stanza two's opening sentence; and the effective use of enjambment (especially in stanza one), which means that although the poem has a predictable rhythm and an obvious rhyme scheme, it still flows freely. Many more details of phrasing, meter, structure, and imagery might be praised by a formalist, but the ones just mentioned suggest how formalists might approach this famous poem.

STRUCTURALIST critics, with their interest in the ways humans use related binary opposites to structure practically everything (including poems), might be intrigued by the sheer number of such opposites here. Thus the fields and poppies seem to symbolize life, while the graves and crosses seem to symbolize death. In the sky, birds sing, while on the ground, guns fire. The living are implicitly contrasted with "the Dead" (6), while an active past (6–8) is contrasted with a static present (8–10). Simply in its first two stanzas, then, the poem is structured around groupings of interconnected opposites. Fields, poppies, life, sky, birds, singing, the living, and an active past are contrasted with graves, crosses, the ground, guns, guns firing, the dead, and a static present. The poem thus seems neatly, almost scientifically structured, although both formalists (with their interest in ironies and paradoxes) and deconstructors (with their interest in irresolvable paradoxes and contradictions) might find this structuralist analysis *too* neat and too simple.

READER-RESPONSE critics could easily imagine a wide variety of possible responses to this poem from numerous possible readers. Many people, when the poem was written, would have known that Britain entered World War I ostensibly to defend Belgium. The fact that Flanders fields are in Belgium, then, would enhance the poem's significance for such readers, although the Belgian location might mean very little to most readers today. For the latter, Flanders fields might simply symbolize any generic battlefield. Some British readers might immediately associate poppies with World War I, whereas many Americans might not make this connection, although most Canadian readers probably would (thanks partly to the popularity of McCrae's poem in Canada). This poem, then, exemplifies how different kinds of readers, in different times and places, are likely to respond differently to the very same stimuli.

Readers especially responsive to McCrae's poem when it was first published would probably have included soldiers, soldiers' loved ones, survivors of dead soldiers, soldiers who had escaped death, and supporters of the war, who would have wanted to see battlefield deaths as meaningful. Christians would probably appreciate the references to crosses; followers of other religions might be bothered by the exclusively Christian emphasis; while atheists might think it unfortunate that any religious symbols are so prominently stressed. Evidence survives that the poem was instantly and strongly popular among McCrae's comrades, who were its first readers and who supposedly saved it when he tossed it away. Yet the poem was rejected when it was first submitted for publication, although when it *was* published, it soon became widely popular. Then, later, its reputation declined, so that today it is remembered mainly because of its historical significance rather than because of its stature as a work of art. In short, McCrae's poem not only *can* be read in significantly different ways by different readers; it actually *has* been variously read.

4

Edward Thomas (1878–1917): "Tears"; "Rain"

TEARS

It seems I have no tears left. They should have fallen—
Their ghosts, if tears have ghosts, did fall—that day
When twenty hounds streamed by me, not yet combed out
But still all equals in their rage of gladness
Upon the scent, made one, like a great dragon   [5]
In Blooming Meadow that bends towards the sun
And once bore hops: and on that other day
When I stepped out from the double-shadowed Tower
Into an April morning, stirring and sweet
And warm. Strange solitude was there and silence.   [10]
A mightier charm than any in the Tower
Possessed the courtyard. They were changing guard,
Soldiers in line, young English countrymen,
Fair-haired and ruddy, in white tunics. Drums
And fifes were playing "The British Grenadiers."   [15]
The men, the music piercing that solitude
And silence, told me truths I had not dreamed
And have forgotten since their beauty passed.

LONGINUS would probably admire this poem for emphasizing noble, powerful emotions rooted in love of beauty, truth, and country. Such emotions contrast with the degraded, materialistic, or selfish passions Longinus despised. The "tears" the speaker now wishes he could weep are associated with sublime feelings, which now seem mostly missing from his life, presumably because the war keeps him from being stirred deeply. Yet desire for deep emotion helps make him admirable. He recalls the joy, vitality, energy, and exultancy he associates with memories of the hounds pursuing their prey. Those vital feelings now seem part of his past, but he ironically recreates them both for himself and for us by creating the present poem. Like the pursuing hounds, people can also be bound together by strong emotions and shared purposes, and memories of such emotions can help inspire and sustain us, especially when those memories are revived through art. The speaker's capacity to remember and be moved by the leaping dogs and marching soldiers suggests his soul's depth and his lofty motives. Like the dogs, the soldiers—glimpsed, apparently, outside the Tower of London—work together as a unit. Their force and energy are disciplined and controlled, making them seem especially admirable. They illustrate the power of music and art to inspire sublime emotions—emotions the speaker explicitly associates with the truth and beauty Longinus loved (17–18).

TRADITIONAL HISTORICAL critics would help readers by supplying various factual details, especially about how these would probably have been perceived in Thomas's day. The poem clearly alludes, for instance, to the English practice of hunting with "hounds" (3), perhaps particularly to hunt foxes. Many people today object to such hunts, seeing them as the cruel pastime of upper-class snobs. A traditional historical critic might comment, however, that during Thomas's day, foxes were widely perceived in the countryside as livestock-killing pests. To feel sympathy for the fox may therefore be anachronistic and sentimental; the speaker, after all, sees the pursuing hounds as beautiful. Some historians have even argued that during Thomas's era foxhunts helped unite members of the upper and lower classes (see Goddard and Martin; Vamplew), and advocates argued that foxhunts helped produce potential members of the cavalry (Underhill, p. 306). Similarities between foxhunters and soldiers have also been stressed by various historians (Colley, p. 190), but a historical critic might find Thomas's statement especially relevant: "I like to see fine horses running at full speed. To see this sight, or hounds running on a good scent, or children dancing, is to me the same as music, and therefore, I suppose, as full of mortality and beauty" (*The Icknield*

Way, p. 104). The best edition of Thomas's poems, in fact, provides similar historical data, especially in one particularly relevant note:

> "White tunics" marks the soldiers' pre-war ceremonial role as custodians of the Tower, but another role seems latent in the image. Guy Cuthbertson calls attention to a passage that Thomas quotes from Richard Jefferies's *The Story of My Heart*: "So subtle is the chord of life that sometimes to watch troops marching in rhythmic order, undulating along the column as the feet are lifted, brings tears in my eyes." (Longley, p. 178)

Traditional historical critics examine the past for solid facts to help make literature more comprehensible.

A FORMALIST might initially note how the brief opening sentence intrigues us, making us want to read further. Its plainness typifies the entire poem's diction. Because the work's phrasing seems unpretentious, we can identify with the speaker and trust him. He frequently interrupts himself, adding detail after detail, as if wanting to be as truthful as possible. Meanwhile, Thomas's effective use of enjambment (only five of eighteen lines end with punctuation) helps give the work strong forward momentum. The brief opening sentence is succeeded by an unusually long one that streams forward like the hounds it describes. The verb "streamed" (3), in fact, is vividly metaphorical, suggesting easy, graceful, speedy movement. Throughout the poem, Thomas emphasizes sensual details of sight, smell, sound, and even touch, as in the implied reference to the speaker's warm skin (10). Alliteration is used effectively (as in "still all equals" [4]), and so are both assonance (as in the way "combed" [3] echoes the double use of "ghosts" [2]) and paradox (as in "rage of gladness" [4]). And, although the poem's lines are unrhymed, much internal rhyme or near-rhyme helps contribute a subtle music. Thus "fallen" is echoed by "fall" and "all" (1–2, 4), "one" by "sun" and "once" (5–7), "day" by "rage," "great," and "day" (2, 4, 5, 7), and so on. Formalists would see all these details, and many more too numerous to mention, as evidence of the work's unity and of the poet's artistic skill.

A MARXIST might condemn foxhunting as an upper-class sport, and so the poem might seem to endorse the life of the rich. The speaker, after all, seems merely a spectator of the hunt, not himself a wealthy, influential participant. Both the dogs and the soldiers can be seen as equally obedient and equally exploited. They merely do as they are told, and the speaker seems unbothered by their blind allegiance. The hounds pursue a frightened, defenseless, usually doomed victim, and the wealthy dog-owners are completely indifferent to the fox's terror and suffering. Another speaker might have challenged, if only implicitly, the power of the rich, but the speaker here seems so focused on his own feelings and on mere formalistic "beauty" that he overlooks the exploitation the poem reveals, almost in spite of itself. The fact that Thomas could create a speaker so naïve and romantic seems all the more ironic since he himself was extremely poor. His interest in a shallow beauty (a Marxist might argue) made him indifferent to advocating the social change that would have benefited him and his entire class. The speaker refers to the Tower of London without ever critiquing it as a symbol of the whole English class system, which had exploited the poor for centuries and which was doing so again by sending men off to fight in an especially senseless war. The soldiers the speaker romanticizes guard a symbol of oppression, and although he calls them "countrymen" (13), that term merely obscures the fact that the English, like people everywhere, were divided by class. Yet these young, mostly poor soldiers are both literally and figuratively "in line" (13): they obey the powers that exploit them. They have succumbed to a brainwashing symbolized both by the music they march to and by the poem itself, which helps perpetuate an unjust system by failing to criticize it. The soldiers play "British" music (15) that implies and encourages their allegiance to a highly exploitative empire.

A PSYCHOANALYTIC critic might approach this poem by noting that tears usually imply strong emotions associated with the subconscious Freudian "id." Tears can imply either intense pleasure or intense pain. Yet this speaker considers himself now incapable of feeling *any* strong emotion. But the poem, paradoxically, expresses and creates the very kinds of intense feelings the speaker both remembers and longs for. The hounds' rapid dashing movement may symbolize the vigor, energy, and vitality that the speaker himself no longer feels. The dogs were full of the strong emotions the speaker remembers and misses. The dogs were united ("made one" [5]), but the speaker now feels psychologically isolated. Jacques Lacan, influenced by Freud, might argue that the speaker yearns for a lost, seemingly irrecoverable wholeness. He once felt connected both to nature (the landscape and the animals) and to other humans (the appealing soldiers), but now he feels alienated from both. The hounds and soldiers symbolize the integration, cooperation, and focus the speaker himself now lacks. To shed tears would at least imply life and the capacity to feel deeply—a capacity he thinks he has presently lost.

RAIN

Rain, midnight rain, nothing but the wild rain
On this bleak hut, and solitude, and me
Remembering again that I shall die
And neither hear the rain nor give it thanks
For washing me cleaner than I have been   [5]
Since I was born into solitude.
Blessed are the dead that the rain rains upon:
But here I pray that none whom once I loved
Is dying tonight or lying still awake
Solitary, listening to the rain,   [10]
Either in pain or thus in sympathy
Helpless among the living and the dead,
Like a cold water among broken reeds,
Myriads of broken reeds all still and stiff,
Like me who have no love which this wild rain   [15]
Has not dissolved except the love of death,
If love it be towards what is perfect and
Cannot, the tempest tells me, disappoint.

ARISTOTLE—or modern Aristotelians—might admire this poem's serious treatment of common human feelings about important common concerns, such as loneliness and death. The poem arouses the tragic feelings of pity and fear—pity for the lonely, suffering speaker and fear of our own vulnerability to loneliness and pain. The poem does not necessarily "purge" us of such emotions, but it does help us understand them. Therefore this text is relevant to a major debate about the meaning of the crucial Aristotelian term *catharsis*. Some translators interpret this word to imply a purging of tragic emotions, but others see it as implying a clarification, or better understanding, of those emotions (Preminger et al., pp. 101–3). The latter interpretation seems the more persuasive, although the former is older and better known. In either case, the poem puts tragic emotions into eloquent, well-structured language that makes them more memorable and thought-provoking.

Clearly Thomas's work results from the deliberate, skilled craftsmanship Aristotle so admired. The key word "rain," for instance, appears repeatedly, both as a noun and a verb. Thus the word "rain" seems as pervasive as rain itself. Moreover, Thomas skillfully employs numerous sound effects (such as the assonance of "rain," "pray," and "pain" in lines 7–8 and 11, the alliteration of line 14, and the repetition of "solitude" in lines 2 and 6, to mention just three examples). He thus satisfies the desire for harmony and rhythm that Aristotle considered a deep human instinct (p. 21), while the constant references to rain, solitude, and death help give the poem the unity Aristotle prized. Death appears at the poem's beginning as something frightening but then appears at the end as something almost appealing. The speaker thus experiences a change accompanied both by an Aristotelian "reversal" of his previous thoughts and an Aristotelian "recognition" of a new kind of truth (p. 26). Moreover, the compassionate speaker seems the "higher" type of human whom Aristotle considered the best subjects of tragedy, while the poet himself seems a "graver spirit" who uses poetry to depict good persons (p. 21). The poem's thought and diction seem appropriate to this speaker; the poem itself is neither too long nor too short; and in these ways and many others, "Rain"—even though it is a lyric poem—satisfies many of Aristotle's requirements for tragic writing.

A THEMATIC critic might note that solitude and death are two key themes of "Tears"; they are openly stated and emphatically repeated. They are also clearly connected; they reinforce one another, especially since death is perhaps the ultimate solitude: it cuts us off from all life. Significantly, the poem does not console us with promises of a happy afterlife. The speaker does use "Blessed" and says he "pray[s]" for others' well-being (7–8), but these religious terms ironically only highlight the relative absence of any kind of religious solace in this poem. The final two lines *might* imply some kind of religious optimism, although that possibility is highly debatable. For that reason alone, thematic critics might admire this work: it not only seems concerned with important *ideas* but also seems designed to provoke thought. We can even read the poem (as a thematic critic might) as teaching various lessons. The poem might imply, for instance, that we should welcome even our darkest hours, since pain can help us perceive life more clearly. Or the poem may suggest that one way to overcome solitude is to contemplate, with sympathy, the solitude of others. Or it may teach that death can seem a source of peace if viewed from the right perspective. However one chooses to interpret this poem, this focus on literature as making or implying arguments is the distinctive feature of thematic criticism.

An ARCHETYPAL critic might note that although rain often symbolizes life and renewal, here it symbolizes darkness, chaos, excess, and discomfort. Almost all humans (an archetypal critic might note) have some experience with excessive rain, which can seem unpleasant and even threatening. This poem, then, arguably taps into various archetypes, including not only our experience with rain in general but with storms and darkness in particular. These are associated with loss of control and with deep instinctual fears. Unwanted isolation (symbolizing vulnerability) is another deeply rooted human fear. Paradoxically, the word "hut" (2) may suggest the presence of other persons (other soldiers, in particular), so that the speaker's isolation may be more psychological than strictly literal. In any case, the poem exploits not only a common human dislike of loneliness but also a common fear of death. This fear is perhaps the most fundamental of all archetypal worries. The poem also plays on various other archetypal emotions, including the desire to be clean; the dislike of feeling dirty; the desire to feel blessed or favored by some greater power; the desire to believe that benevolent higher powers even exist; the fear of pain; the desire for sleep; the fear of helplessness; and, above all, the desire to feel others' love and express love for others. The poem speaks in accessible language about very basic human emotions, and, for both reasons, it would greatly interest archetypal critics.

A STRUCTURALIST might argue that this poem works largely through implication: it emphasizes only one side of a binary structure and thereby implies the opposite side mainly through that side's absence. Thus the poem explicitly emphasizes rain, so that the opposite (dry weather) is only implied. Similar, related binaries, which together help form the poem's core structure, are as follows, with the implied term in square brackets: midnight/[noon]; wild rain/[mild rain]; darkness/[light]; bleakness/[something appealing]; hut/[home]; solitude/[companionship]; death/[life]; silence/[sound]; unable to give thanks/[able to give thanks]; [death in the present or near future]/birth in the past; [lack of blessings]/blessedness; absence of loved ones/[presence of loved ones]; the present (and distance from loved ones)/[the past, and closeness to loved ones]; pain/[pleasure]; helplessness/[strength]; cold water/[water at a comfortable temperature]; broken reeds/[sturdy reeds]; stiffness/[flexibility]; absence of love/[presence of love]; love of death/[love of life]; disappointment/[satisfaction]. In this list, nearly all the terms explicitly mentioned (the ones not inside square brackets) are negative; nearly all the terms merely implied (the ones inside square brackets) are positive. The poem is very clearly structured, then, to emphasize negative experiences. A structuralist could hardly find a better example than "Rain" of how we tend to structure experience—and art—in terms of binary opposites.

An ECOCRITIC might note that Thomas had an especially strong interest in nature. He was far better known in his own lifetime as a writer about nature than as a poet. An ecocritic might further note that rain is mentioned extremely often in memoirs of World War I—a war that exposed soldiers not only to danger from other humans but also, and especially, to bad weather in open trenches. Thomas, of course, does not mention trenches in "Tears." But he does illustrate how the environment can strongly influence thoughts and emotions. The poem exemplifies how we tend to treat nature symbolically. We often place ourselves front and center when discussing or depicting nature. We often treat the environment as merely a backdrop to human self-preoccupations. When Thomas wrote, human power over nature was growing but had not yet become potentially catastrophic, as it is today. In this lyric, nature still seems ultimately in control: nature is permanent while individual human lives are merely fleeting. Significantly, no "supernatural" power (including God) is mentioned. Such powers (arguably invented by humans) are not present to make nature seem wholly benign or comprehensible. Instead, the nature emphasized here is uncontrollable. We can control or alter the landscape; we can control animals and plants; we can depend upon the predictable alteration of night and day; but we have almost no control over (but can merely seek shelter from) rain and storms. The poem thus presents humans at their most vulnerable in dealing with nature.

Eleanor Farjeon (1881–1965): "Now that you too must shortly go the way"

NOW THAT YOU TOO MUST SHORTLY GO THE WAY

Now that you too must shortly go the way
Which in these bloodshot years uncounted men
Have gone in vanishing armies day by day,
And in their numbers will not come again:
I must not strain the moments of our meeting   [5]
Striving each look, each accent, not to miss,
Or question of our parting and our greeting,
Is this the last of all? is this—or this?

Last sight of all it may be with these eyes,
Last touch, last hearing, since eyes, hands, and ears,   [10]
Even serving love, are our mortalities,
And cling to what they own in mortal fears:—
But oh, let end what will, I hold you fast
By immortal love, which has no first or last.

A reader influenced by PLATO might admire how the soldiers
mentioned here perform their duties, and also how the female
speaker supports her dutiful man. She tries to control her emotions
and behave rationally (an attempt Plato would have praised),
and she also seems to assume there is an eternal realm (beyond
this earthly, mortal life) far more important than mere temporal
existence. The speaker demonstrates her morality not only by
supporting her nation's cause but especially by showing her concern
for her loved one. She does not want to upset him or provoke *him*
to feel emotional weakness. Although she begins by mentioning
"bloodshot years" and "vanishing armies" (2–3)—terms that can
seem somewhat emotional—she soon drops such language. Instead,
the poem mostly concerns her efforts to control her emotions,
even as she implies how emotional she feels. She sometimes speaks

emotionally, especially in lines 8 and 13, but in the first case she mimics emotion while saying that she must restrain her feelings, while in the second case she uses emotion to express a positive good that Plato would have admired: genuine love. The poem develops away from a concern with physical closeness and toward a concern with a spiritual bond. Ultimately the body seems less important than the soul—an emphasis Plato would have approved.

A FEMINIST reader might note that poems about World War I by women poets have only recently begun to receive much attention. Part of this new attention has resulted from the rise of feminism as a force in society and in academe. One major purpose of some feminist critics has been precisely to "recover" the work of "lost" women writers such as Farjeon. Some feminists might argue, however, that Farjeon's poem almost inevitably reinforces some of her era's stereotypes about women. The poem presents men as active and women as relatively passive, partly because women were considered too weak, both physically and psychologically, to do any actual fighting. Yet while men were often imagined and presented in this period as protectors of women, in this poem the woman tries, to some degree, to protect her man. She wants to keep her strong emotions under check for his sake. In a sense, she acts "like a man" by not displaying her emotional vulnerability; but she does so partly to avoid provoking vulnerability in *him*. Yet the poem not only relies on stereotypes about women (see especially the emotional "oh" of line 14); it also, inevitably, helps perpetuate and reinforce them. Merely by writing a sonnet (rather than some other, less conventional poem), Farjeon arguably conforms to traditional stereotypes regarding gender and literary genres. During a period when modernist writing (associated mostly with males) was challenging and undermining literary traditions, Farjeon chose to write a sonnet—a "safe" choice for any writer, but especially for a woman.

A DIALOGICAL critic might note that this poem is *literally* dialogical: the speaker overtly addresses another person. As readers, we seem to be eavesdropping. Of course, the poem also engages the reader in dialogue. The person the speaker addresses may or may not be "real," but readers definitely are, and Farjeon had to take their potential reactions into account when writing the sonnet. Readers (according to dialogical critics) help shape literary works because writers almost inevitably consider readers' potential reactions as they write their texts. Even an author who chooses to violate or reject readers' expectations thereby responds to them. Thus, various expectations may have helped shape Farjeon's poem. These (to mention just a few) probably included (1) expectation of a familiar or at least accessible form (such as the sonnet form); (2) expectation of clear and accessible language (which this poem definitely provides); (3) expectation that the poem would conform to conventional political, social, and gender standards (as the poem actually seems to do); and so on. Farjeon conforms to these expectations in practically every way, whether through conscious choice, through influences she did not even think about, or perhaps a bit of both. By speaking conventionally, the poem's speaker encourages readers to speak (and think) conventionally, too. Thus the poem is both influenced by and has influence on potential readers. The relationship between the work and its readers is dialogical.

Even though the male the speaker addresses is silent (or may not even be present), nevertheless *his* expectations also influence what and how she speaks. She must walk a thin emotional line: she must seem sufficiently emotional to let him know she really does love him, but she must not be *so* emotional that she upsets him or seems weak or selfish. Furthermore, Farjeon herself must be sensitive to the expectations of her own audience, especially those who have already lost loved ones in the war. If Farjeon's speaker had seemed concerned only with the welfare of one particular man, she might seem repulsively self-centered. There are, then, a multitude of real or implied participants in the "dialogue" this poem embodies, including, of course, previous sonnet writers, who helped shape both the form and the expectations readers bring to their reading of sonnets. Farjeon was also inevitably engaged in dialogue with other poets of her time. Thus her choice of a relatively conventional form may imply either a rejection of modernism or perhaps an unawareness of its growing influence.

A POSTMODERNIST might argue that the speaker implies, accepts, and implicitly restates various "grand narratives": broad, simplistic explanations that impose order on life's real complexities and incoherences. These monolithic, totalizing ways of thinking almost inevitably limit freedoms and eliminate options—reason enough to make postmodernists resist them. The speaker assumes that the male soldier simply "must" head off to war (1), and in one sense she is right: he might be punished if he refused to serve. This, however, is one way grand narratives work: through force and coercion, whether subtle or direct. Patriotism, for instance, may seem natural when it is merely a social construct. Ironically, a war that involved conflict among competing grand narratives ultimately resulted in the destruction of several, including the narratives that helped sustain (and were imposed by) the German, Russian, and Austro-Hungarian empires. In her choices of social values, poetic form, gender behavior, and in most other ways, this poem's speaker succumbs to conservative pressures. Her choices, in other words, are not really free at all. In any number of ways, neither the speaker nor her creator seems to think or act independently, and so this poem would not be considered "postmodernist" in any meaningful sense.

Whereas postmodernists might see the heterosexual relationship this poem depicts as merely one among many possible choices, a DARWINIAN might instead argue that heterosexuality is (for humans at least) a biological norm essential for humanity's continued existence. In fact, both the male and the female in this poem behave precisely as a Darwinian might predict. Men, in general, are physically stronger than women, and therefore men have almost always been fighters and soldiers, with women playing (as in this poem) more passive roles. Among most animals, too, males fight other males, often in competition for females. However, because it takes years for human offspring to mature, women usually favor mates who will make reliable commitments to long-term relationships—relationships of the sort this poem implies. Farjeon's female speaker seems committed to the man she addresses and seems to assume that he (if he survives) will remain committed to her. He also seems, in other ways, the kind of man who might appeal to most women, at least according to Darwinian predictions: presumably he is strong enough to serve in the military, and, if he volunteered for service, then presumably he is also courageous. For these two reasons alone he might make a good, protective husband and father. Yet the poem never mentions children, and if he were to die before passing on his genes, his death would strike most Darwinians as especially wasteful. The female speaker alludes, idealistically, to their "immortal love" (14), but from a Darwinian perspective the only real form of immortality is genetic.

5

Margaret Sackville (1881–1963): "A memory"

A MEMORY

There was no sound at all, no crying in the village,
 Nothing you would count as sound, that is, after
 the shells;
Only behind a wall the low sobbing of women,
 The creaking of a door, a lost dog—nothing else.

Silence which might be felt, no pity in the silence,   [5]
 Horrible, soft like blood, down all the blood-stained
 ways;
In the middle of the street two corpses lie unburied,
 And a bayoneted woman stares in the market-place.

Humble and ruined folk—for these no pride of conquest,
 Their only prayer: "O Lord, give us our
 daily bread!"   [10]
Not by the battle fires, the shrapnel are we haunted;
 Who shall deliver us from the memory of these dead?

A critic influenced by HORACE might praise this poem for various
reasons, including its simple, clear phrasing (pp. 51–2), the ways
it mixes fiction with truth (p. 53), the ways it begins by plunging
us into the midst of things (*in medias res* [p. 53]); and its general
lack of inconsistencies. The poem is also written in a style anyone
might hope to achieve (p. 55); all its parts are carefully integrated

(p. 55); and it skillfully uses meter (as, for example, in the ways "low sob" and "lost dog" are metrically emphasized in lines 3–4). Horace might, however, find its descriptions of brutalities excessive, especially in lines 7–8, and he might worry that such excess could offend some readers (p. 55). But he might admire how the poem is unified both in its themes (such as silence, nothingness, blood, humility, and death) and in its careful use of repetition.

TRADITIONAL HISTORICAL critics might approach this poem by asking specific historical questions. They might wonder, for instance, how World War I compared to previous conflicts in the number and nature of civilian casualties. They might want to know how common it actually was for civilians in general—and women in particular—to be bayoneted, and what possible justification there could have been for such behavior if it did indeed occur. (In some cases, Germans suspected enemy civilians of being guerillas or of offering other kinds of secret resistance.) Traditional historical critics might wonder whether civilian casualties were caused disproportionately by one side or the other and, if so, why. In short, such critics would be interested in any hard, factual information that might help us interpret the poem. Yet discovering such information about civilian casualties is exceptionally difficult, for reasons Lance Janda explains (pp. 444–6). For most countries, accurate numbers of such casualties are unknown, although Janda notes that in France civilian losses were "heavy" (p. 445). A traditional historical critic would not be surprised, however, to learn that Margaret Sackville was a pacifist who strongly opposed the war (Khan, p. 31), as this poem itself clearly suggests. Yet it is easy to imagine how this poem could ironically have been used by war supporters as anti-German propaganda.

FEMINIST readers might be especially interested in this poem's unusual focus on women as the victims of war. Most depictions of the war—at the time and also since then—focus on male casualties. Women have usually been presented as somewhat distant (both literally and psychologically) from the actual deaths the war produced; Sackville's poem, in contrast, strongly emphasizes a female victim. At first, the poem describes women as "sobbing" in a somewhat stereotypical way (3); later, however, we see one woman who has died in an especially brutal manner, almost in a kind of symbolic rape (8). Presumably this victim, whose corpse lies in the "market-place" (8), was going about the stereotypical business of a woman at the time (grocery shopping) when she was killed. Nothing suggests that she was a combatant. The fact that she died from a bayonet thrust, rather than being killed, say, by an artillery shell, makes her death seem especially vicious. Yet Sackville does not present this death in excessively sentimental terms, as many readers might have expected a woman poet of the time to do. Instead, Sackville shows stereotypically "male" restraint, reminding us that although women usually have nothing to do with starting wars, they are quite often victims of them, both directly and indirectly. A woman poet describes a female victim in a poem that resists the sentimentality often associated, at the time, with writings by women authors.

A DECONSTRUCTIVE critic might emphasize all the potential contradictions, paradoxes, and instabilities the poem manifests. For example, although the poem may have been intended to protest war, it could easily have been used as anti-German propaganda and thus might actually have led to continued conflict. Similarly, although the prayer quoted in line 10 might suggest deep Christian faith, the events the poem describes might easily lead some readers to doubt the very existence of a loving, protective God. Thus a poem perhaps intended to promote confidence in God might, for some readers, undermine such confidence. Whatever Sackville's intentions may have been in writing line 10, her intentions (a deconstructor would say) cannot control how line 10 might be interpreted. Line 12, in fact, might easily be read as further undermining our sense of God's power, whether or not such irony was at all intentional. For deconstructors, an author's intentions cannot determine how a text is read, and this poem, like all texts, is potentially open to radically different readings, so that its "real" meaning seems ultimately impossible to pin down.

A NEW HISTORICIST critic might call attention to the ways this poem differs from many previous poems about war. By emphasizing civilian (and civilian women) casualties, the poem focuses on groups usually "marginalized" or overlooked in writings about war. Most conventional histories of war from Sackville's era focused on male soldiers, particularly prominent males such as generals, admirals, and other commanding officers. Sackville's poem, written when democracy was becoming increasingly influential, both reflects and contributes to this democratizing process. In an era of growing calls for women's rights (especially the right to vote), Sackville's poem reminded its readers that women, too, were often war's victims. In an era of growing emphasis on rights for the poor and the middle classes, Sackville's poem emphasized that such persons were themselves often affected by war, not only by being drafted as soldiers but simply while going about their daily lives as civilians. The poem both implies and reflects complex power relationships. It was written by an aristocratic woman who displays her sympathies for the poor; it was written by a woman who had an affair with Ramsay MacDonald (an influential leader of the British Labour Party), whose antiwar views led at first to political defeat before he later became prime minister; and it was written by a woman whose Catholicism made her reluctant to marry the Presbyterian MacDonald. As a pacifist, woman, and Catholic, Sackville was a member of three relatively powerless groups in the British society of her time, while as an aristocrat, writer, and lover of a powerful man, she enjoyed unusual prominence. Both her life and her poem reflect the complexities of her social standing—complexities that would definitely interest any new historicist.

Sara Teasdale (1884–1933): "There will come soft rains"

THERE WILL COME SOFT RAINS

There will come soft rains and the smell of the ground,
And swallows circling with their shimmering sound;

And frogs in the pools singing at night,
And wild plum trees in tremulous white;

Robins will wear their feathery fire,   [5]
Whistling their whims on a low fence-wire;

And not one will know of the war, not one
Will care at last when it is done.

Not one would mind, neither bird nor tree,
If mankind perished utterly;   [10]

And Spring herself, when she woke at dawn
Would scarcely know that we were gone.

A reader influenced by LONGINUS would probably admire this poem's emphasis on nature as a source of elevation, inspiration, and beauty. The poem implies the loftiness or sublimity not only of the speaker and landscape but also of the reader capable of appreciating sublimity. Although the poem implies that humans destroy beauty by making war, the speaker also shows that only humans can fully appreciate nature's beauty by articulating and celebrating it. Ironically, humans are not only uniquely capable of perceiving and appreciating the sublime but are also uniquely capable of destroying it.

By personifying Spring, Teasdale treats it almost as if it were human or a kind of goddess. The poem celebrates nature, but it also implicitly pleads with humans to respect nature and thus exemplify their own beauty and loftiness. Anaphora (in the repeated use of "And") contributes to the poem's chant-like, emotional, and compelling rhythm, so that the work both implies and evokes strong feelings. Just as Longinus's treatise *On the Sublime* ultimately condemns humans who fall short of their full spiritual potential—or who ignore or reject that potential altogether—so Teasdale's poem implies the same kind of condemnation. Her poem, however, is all the more effective for being so understated, especially since the idea of the total extinction of humanity is so powerful partly because it is so surprising.

An ARCHETYPAL critic might note that practically all the details mentioned until line 7 are associated with vitality and with the pleasant aspects of life and nature. The poem almost depicts a kind of paradise. Until line 7, it presents nature as man's comfortable home, providing both nourishment and beauty. Everything seems balanced; there is no hint of unappealing excess. All the traditional aspects of nature—air, water, earth, and sky—seem in harmony, and the coming of the seasons seems part of the predictable, reassuring rhythm of life. In short, the poem appeals to many of our deepest archetypal instincts about what is desirable in life, and then it suddenly deals with perhaps the greatest of all archetypal fears— fear of death. In this case that fear involves not merely the deaths of individuals but of the whole human race. Yet the poem implies that nature might be better off if humans disappeared. Humans are presented as the disruptive, destructive force on a planet that might seem Edenic if we were absent. Ironically, the poem appeals to archetypal human instincts in a way that makes us almost wish that humans did not exist.

A FEMINIST critic might note that Teasdale was and is a generally admired woman poet. She helped contribute to a feminine literary tradition and is still an important representative figure. Her poem—with its initially pleasant lyricism—might at first seem a stereotypically "feminine" work of her era (the kind of work one might "expect a woman to write"), but the ironic sting of its second half undercuts that impression. Yet Teasdale does present Spring in feminine terms, almost as a female goddess. Spring is depicted as a source of life, nurture, and nourishment and is implicitly associated with those stereotypical traits of human females. One can read the poem, in fact, as an implied feminine protest against the destructiveness (especially war) caused by men. It does not seem accidental that Teasdale refers to destructive humans as "mankind"

(10). The word "people" would have fit the poem's meter just as well and would even have alliterated with "perished." Yet despite the poem's irony and sarcasm, many readers may still find it too soft, too tame, and thus too stereotypically "feminine" in the old-fashioned senses of that word.

An ECOCRITIC might note that in the early twentieth century, the idea that humans might indeed be extinguished from the earth probably would have seemed merely figurative and imaginative. It might have seemed simply a bit of poetic exaggeration. Today, however, the idea of literal human extinction strikes many as a very realistic possibility, whether from atomic warfare, biological warfare, or some other catastrophe caused by humans themselves. This change in the way we are now likely to read the poem illustrates the relevance of historical criticism (since the same words can have different significances for different generations). But the poem also seems highly relevant to ecocriticism, since it implies that earth might be better without humans. Yet the poem can also be read by ecocritics as too optimistic: it suggests that nature would survive a catastrophe wrought by humans, even though it is entirely possible that such a catastrophe (especially a so-called nuclear winter) might also destroy almost all life on earth. In any case, ecocritics might argue that war, in its destructiveness, is merely an exaggerated version of how humans generally interact with the planet and with other forms of life. The poem can imply that in general we need to be better stewards of nature, even if we somehow manage to avoid actual war.

DARWINIAN critics resemble ecocritics in the sense that both kinds of theorists emphasize humanity's relationship with the natural environment and with other species. Darwinian critics, moreover, would not be at all surprised by the idea of mass extinctions of species on a global scale, since such events have of course occurred previously on our planet. Yet those earlier extinctions resulted from natural events (such as asteroid impacts, the coming of ice ages, or other sudden climate changes) rather than from deliberate behavior. Only humans, ironically, have evolved fully enough to potentially destroy themselves and most other life on earth. But this also means that only humans have developed fully enough to prevent such destruction if they choose to do so.

Some Darwinian critics might find Teasdale's poem romantically naïve, since it emphasizes only aspects of nature that seem appealing and comforting to humans. Nothing here implies anything about "nature red in tooth and claw," but the poem does imply—especially in its emphasis on birdsong and the bright colors of plants and animals—a basic Darwinian assumption: that the fundamental impulse of all living things is to reproduce. Other creatures, of course, do kill to survive, and perhaps some (one thinks of certain insects) even engage in something resembling wars. Only humans, however, have evolved to the point that our wars could potentially lead to our own extinction. Teasdale's poem attempts to use human intelligence to make such an outcome less likely. She seems undeniably correct, however, in assuming that if humans ever did disappear, the basic natural processes of sex and reproduction would go blissfully on without us.

6

Siegfried Sassoon (1886–1967): "They"; "The rear-guard"; "The glory of women"; "Atrocities"

THEY

The Bishop tells us: "When the boys come back
"They will not be the same; for they'll have fought
"In a just cause: they lead the last attack
"On Anti-Christ; their comrades' blood has bought
"New right to breed an honourable race,   [5]
"They have challenged Death and dared him face to face."

 "We're none of us the same!" the boys reply.
"For George lost both his legs; and Bill's stone blind;
"Poor Jim's shot through the lungs and like to die;
"And Bert's gone syphilitic: you'll not find   [10]
"A chap who's served that hasn't found *some* change."
And the Bishop said: "The ways of God are strange!"

A reader influenced by HORACE might be troubled by this poem, since it is not safely conservative or conventional, particularly in its "message." It might potentially offend various readers, including civilians, religious persons, and especially the religious hierarchy. It does try to teach a lesson (an objective Horace favored), but it does so not by pleasing its audience, as Horace would prefer, but instead by shocking and even mocking them. Horace *would* probably admire the poem's simplicity, unity, and craftsmanship (as in the way the first stanza is devoted to the bishop and the second to the soldiers, and in the way the poem both opens and closes with the bishop speaking). And Horace might also admire how Sassoon skillfully mimics two different styles of speech and assigns each one to the appropriate characters, thus demonstrating "decorum" (pp. 51–3). The resulting lyric is clear and straightforward and could thus be read and understood by practically anyone. Sassoon has obviously chosen a topic within his powers (as Horace advises writers to do [p. 51]), and the final line of the poem gives novelty to a familiar phrase by means of a skillful setting (p. 52). Nothing about the poem's language seems outdated (p. 52); the work exhibits consistency (p. 53); and it mixes fiction with truth by presenting invented characters who nevertheless function as typical, representative imitations of real human beings (p. 53). The details mentioned in stanza two are gruesome but are not excessively emphasized (p. 54), and nothing in this work might make the poet seem laughable or ridiculous (the fate Horace fears the most for the young poets he advises). In all these ways, then, the poem satisfies many of Horace's criteria for a good poem. Only in its potential offensiveness might it risk his disapproval.

A MARXIST would probably greatly admire this poem. Since Marx considered religion the "opiate of the masses," the poem's mockery of religious justifications of the war would surely please a Marxist. Marxists believe(d) that this war, like most wars, benefited only the elites who profited from them. The war was another way capitalists exploited workers, and the church—which in England was officially connected with the state—helped promote and justify such exploitation. Humble, individual priests often served heroically alongside soldiers in the trenches and were often deeply respected. It is not surprising, therefore, that Sassoon makes a *bishop* the spokesman for an especially fatuous, hypocritical sort of Christianity. Bishops, by definition, were themselves members of the European ruling elite. Of course, one great paradox of World War I was that elite churchmen often justified the war by proclaiming that it was *their* nation, rather than their Christian enemies, that was truly fighting for God. The war was not only a conflict between

Europeans but between different national churches. The poor and weak suffered the most, while people such as bishops rarely suffered at all (at least according to Marxists). The men mentioned in stanza two are clearly not aristocrats or wealthy. They are almost certainly members of the exploited classes, who always suffer the most from wars, whether as soldiers or civilians. Of course, one great irony of the war was that it eventually weakened and/or destroyed most of the exploitative regimes who hoped to benefit from it, especially in Russia, Germany, and Austria-Hungary. And, at least in the case of Russia, the war also essentially destroyed the power of the Russian Orthodox Church, which soon found itself under the thumb of Soviet Marxism.

DIALOGICAL critics might note that Sassoon's poem is quite literally dialogical: it features more than one "voice," and the second stanza is an explicit "reply" to the first (7). Of course, the poem's speaker is yet another voice, as is the implied voice of the poet, who created all three other voices. The poem, moreover, addresses readers and is shaped by their various possible responses—responses that might have been negative from some Christians (but not all) and positive from atheists or agnostics. Finally, the text concludes with the bishop alluding either to the Bible itself or to a common interpretation of various biblical passages. His precise phrasing ("The ways of God are strange" [12]) seems to echo Robert Louis Stevenson's poem beginning "Strange are the ways of men, / And strange the ways of God." In short, Sassoon's poem features or implies numerous voices, all in a kind of complex, even intertextual dialogue.

Ironically, the bishop does not even attempt real dialogue; he merely "tells" what he thinks, and he takes an entire stanza to do so (1), unlike the individual men, who somehow speak collectively, as if one speaks for all. Although the bishop has literally the first and last quoted word, his final comment again does not really engage the men in any genuine dialogue; instead, he ends with a trite cliché—voicing words that are somehow his but not deeply his; instead, they are almost proverbial. The poem can be read as a kind of challenge to the voices of the imagined bishop, to any real bishops and other church figures who resembled him, to the church as an institution, to individual Christians who accepted such views, and to individual Christians who opposed the war in insufficiently vocal or forceful ways.

The bishop speaks in bland generalities; the "boys" (7) speak by referring to real, specific facts. The poem "speaks for" the common soldiers of the war. It gives their imagined voices a prominence they would otherwise lack. The ways the two main voices speak are significant, as in the Bishop's chummy use of "boys" (1), his naïve use of the cliché in the first half of line 2, his adoption of official church rhetoric in lines 3–4, and even his adoption of conventional militaristic rhetoric in line 6. In that line, it is almost as if he is trying to sound like a military officer. The bishop, however, is just a talker; he has no real personal experience with the things he merely talks about. In contrast, the "boys" speak in a collective voice; they deal with grim specifics, not abstract platitudes. Their tone is familiar, colloquial, unsophisticated, and unpretentious. They are brutally honest, as when referring to Bert (10). Yet the boys do not seem bitter, accusatory, or angry, although anger and contempt may be implied by the poet or speaker. The bishop concludes with a trite cliché that ironically exposes the limitations of such language.

The first stanza of Sassoon's poem shows the inevitable limits involved in trying to speak for others rather than letting them speak for themselves; in this sense, both the speaker of the poem and the poet himself are unlike the bishop. The poet and speaker give the common soldiers a voice and let them speak for themselves. The bishop ends with a cliché that in this context seems highly ironic: its trite language is subverted by the rest of stanza two. The bishop is here speaking words that are not even really his, even though he speaks them. His words are official church rhetoric, for which he is merely the mouthpiece. Is there, perhaps, any suggestion that he begins to intuit their inadequacy? Does he begin to doubt the platitudes he mouths? For dialogical critics, the best literary works are full of possibilities because they contain more voices than merely one.

NEW HISTORICIST critics might argue that traditional histories of World War I (and of wars in general) have often paid less attention to "marginal" voices than this poem does. In Sassoon's text, common soldiers are not merely talked *about* but are given a chance to speak for themselves. In this way, the poem reflects the historical fact that World War I saw an enormous proliferation of war poetry and other kinds of war writing done by actual common soldiers. British newspapers and magazines were flooded with submissions of war poetry composed by fighting men. Eventually some periodicals felt overwhelmed and even discouraged further submissions. Ironically, much of the verse was highly conventional, predictable, and patriotic (as if the soldiers' "discourse" had been shaped *for* them by the larger culture). Yet the mere fact that so many participants were writing and submitting poetry would seem, to a new historicist, historically significant. That fact implies the growing democratization of British culture. More and more people were able to read and write and felt entitled to express themselves.

The war itself promoted democratization. Sassoon's poem, written by a member of the upper class, expresses real sympathy and understanding for men much lower in the social scale—men with whom Sassoon, as a brave officer, had come to share mutual respect. The poem, moreover, may be partly rooted in Sassoon's sense of his own limited power: as a homosexual with Jewish ancestry, Sassoon, although from a wealthy, educated background, embodied many complexities of English society at his time. In one sense a member of the ruling class, he was in other senses a deeply marginal figure and could thus "relate" to other such figures, such as the "boys" in this poem. Although plentiful in their sheer numbers, such people were still relatively powerless politically. Yet their power was growing and would continue to grow, and Sassoon's poem not only lets them speak but also, thereby, contributes to their increasing assertiveness. Bishops' voices were mattering less and less.

POSTMODERNIST critics might argue that the bishop voices a grand religious narrative that claims to make sense of literally everything. The very word "bishop" literally means "overseer": he watches over the church, but he is also merely an observer of—rather than a real participant in—the war. As a senior churchman, he is supposed to see the "big picture" of all of existence and be able to explain it clearly, but his concluding comment is almost pre-postmodern in its inconclusiveness. Meanwhile, in stanza two, Sassoon lets common soldiers speak for themselves and (thereby) implicitly challenge the grand narrative that the bishop accepts, supports, and voices. The painful details they mention complicate and undercut the bishop's blithe optimism. They offer "local" narratives, concerned with individual facts that are difficult to integrate into the grand story the bishop tries to tell.

The bishop speaks of "the boys" in general; the boys themselves respond with particular names and specific instances, although those instances are also variously representative. The fates of George, Jim, Bill, and Bert have also befallen countless others. The bishop speaks *of* others; in Sassoon's poem, the others speak for themselves, thereby complicating and undermining the bishop's grand narrative. Various phrases used by the bishop are especially susceptible to postmodern skepticism. Thus the words "just cause" would mean one thing to the rulers of England and another to the rulers of Germany: identical words have diametrically opposite meanings, so that the language the bishop uses seems, in typically postmodern fashion, slippery in more ways than one. Ultimately the bishop tries to impose yet another grand narrative, but this new narrative is at least as inadequate as the first.

THE REAR-GUARD

Groping along the tunnel, step by step,
He winked his prying torch with patching glare
From side to side, and sniffed the unwholesome air.

Tins, boxes, bottles, shapes too vague to know,
A mirror smashed, the mattress from a bed;   [5]
And he, exploring fifty feet below
The rosy gloom of battle overhead.

Tripping, he grabbed the wall; saw someone lie
Humped at his feet, half-hidden by a rug,
And stooped to give the sleeper's arm a tug.   [10]
"I'm looking for headquarters." No reply.
"God blast your neck!" (For days he'd had no sleep.)
"Get up and guide me through this stinking place."
Savage, he kicked a soft, unanswering heap,
And flashed his beam across the livid face   [15]
Terribly glaring up, whose eyes yet wore
Agony dying hard ten days before;
And fists of fingers clutched a blackening wound.
Alone he staggered on until he found
Dawn's ghost that filtered down a shafted stair   [20]
To the dazed, muttering creatures underground
Who hear the boom of shells in muffled sound.
At last, with sweat of horror in his hair,
He climbed through darkness to the twilight air,
Unloading hell behind him step by step.   [25]

A critic influenced by ARISTOTLE might first want to determine this poem's genre—the "kind" of work it is. Aristotle believed that literary works are inevitably certain *kinds* of work, such as tragedy, comedy, epic, and the like. His own *Poetics* focuses mainly on tragedy, although he mentions comedy and epic in passing. Tragedy (he says) emphasizes central characters who are morally better than most people, while comedy deals with people who are of a lower type than most persons (p. 20). Sassoon's poem, although technically a lyric, seems, despite its relative brevity, to exhibit many traits that Aristotle associated with epic. It is a third-person narrative; it deals with war; its lines are relatively long; its stanzas are not regular in numbers of lines; and it deals with human beings who are neither better nor worse than average. Its tone is serious, and its details are grimly realistic (pp. 35–6). Indeed, part of Sassoon's purpose in writing such poetry must have been to help his audience learn through his literary imitation of a coherent, unified "action," and his imitation of that action does give us a kind of unexpected pleasure, despite the horrific details of the description (p. 21). Sassoon has created a character appropriate to the kind of "plot" the poem presents, and the poem itself has a high degree of unity, with a clear beginning, middle, and end. It begins by jumping into the midst of things (*in medias res*); it provides the pleasures associated with a skillful use of meter; and it also offers a complex plot involving both reversal and recognition, especially in lines 15–18. The poem uses a specific, particular action to illustrate general, universal truths. In all these ways, Sassoon's lyric—although not a tragedy in the strict Aristotelian sense—exhibits many of the elements that Aristotle associated with successful tragic writing.

A TRADITIONAL HISTORICAL critic might want to discuss the poem by exploring the use of tunnels during World War I. Although tunnels had been used in previous conflicts, they were especially common—and unusually massive—during World War I. Partly, of course, this was due to the development of industrial machines and techniques, which made tunneling far easier than in the past. Some tunnels, which were used for shelter and storage, were enormous, although most, obviously, were not. Smaller tunnels were sometimes dug directly beneath enemy positions; they were then filled with explosives which, when detonated, not only literally undermined the enemy but killed many thousands all at once. (In the Battle of Messines, nineteen British mines abruptly destroyed roughly 10,000 German soldiers.) Sassoon's depiction of a tunnel is thus historically realistic, as is his use of the word "torch" (2) to designate what most American readers, at least, would today call a "flashlight." Perhaps the poem's most surprising aspect, from the perspective of a historical critic, is the exclamation "God blast your neck!" (12), which might sound like a common British oath. If Google Books can be trusted, "God blast your [fill in favorite word, often 'soul']" was not an uncommon phrase, but "God blast your neck" is apparently Sassoon's own invention. However, descriptions of coming across corpses are quite common in memoirs of World War I, so that the incident depicted in this poem has a real basis in solid historical fact.

An ARCHETYPAL critic, concerned with fundamental, widely shared responses deeply rooted in a basic "human nature," might argue that this poem exploits very common human fears. These include not only the fear of pain and death but also the fears of vulnerability and loss of control. The latter can be manifested in very simple fears of losing balance, tripping, and falling. The poem also exploits common human fears of hidden danger, of darkness, of being trapped and confined, and of chaos and uncertainty. It additionally suggests an almost universal dislike of bad smells, especially the smell of dead, decaying flesh. Yet the poem also implies other common, deep-seated reactions, such as anger at being ignored by a person whom one has directly questioned; frustration with disobedience from subordinates; an archetypal impulse to curse when frustrated; a fundamental need for sleep, and frustration when sleep is long delayed or denied; and frustration with the sense of losing control of one's body, environment, and/ or mind. Sassoon's poem, an archetypal critic might contend, is immensely effective not only because it alludes to all these various fears and frustrations but especially because it compounds and combines them.

A STRUCTURALIST critic, concerned with the binary opposites by which humans structure existence, might note the numerous binaries (stated or implied) that help structure Sassoon's poem. These include life versus death, light versus darkness, sight versus blindness, and ease of movement versus difficult movement. They also include good smells versus bad smells, order versus chaos, wholeness versus brokenness, and steadiness versus unsteadiness. Yet the list can easily be lengthened to include control versus lack of control, authority versus absence of authority, freedom from pain versus pain, speech versus silence, health versus injury, and companionship versus loneliness. All the terms mentioned first in each of the pairings just listed are positive; all the terms mentioned second in the pairings are negative. The existence in Sassoon's poem of these underlying, reinforcing patterns would not surprise structuralists because structuralists believe that humans almost inevitably impose such structures on every aspect of their lives. Thus, life is to death as light is to darkness, and so on. The patterns underlying Sassoon's poem resemble similar (or even identical) structures underlying many other examples of the ordering of experience by human thought. Studying such interlocking opposites can help us understand how we tend to think by imposing structures, while studying common structural patterns can help us perceive how particular aspects of culture (such as Sassoon's poem) achieve coherence and meaning.

A critic influenced by DECONSTRUCTION might examine all the binary opposites just discussed and then try to "deconstruct" them—that is, try to show how they blend and bleed into one another, how they are far less stable than they seem. The opposition between life and death, for instance, can be deconstructed by arguing that the poem's central character is living a kind of metaphorical death as he moves through the tunnel. Although death is often imagined as the worst that can happen to a living thing, in a sense the speaker's condition—confused, frustrated, suffering, terrified, and conscious of it all—may indeed be worse than death. On the other hand, one could argue that life is better than death in even the most trying circumstances, since life at least implies potential for improvement. Thus any clear distinction between life and death breaks down or is deconstructed. Although the two concepts help define one another (since they seem to be obvious opposites), no hard-and-fast distinction between them can be maintained. Similarly, the tunnel itself is fundamentally ambiguous. On the one hand it is relatively safe—preferable, in some ways, to aboveground battlefields with their whistling bullets and exploding shells. On the other hand, it resembles a grave or tomb and cannot offer complete protection, as the existence of the corpse 50 feet below ground clearly shows. And, no matter how much protection the tunnel may sometimes provide, that protection can only be temporary: as the poem's final lines suggest, emergence from the tunnel is inevitably necessary.

Thus any clear distinction between aboveground and belowground cannot be maintained.

THE GLORY OF WOMEN

You love us when we're heroes, home on leave,
Or wounded in a mentionable place.
You worship decorations; you believe
That chivalry redeems the war's disgrace.
You make us shells. You listen with delight,   [5]
By tales of dirt and danger fondly thrilled.
You crown our distant ardours while we fight,
And mourn our laurelled memories when we're killed.
You can't believe that British troops "retire"
When hell's last horror breaks them, and they run,   [10]
Trampling the terrible corpses—blind with blood.
O German mother dreaming by the fire,
While you are knitting socks to send your son
His face is trodden deeper in the mud.

If one assumes that PLATO would have supported the British cause in World War I (a big assumption), one can easily imagine him objecting to this poem for various reasons. Because Plato believed that literature should serve the best interests of the state, he might, in the first place, argue that poems like this could weaken the war effort and thus expose the nation to danger and destruction. Such poems could damage national unity among civilians and promote fear and self-concern in soldiers, who should ideally offer themselves in selfless sacrifice and serve the best interests of their nation. Plato might also argue that although the poem implies that women are emotional and irrational, it is itself guilty of these same traits—traits he would have regarded as major flaws. In Book 3 of *The Republic*, Socrates (Plato's spokesman) praises courage and criticizes fear of death. He argues that a good man should "not consider death terrible to any other good man who is his comrade." He contends that the loss of a son or brother who fights for a good cause is not to be regretted and says that women, not men, can be left to mourn such losses (Preminger et al., p. 50). Young soldiers, he felt, should be temperate: they should obey their commanders and be in command of themselves (Preminger et al., p. 52). Plato, therefore, would arguably have had little sympathy for Sassoon's poem. In any case, he would have been concerned above all with the *message* it conveys rather than with its technical features or artistry.

THEMATIC critics, concerned primarily with the ideas literature conveys, might see in this poem a general tendency of Sassoon's later war poetry. By 1917 he strongly opposed the war. He felt it was being waged, by both sides, to win wealth, land, and power, not freedom. This poem is, therefore, an implied argument, interesting mainly for the claims it suggests rather than the way those claims are phrased. In fact, one criticism of Sassoon's poems is that they are *too* argumentative, too propagandistic, and therefore often unsubtle and insufficiently complex. Sassoon would have justified such poems by asserting that arguments against the war were needed: both soldiers and civilians were suffering and dying wastefully and pointlessly. British civilians needed to hear the truth, not official lies. By accusing women of naive and even callous attitudes, Sassoon seeks to influence half the British population (although, in the process, he also risks offending them). Overtly and implicitly, the poem explores such themes as the nature of true patriotism, the nature of true concern for others, and the contrast between naïve ideals and grim realities. The poem's "message" is fairly obvious, although the concluding sympathy for German mothers adds effective surprise. One theme of the poem would thus seem to be that women on both sides suffer *from* the war by supporting the war.

PSYCHOANLYTIC critics are often interested in tensions between the id (the seat of emotions), the ego (the seat of reason), and the superego (the seat of conscience or morality). A psychoanalytic critic might therefore see Sassoon's poem as strongly expressing the speaker's id but perhaps also as expressing his superego as well. The poem also tries to appeal both to the audience's feelings and to their ethics. In a way, it tries to shame its readers, especially women, by implying that they are at best naïve and at worst unethical. The speaker indeed suggests that female supporters of the war have succumbed to their ids; they seek selfish pleasures, especially when they "listen with delight, / By tales of dirt and danger fondly thrilled" (5–6). As the poem develops, its own expressions of emotion become increasingly overt. At first, for instance, it mimics the genteel restraint of the women it addresses by referring politely (if ironically) to men "wounded in a mentionable place" (2). But lines 10–14 (especially 14) are overtly emotional, expressing the speaker's id while arousing the ids of readers.

A psychoanalytic critic might also be interested in exploring the poem's sexual dimensions. Sexuality is already suggested by the allusion to wounds in "mentionable" places' (2), but the whole poem can be read as an implied critique of heterosexual women by Sassoon, who was himself a homosexual. The poem may express his frustration with the relatively privileged position such women enjoyed: they could support wars without risking any real physical dangers themselves. Their love and concern for soldiers could seem shallow compared to the real risks Sassoon was facing, not only on the battlefield (he was a very heroic soldier) but also simply by publishing poems like this one. His poem might be read, by a psychoanalytic critic, as partly fueled by his disgust with the maiming and death of selfless young men while women sat by as relatively safe (and often uniformed) spectators. It is as if, especially in the final lines, he means to give his readers (especially females) nightmares, forcing them to confront at least imaginatively the kinds of horrors young male soldiers had to endure constantly in real life.

FEMINIST critics might note that annoyance and even anger at civilian women was not uncommon among male soldiers during World War I. In Britain, many women even gave white feathers to men they considered too selfish or frightened to volunteer. Many men, of course, resented such shaming and intimidation, especially since most British women faced no real danger at all from the war. Feminists might argue that such resentment might not have existed if females had been permitted, encouraged, or perhaps even compelled to serve. Of course, if universal service had been compelled, the war might not even have begun or might not have lasted nearly as long. The prospect of millions of killed or wounded women might have concentrated the minds of leaders and civilian populations on both sides of the conflict. As it was, the only pressure women could realistically impose on elected leaders of the time was moral pressure, since in most of the major European countries (and in America as well), women still could not vote. There were also few female journalists, editors, professors, business leaders, religious leaders, or political agitators. Few women could influence public opinion. Indeed, since women's opinions were mostly shaped by men, Sassoon's criticism of women might strike a feminist as unfair. Women, from this perspective, were a far too easy a target of Sassoon's satire. It was men, not women, who enjoyed massive special privileges, and it was mostly men who could end the war if they wanted to. The war itself could in fact seem an expression of "macho" competitiveness. No leaders of the countries at war were women.

A feminist might argue, as well, that Sassoon's poem is unfair to the women who did try to do their parts during the war. The poem does mention that some women factory workers made artillery "shells" (5) and that many women knitted millions upon millions of socks for soldiers (13). The poem omits reference to the dedicated service of such women as nurses and Red Cross volunteers. Nor (a feminist might assert) does the poem do any justice to the real fear and grief women felt for their endangered, injured, or slain sons, brothers, husbands, and fathers. In short, from a feminist perspective, the poem's righteous indignation might seem very shallow and shortsighted.

The MULTICULTURAL critics known as "Queer theorists" might be especially interested in this poem: its author was gay, and it implies tension between men and heterosexual women. Unlike psychoanalytic critics, however, queer theorists would be less interested in Sassoon's personal psychology than in what the poem suggests about gender when the poem was written. Queer theorists might argue that although heterosexual women in Sassoon's time were themselves disadvantaged, they were not nearly as oppressed as homosexuals. Homosexual relations were technically illegal then, and penalties (especially for gays in the military) could be severe. If disadvantaged women had supported oppressed gays, progress for both groups might have been speedier, but gays then could rarely if ever speak openly to defend themselves. In fact, a bogus claim that Britain's government was riddled with gays (who could be blackmailed by German agents) was a major scandal of the war. Evidence for the claim was minimal, to say the least, but the mere fact that it was asserted suggests how dangerous being gay could be in Britain at this time. If Sassoon had written as an open, defiant homosexual, he would have been ridiculed at the very least and perhaps even court-martialed and imprisoned. Women could and did march to demand greater political power; gays at the time could never have done the same.

ATROCITIES

You told me, in your drunken-boasting mood,
How once you butchered prisoners. That was good!
I'm sure you felt no pity while they stood
Patient and cowed and scared, as prisoners should.

How did you do them in? Come, don't be shy: [5]
You know I love to hear how Germans die,
Downstairs in dug-outs. "Camerad!" they cry;
Then squeal like stoats when bombs begin to fly.

And you? I know your record. You went sick
When orders looked unwholesome: then, with trick   [10]
And lie, you wangled home. And here you are,
Still talking big and boozing in a bar.

LONGINUS might respond to this poem by suggesting that although it deals with an ugly, revolting subject, it implicitly appeals to our noblest, most sublime instincts. Longinus attributes lack of sublimity (or moral elevation) to avarice and to love of the lowest pleasures. Certainly the man addressed here exhibits such traits. They are reflected in his drinking, his self-concern, his deceptive, ignoble efforts to return home, and of course his very commission of battlefield atrocities. Longinus himself refers to "insolence, lawlessness, and shamelessness" as "inexorable tyrants of the soul" (p. 75), and certainly the corrupt soldier addressed here is immoral in these ways. Many first readers of Sassoon's poem would not have wanted to believe that British soldiers could commit atrocities. The idea would have disgusted them. In fact, the common belief that Germans had brutalized civilians had helped prompt Britain to enter (and stay in) the war. Disgust with atrocities suggests (Longinus might argue) that humans innately want to feel noble and sublime and are repelled by base motives and behavior. In that sense, this poem implies the sublimity of Sassoon and his speaker and implicitly appeals to the sublimity of the poem's readers.

A TRADITIONAL HISTORICAL critic might emphasize that one reason the British went to war was because of real and alleged German atrocities, especially against Belgian civilians. Sassoon's poem therefore seems especially ironic. In fact, a traditional historical critic might note that the poem could not even be included in the first published edition of Sassoon's war poems; the book's publisher considered this particular work simply too provocative. Only recently, indeed, has the poem's first draft come to light—a draft that includes such phrases "you're great at murder" and "gulp their blood in ghoulish dreams," which were deleted when the poem was eventually published (Alberge). In line 5, the question "How did you kill them?" was toned down to the present "How did you do them in?" Historical investigation thus reveals much about the era when the poem was written, the practical pressures felt by both the author and publisher, and even the nuances of the published text. By comparing and contrasting the poem-as-published with the original draft, we gain fuller insights into the published work.

A historical critic might also explore other issues concerning the poem in the contexts of its time. These might include how it reflects changes in the kinds of literature considered acceptable in the early twentieth century; the precise meaning of "Camerad!" (an expression Germans often used when trying to surrender); whether stories about widespread German atrocities were credible; how often British soldiers committed atrocities; and whether Sassoon may have had any particular person in mind when crafting this poem. A historical critic would know that Sassoon himself was particularly brave and daring and thus would have had real personal reasons to feel contempt for bragging, ignoble cowards.

READER-RESPONSE critics would probably note that different kinds of readers might respond to this poem in significantly different ways. Some readers might argue, for instance, that since Germans had been the first to commit wartime atrocities, they could not complain if they suffered the same fate. A German reader, however, might have read the poem as evidence of English barbarity, and one can readily imagine how the poem—if it had indeed been published before the war had ended—could easily have been exploited by German propagandists. Many British readers might not have believed (or wanted to believe) that "their" soldiers were capable of such atrocities. At the very least, they may have felt it would be imprudent to publish such a poem before the war ended. Soldiers who had committed or witnessed atrocities might have been deeply disturbed by the poem, or, alternatively, they might have felt defensive and tried to justify such behavior. In short, the number of possible responses to the poem is almost as large as the number of possible readers, thus implying that works of literature cannot dictate single, simple reactions. The meanings of literary works (a reader-response theorist might contend) are ultimately determined by the varied people who read them.

NEW HISTORICIST critics are often interested in depictions of marginal groups who lack great power. They are also often interested in unexpected, unconventional views of history that complicate and even undermine simplistic narratives. They believe that historical events can be extraordinarily complex, especially in the ways power is distributed and exercised. Finally, new historicists are intrigued by the ways literature is not only shaped by historical forces but is itself a historical force, capable of influencing present and future events and attitudes. For all these reasons, new historicists might be particularly intrigued by Sassoon's poem. Certainly it deals with an exceptionally marginal, powerless group (prisoners of war), and it challenges standard notions of the war. Such notions were not only current at the time but are still current today. This poem reflects the views of a small, exceptionally powerless group (vocal opponents of the war). And, because the poem was essentially self-censored by Sassoon's publisher, it exemplifies how power often operates in society—less by overt repression than by more subtle means, so that the powerless often feel forced to cooperate even as they try to resist. Sassoon's own power, not only economically and socially but also as a respected soldier, gave him the means and self-confidence needed to write and (try to) publish such works. But a less influential, less socially secure writer might never even have made the attempt. In short, this poem suggests much about the complex, unpredictable ways power was distributed, used, and negotiated in Sassoon's era. It depicts the war not as a traditional historical critic might depict it (as a matter of strategies designed by politicians and generals and as the story of battlefield triumphs and defeats). Instead, this poem is an example of microhistory—the kind that focuses on the thoughts and behavior of relatively obscure individuals. Yet these are the people, of course, who make up most of the human population. Their stories (a new historicist would argue) need to be told.

POSTMODERNIST critics, skeptical of "grand narratives" that seek to impose order on history, would probably be very interested in Sassoon's poem. This work, after all, tends to undercut the view (popular during and after the so-called Enlightenment) that history was basically a narrative of increasing progress toward ideal goals. The Germans and English considered themselves especially civilized, and indeed the Germans even boasted of their impressive "kultur." A postmodernist might be intrigued by the ways this poem undermines simple binaries, especially any automatically associating Britain with morality and Germany with immorality. Indeed, the poem even suggests how a strong sense of morality can ironically lead to self-contradictory behavior: any British soldiers who did commit atrocities probably felt justified in doing so as punishment for atrocities allegedly committed by the Germans. Disgust with immoral behavior might thus itself lead to immoral behavior. This sort of paradox would fascinate a postmodernist. Of course, one alleged problem with postmodern skepticism is that it can actually undermine or destroy firm notions of what is right and wrong. Sassoon's implied criticism of English atrocities suggests that atrocities are immoral. Some critics of postmodernism claim that postmodernists have abandoned the means—and the right—to distinguish the moral from the immoral.

7

Rupert Brooke (1887–1915): "Nineteen fourteen: The soldier"; "Nineteen fourteen: The dead"

NINETEEN FOURTEEN: THE SOLDIER

If I should die, think only this of me:
  That there's some corner of a foreign field
That is for ever England. There shall be
  In that rich earth a richer dust concealed;
A dust whom England bore, shaped, made aware,   [5]
  Gave, once, her flowers to love, her ways to roam;
A body of England's, breathing English air,
  Washed by the rivers, blest by suns of home.

And think, this heart, all evil shed away,
  A pulse in the eternal mind, no less   [10]
    Gives somewhere back the thoughts
     by England given;
Her sights and sounds; dreams happy as her day;
  And laughter, learnt of friends; and gentleness,
    In hearts at peace, under an English heaven.

PLATO might admire this poem because its speaker seems totally devoted to lofty ideals. (Longinus would admire the poem for the same reason.) The speaker seems unafraid of death and seems instead focused on an afterlife (whether literal or metaphorical) far more important to him than his life on earth. He seems reasonable, and his emotions seem elevated and inspirational rather than selfish or degrading. This poem endorses a cause promoted by the government, and indeed this poem quickly became a kind of unofficial piece of government propaganda. If the government and its cause were virtuous, Plato would admire this poem and this use of poetry. Yet Plato would probably admire the poem's speaker for other reasons, too: he seems concerned with becoming and being good (9); he assumes that there is some kind of god or higher power (10); he displays the military discipline, temperance, and courage that Plato explicitly endorsed; and he is an inspiring example of men enduring ills while pursuing high ideals (Preminger et al., pp. 52–3). Plato was especially interested in poetry that might encourage soldiers (Preminger et al., p. 60), and it is hard to imagine a better example of such poetry than Brooke's sonnet.

Even the poem's style, form, and rhythms might have appealed to Plato. Brooke uses a traditional, long-accepted genre (the sonnet); his style reflects what Plato called the "true simplicity of a rightly and nobly ordered mind and character" (Preminger et al., p. 62); and the work also displays the kind of "grace and harmony [that] are the twin sisters of goodness and self-restraint and bear their likeness" (Preminger et al., p. 63). For all these reasons, Plato would almost surely have valued Brooke's sonnet as much as it was valued both by influential and common readers of its day.

A PSYCHOANALYTIC critic might argue that Brooke's poem displays the heavy influence of the superego, the part of the mind concerned with morality, conscience, and ideal, selfless behavior. The speaker's id (the seat of self-interested emotions) seems firmly under control, and indeed the poem helps inspire others to discipline their own emotions. The speaker functions as a psychological role model; he neither fears death nor displays an excessive desire for pleasure. The only pleasures that interest him are socially sanctioned. A Freudian might regard him as mature, responsible, and well adjusted to reality. The speaker considers England a kind of parent, and he presents himself as a nearly perfect child—happy with his upbringing, loyal to the people who raised him, yet perfectly willing and capable of meeting adult responsibilities. Jacques Lacan, an influential recent Freudian, might say that the speaker has smoothly entered the "symbolic" realm of the father: he has accepted external laws. But he also displays the psychological unity, completeness, and harmony Lacan links to attachment to the mother. Brooke's speaker *seems* remarkably mature and undisturbed, but a Freudian might wonder if this is merely naïve—merely a pose or an example of wishful thinking.

A MARXIST might be disturbed by the speaker's self-focus. Admittedly, he seems devoted to "England," but a Marxist might regard "England" either as a mere abstraction or as a conventional name for the current bourgeois power structure, devoted to nationalism, capitalism, and ruling-class interests. Although the speaker may at first seem selfless and noble, he promotes a jingoism that subverts the real interests of a united, international working class. He implicitly presents himself as a noble individual hero rather than as a spokesman for common, suffering humanity. He depicts England as a rural paradise rather than as a grimy industrial power, and he presents it in idyllic terms rather than emphasizing its role as the seat of a gigantic exploitative empire. Even his emphasis on "England" might seem suspicious to some readers from the larger British Isles. He never mentions soldiers from Scotland, Wales, or Northern Ireland (parts of "Great Britain" that themselves have often felt dominated by the English). Despite the speaker's apparently selfless patriotism, he implicitly endorses a war whose main beneficiaries were profiteers on both sides, and even his notion that his grave will forever be a part of England might remind a Marxist reader of England's history as a colonial power, seizing territory from other nations. Finally, the speaker's reference to an "eternal mind" (10) can be read as an example of naïve, delusive, and self-delusive spiritualism that seems absurd from a materialist point of view. The poem, a Marxist might argue, reflects Brooke's own privileged social status; it would appeal especially to others of his class; but it could be (and was) used as an effective tool of government propaganda.

Readers influenced by ECOCRITICISM might argue that this poem displays strong attachment not only to England in general but to an ideal, rural English landscape in particular. The poem does not mention English towns or, especially, English cities. The latter were often crowded, filthy, and polluted. It implies that an ideal aspect of English life is the land's natural beauty. The poem might thus help promote pride in, and protection of, rural England. The poem imagines a future in which the speaker not only becomes part of the earth but also transforms that small plot of land (his grave) into something permanently English. The speaker may die, but he tries to immortalize England as Eng*land*—a place worth loving partly for its rural beauty. Brooke's celebration of this beauty would have seemed especially valuable during wartime, when other rural areas—especially in northern France—were being transformed into hellish moonscapes, pockmarked with craters and oozing with mud. The war, in a sense, merely exaggerated the ways modern industrialism could destroy natural beauty and the natural ecosystem. Paradoxically, of course, the poem's speaker could be seen as a willing participant in such destruction since he does not resist the war. But this speaker—and others who shared his views—seems to have assumed that ultimately there are values higher than earthly values. Those values are most eternal not in a literal landscape but in an ideal "English heaven" (14).

DARWINIAN critics might argue that this poem reflects a genetic predisposition of humans (especially males) to fight, especially in perceived defense of their own property, tribe, and values. Such a predisposition would have been favored through natural selection: males who were reluctant to fight might not survive and might not be attractive mating partners. On the other hand, males who did fight risked being killed. If they had reproduced before dying, their genes would be passed on to the next generation. Of course, many young men, like Brooke, died before they could reproduce. Yet Brooke survives partly through this poem, which functions as a kind of "meme" (in Richard Dawkins' sense of the word)—a bit of thought competing with other bits for a place in an "eternal mind" (10). For Dawkins, this is not the mind of a real God but the collective intellectual heritage of a people or of humanity as a whole.

However much the views this poem expresses might strike a Darwinian as rooted in a biological "human nature," Darwinians might also note that World War I differed substantially from any war ever waged before. Millions upon millions died, and many were young men (like Brooke) in the prime of young manhood, who had not yet passed on their genes. This war was, then, particularly wasteful from a Darwinian viewpoint. Yet Brooke's poem might be seen as promoting survival values, especially in the way it encourages self-sacrificing devotion to one's community. A poem like this would (and did) make its author romantically attractive, both to women and to men. Its speaker seems both brave and selfless; he seems strong both physically and psychologically. He is devoted to the survival of his culture even if he cannot ensure his own survival. For all these reasons, he seems an ideal specimen of Darwinian manhood.

NINETEEN FOURTEEN: THE DEAD

These hearts were woven of human joys and cares,
Washed marvelously with sorrow, swift to mirth.
The years had given them kindness. Dawn was theirs,
And sunset, and the colours of the earth.
These had seen movement, and heard music; known   [5]
Slumber and waking; loved; gone proudly friended;
Felt the quick stir of wonder; sat alone;
Touched flowers and furs and cheeks. All this is ended.

There are waters blown by changing winds to laughter
And lit by the rich skies, all day. And after,   [10]
Frost, with a gesture, stays the waves that dance
And wandering loveliness. He leaves a white
Unbroken glory, a gathered radiance,
A width, a shining peace, under the night.

LONGINUS, who emphasized moral and spiritual elevation, might variously admire this poem's style. He believed that only effective language could achieve a truly "sublime" or elevated impact. This poem's diction, for instance, is not inflated or pompous—failings especially likely to afflict writers aiming for greatness. If anything, its wording is understated, but it is also uplifting (Preminger et al., pp. 193–4), as when the speaker says that "The years had given them kindness" (3). The poem displays appropriately moderate emotion but is not frigid (Preminger et al., p. 194), and it reveals no lapses from dignity resulting from a desire to seem original (Preminger et al., p. 195). Like any truly sublime work, it leaves us with much to ponder, especially since it provides no easy, simple responses to the fact of death (Preminger et al., p. 196). Its phrasing seems noble (see especially lines 6–7); nothing seems low, trivial, or servile

(Preminger et al., p. 197). In attempting to appreciate and honor the dead, the speaker expresses noble thoughts, and Longinus believes that "[w]ords will be great if thoughts are weighty" (Preminger et al., p. 197). The poem celebrates love, friendship, beauty, and nature. There is no extended, melodramatic dwelling on death but instead a simple, brief statement. Indeed, the sestet presents death as part of a larger natural cycle and, by implication, as nothing to greatly fear. The poem thus endorses courage, temperance, and stoicism—all lofty, sublime reactions to the pains of life, including death itself.

ARCHETYPAL critics assume there is a basic human nature. They think most people share the same desires and fears, the same joys and sorrows. They assume that humans live in real physical environments (not concerned only with ideas or intellectual abstractions) and that death is perhaps the ultimate fact we must face. It is the most important of all shared realities. Brooke's speaker lists, phrase by phrase, one common human experience after another, so that almost every reader will be able to "relate" to many if not most of the poem's details. Ironically, of all the common experiences listed, experience with frost (11–14) might actually be the least common for a worldwide audience, but certainly it is common enough to make the poem widely effective. Even more "archetypal," though, are the references to such experiences as joys, cares, sorrow, mirth, dawn, sunset, slumber, waking, and, especially, love and friendship—two phenomena almost universally desired. Is there, or has there ever been, any culture in which most people have not wanted to be loved and to have friends? If not, then poems on these topics are likely to be of universal interest. Even this poem's phrasing seems somehow universal: it is easy to comprehend and highly accessible; the speaker uses no terms that seem strange, forbidding, or self-indulgent. He speaks plainly and simply of matters (especially death) that concern almost everyone, and so (an archetypal critic might argue) this poem's appeal is likely to transcend any differences of race, culture, gender, nationality, ethnicity, or particular historical circumstances.

A READER-RESPONSE critic, interested in the potential diversity of reactions to any literary work, might imagine a wide variety of possible responses to this poem. These responses might be especially affected by different attitudes toward death. Thus persons grieving over the recent deaths of loved ones might respond to this sonnet both powerfully and variously. Some readers might be comforted, while others might find the poem naïve and romantic, arguing that it fails to convey (or deal with) the true pain of loss. Some might find the first half of line 2 ("Washed marvelously with sorrow") nonsensical, while others might see it as especially thought-provoking and profound. Some might regard this poem as a wholly secular response to death, and therefore might find it either satisfying or disappointing. After all, the poem never mentions God or an afterlife. This might please some readers and dissatisfy others. Meanwhile, readers who have suffered severe, persistent physical pain (or who have watched their children or other loved ones suffer) might consider this sonnet pollyannish. And it is easy to imagine that a Marxist might see it as predictable work by a bourgeois or privileged writer who has enjoyed a relatively pleasant life and who has known very little real, grinding, crushing sorrow. A psychoanalytic critic, with some knowledge of Brooke's personal life, might find it intriguing that he is so general and imprecise in referring to love and friendship; nothing in this poem, for instance, suggests anything about Brooke's homoeroticism. A gay reader, meanwhile, might say that this reticence is understandable given the persecution Brooke would have suffered if he had been frank. On the other hand, anyone who has ever been in love, had friends, or had to deal with death might respond in highly personal ways to this poem. (Imagine, for instance, the responses of someone who had faced grief again and again, as opposed to someone who had faced it relatively rarely.) For a reader-response critic, no reaction mentioned so far would be inappropriate or (on the other hand) especially valuable; each would be legitimate and valuable in its own terms. One's responses to the sonnet might change from year to year or from even week to week, depending on changes in one's experiences. Brooke's own poetic reputation is the best possible illustration, one might argue, of the undeniable fact that reader responses widely vary. Immediately after his death, his work was immensely praised and valued; today, however, it arouses much less interest.

STRUCTURALIST critics are interested in the ways humans create order by imposing structures on reality. Often these consist of related pairs of opposites, or "binaries." In this poem, the linked binaries are especially obvious. At the same time, the poem also reveals how difficult it sometimes is to define binaries and to link them—a difficulty that critics of structuralism (including deconstructors) often emphasize. Some binaries in Brooke's poem seem, at least at first glance, difficult to dispute, and it is also easy to see how they reinforce one another. Thus the poem juxtaposes, either explicitly or implicitly, joys and cares, happiness and sorrow, mirth and unhappiness, kindness and unkindness, color and colorlessness, music and silence, love and hate, wonder and boredom, peace and disturbance, and so on. In this list, all the terms mentioned first are positive, and they help define (and are themselves partly defined by) their opposites (the terms mentioned second) as negative. This, according to structuralists, is how humans usually make sense of experiences: by seeing them as structures of related opposites.

Critics of structuralism, such as deconstructors (see the following paragraph) suggest that attempts to structure reality are almost inevitably imperfect and laden with unintended contradictions, ironies, and ambiguities. Structuralists might reply, however, that it is still necessary to learn and know the various "codes" cultures impose upon reality if we hope to make sense of the artifacts any culture produces. The opening line of Brooke's poem, for instance, associates the human heart with human emotions; the poem is thus part of a long tradition in Western culture of making such an association. However, in ancient Egyptian culture the heart was often associated with the intellect (Jobes, p. 737). It was considered the seat of intelligence. Thus the same biological fact—the heart—could be given radically different meanings in two different cultures. One would need to know a culture's "codes" to make sense of anything (such as a poem) that culture produced. At the very least, one would need to know a culture's actual spoken and written language in order to understand its literature. This argument—that distinct cultures have distinct codes or languages—is the central argument of structuralism.

DECONSTRUCTORS assume that cultural codes are inevitably full of gaps, contradictions, and irresolvable paradoxes. Interpretations, therefore, are never likely to be free of such problems themselves. Deconstructors also assume that in any apparently simple pair of opposites, such as love/hate, one element tends to be "privileged" over the other, whether explicitly or implicitly. In the love/hate pairing, for instance, love is usually privileged. A deconstructor would try to show how distinctions can never be clear-cut. War, in fact, involves an almost inevitable blurring of the opposition between love and hate, since soldiers are usually expected to love their countries, families, and comrades but feel murderous hate for the enemy. Thus, in this case, love produces hate rather than being its simple opposite. The clear distinction between love and hate has been "deconstructed."

In Brooke's poem, apparently simple contrasts can often be deconstructed. Does the poem, for instance, privilege joys over cares? It may, but by the end of the poem, cares have helped produce the joy the poem engenders (by its beauty and its especially beautiful final imagery). Yet this joy cannot really compensate for the cares, especially the pain caused by death, the poem emphasizes. But we do achieve some happiness from the poem's beautiful exploration of sorrow. Another example of the difficulty of making clear distinctions involves the men whose deaths the poem laments. They were raised to show "kindness" (3), but their kindness and concern for their friends and countrymen ultimately led them to become killers and be killed. For deconstructors, apparent opposites almost inevitably bleed into one another. Black and white become gray or, at the very least, they wobble so much that it is difficult to see and maintain any clear difference between them.

Teresa Hooley (1888–1973): "A war film"

A WAR FILM

I saw,
With a catch of the breath and the heart's uplifting,
Sorrow and pride,
The "week's great draw"—
The Mons Retreat;   [5]
The "Old Contemptibles" who fought, and died,
The horror and the anguish and the glory.

As in a dream,
Still hearing machine-guns rattle and shells scream,
I came out into the street.   [10]

When the day was done,
My little son
Wondered at bath-time why I kissed him so,
Naked upon my knee.
How could he know   [15]
The sudden terror that assaulted me? . . .
The body I had borne
Nine moons beneath my heart,
A part of me . . .
If, someday,   [20]
It should be taken away
To war. Tortured. Torn.
Slain.
Rotting in No Man's Land, out in the rain –
My little son . . .   [25]
Yet all those men had mothers, every one.

How should he know
Why I kissed and kissed and kissed him, crooning his name?
He thought that I was daft.
He thought it was a game,   [30]
And laughed, and laughed.

A critic influenced by HORACE, who emphasized the writer's need to please an audience, might praise this poem for various reasons. This text, for instance, does use words appropriate to its subject matter, and it does arrange them clearly. It says "only what needs to be said," and, especially in lines 22–3, it gives novelty to "familiar words by a skillful setting" (p. 52). Above all, it exemplifies Horace's assertion that it "is not enough for poems to be beautiful; they must be affecting, and must lead the heart of the hearer as they will" (pp. 52–3). "If you wish me to weep," he later writes, "you must first feel grief yourself" (p. 53). Hooley's poem also marks "the characteristics of each period of life" and presents "what is fitting to the various natures and ages" of different persons—in this case the mature mother and the immature child (p. 53). The ideal poetic style, Horace maintains, should "mold familiar material with such skill that anyone might hope to achieve the same feat" (p. 55), and Hooley's poem, with its simple diction and straightforward structure, clearly satisfies these criteria.

A THEMATIC critic, interested in how literary works emphasize (and are organized by) key ideas, might say that one major theme of Hooley's lyric is the idea that different people perceive and interpret the same event from different viewpoints. This theme of varied perceptions is implied immediately, and indeed much of the rest of the poem deals with the speaker's perceptions, which are clearly the most important perceptions the poem records and expresses. Right from the start the speaker's reactions are complex, mingling "Sorrow and pride" (3), although as the poem develops sorrow is emphasized more than pride. Meanwhile, other persons' perceptions are also implied: the owners of the theater see this filmed news about the war as "The 'week's great draw'" (4) that will attract paying customers, while the reference to the English army as "Contemptibles" (6) alludes to the German Kaiser's dismissive perception of British forces. Yet those very forces proudly adopted the Kaiser's term and nick-named themselves the "Old Contemptibles," thereby offering yet another of the many different perceptions implied even within the poem's first few lines. Of course, the contrasting perceptions of the mother and son are the perceptions that matter most, but the whole text (a thematic critic might argue) stresses and is partly structured by this key idea: that different kinds of people often perceive the same facts in distinct ways.

Yet the issue of perceptions is also implied in other ways. Thus lines 8–10 juxtapose imagined perceptions with real perceptions;

and although one purpose of newsreels was to promote patriotic reactions to the war, the poem shows that different individuals might react to such films in distinct ways, from their specific, personal viewpoints. Anyone seeing this mother repeatedly kissing her son, for instance, might interpret her behavior as motivated merely by maternal affection, whereas she (as speaker) and we (as readers) have clearer insight into her deeper motivations. Thus the poem can be read as an extended meditation on the sheer variety and complexity of perceptions.

A FORMALIST, interested in the poem's artistic success or failure, would pay very close attention to all its complicated details. A formalist would want to see if and how those details work together to make the poem effective. A formalist might claim, for instance, that the opening line is effectively brief. It surprises us and immediately creates interest. Also effective is the juxtaposition of the very short opening line and the much longer succeeding line: each line receives extra emphasis because of this striking contrast. Contrasts, in fact, help organize the poem in other ways. Thus, line 3 complexly contrasts (and combines) sorrow with pride, and the superficial perceptions implied by line 4 contrast with the deadly serious event mentioned in line 5. In all these ways, the poem already begins to demonstrate the kind of "complex unity" formalists greatly prize.

Formalists might also appreciate many other specific details of this poem's phrasing, including such matters as (1) the irony of the term "Old Contemptibles" (since British soldiers were mostly young and were anything but contemptible on the battlefield); (2) the ways the poem's rhymes give it greater unity than if it were unrhymed; (3) the way the comma in "fought, and died" gives each verb special emphasis; and (4) the ways each noun in line 7 receives special emphasis thanks to the repeated use of "and." This list could easily be extended, but by now the main point is clear: for formalists, a work's success depends less on its paraphraseable "message" or "meaning" than on the very precise details of its phrasing and structure.

A PSYCHOANALYTIC critic, interested in the complexity of human minds, might be interested in the ways Hooley's poem implies such complexity in its speaker, internal characters, and readers. Complications are already implied, for instance, in line 2's reference to sorrow mixed with pride, where sorrow seems a response mainly rooted in the emotional id while pride in others' achievements seems basically a moral response, rooted in the conscience or superego. Meanwhile, the reference to newsreels about the war constituting the "week's great draw" at the movies might be interpreted as alluding to all three basic aspects of the psyche: to an interest in facing facts (associated with the rational ego); to an interest in the emotions of fear and anger (associated with the id); and to an interest in patriotism and moral idealism (associated with the superego). Line 7's reference to "The horror and the anguish and the glory" implies the speaker's psychological maturity: she can face grim facts and the pain they provoke while also connecting them to something higher than mere pain. In general, the speaker seems psychologically well balanced and thus seems a worthy role model for her child. Thus, rather than expressing her concern for him by breaking down and crying and in the process upsetting him, she instead expresses her love and fear in positive ways, by kissing him and making him feel valued and secure, no matter how insecure the speaker herself may feel. Of course, Jacques Lacan would say that eventually the child will need to move from this comforting realm or "mirror stage" associated with his mother's love to the "symbolic order" (associated with the father) that adults must inhabit. The child's mother is aware of the eventual loss of her close bond with her child and of his inevitable entry, as he ages, into a new world of rules, laws, and cultural expectations, some of them cultural norms involving patriotism, proper "masculine" behavior, and the risk of killing and death.

A FEMINIST might note all the ways in which this poem conforms to (and thus reinforces) standard gender stereotypes of its time. This is particularly true of its implication that while men are off fighting, women stay at home and care for children. Interestingly, however, no clear reference is made to the speaker's husband. Has he already been killed? Is he still alive but constantly risking death on battlefields? Is the female speaker a widow? A single mother? The absence of any reference or even allusion to the child's father is striking, especially since the poem was written when men were nominally any family's key figures. This poem, however, clearly focuses on the mother and on her status *as* a mother. Mothers carry children during the nine months of pregnancy (18) and then usually care for children both physically and emotionally. The newsreel the speaker views focuses on male suffering on the battlefield, and, in a way not previously possible, it brings that suffering home to the women left behind. Hooley's poem, however, reminds us of the special suffering of women and mothers during war. Unable to live as completely as men could live, women of this era would spend years raising and loving children and then often see their grown sons die in wars concocted, directed, and continued by powerful men. Hooley's poem reminds us that mothers on both sides of any conflict are important victims of any war, yet her poem does this without perpetuating any stereotypes of women as weak, flighty, and excessively sentimental. This text implies strong feelings, but its speaker never seems hyperemotional. This work is one of the often-neglected war poems by women that feminist critics have helped us recover and appreciate.

Claude McKay (1889–1948): "The little peoples"

THE LITTLE PEOPLES

The little peoples of the troubled earth,
The little nations that are weak and white;—
For them the glory of another birth,
For them the lifting of the veil of night.
The big men of the world in concert met,   [5]
Have sent forth in their power a new decree:
Upon the old harsh wrongs the sun must set,
Henceforth the little peoples must be free!

But, we, the blacks, less than the trampled dust,
Who walk the new ways with the old dim eyes,—   [10]
We to the ancient gods of greed and lust
Must still be offered up as sacrifice:
Oh, we who deign to live but will not dare,
The white world's burden must forever bear!

Readers influenced by LONGINUS, who emphasized basic human desires for moral and spiritual elevation, might especially appreciate this poem by Claude McKay. After all, it implicitly condemns war and materialism as well as economic and especially racial oppression. The "big men" who met after World War I to hammer out the details of the postwar world were the victorious politicians (largely controlled by the rich) who ostensibly opposed the oppression imposed by large European empires on the small white nations of Europe. Of course, the empires the victors dissolved were those that had lost the war (Germany, Austro-Hungary, and Russia). No efforts were made to dismantle the empires of Britain, France, Italy, or even America, not only because those nations had triumphed in battle but also because they oppressed mainly peoples of color, both abroad and also (especially in the case of the United States) at home. It is little wonder, then, that McKay and many other blacks felt cheated when the war ended: they were still as oppressed as ever (especially in Africa, India, and the United States). Although people of color might feel the elevated moral and spiritual longings praised by Longinus, they were still as beaten-down, economically, socially, and psychologically, as before.

In his treatise *On the Sublime*, Longinus explicitly condemns "unlimited war which lays hold of our desires," and he calls avarice or greed "the insatiable disease from which we all suffer," saying that he "cannot see how we can honor, or rather deify, unlimited wealth as we do without admitting into our souls the evils which attach to it" (Preminger et al., p. 224). McKay would have seen the "big men" his poem attacks as almost inevitably either wealthy themselves or as mere tools of the rich. In this sense, they would actually be "little men" when seen from a moral, Longinian point of view.

A MARXIST, ostensibly concerned with economic justice for the poor, might respond to McKay's poem by noting that the rich have always oppressed "little people" (singular): one way the poor have in fact been exploited has been by being carved up into warring nations—"little peoples" (plural). They have thus long been pitted against each other in ways that serve the ruling classes. If the earth's "little peoples" ever united, the power of the wealthy would be unsustainable. The earth has long been troubled by conflicts between and among economic elites, and "little people" have always suffered most from those disputes. A Marxist of McKay's era might argue that there were, of course, many weak white people—that, in fact, most white workers were weak when compared with the economic and social elite, most of whom happened also to be white. But not every powerful exploiter, a Marxist might remind us, was white; China, India, and Japan, for instance, had exploitative ruling classes of their own (even though those nations were themselves negatively affected by the imperialism of rich whites). A Marxist might contend that just as ruling classes divide the weak of one nation against the weak of another, so they similarly divide the races and exploit any divisions between them. White, black, brown, yellow, and red workers should, from a Marxist viewpoint, all make common cause and oppose their common exploiters, just as workers from England, France, Germany, Austria, Russia, and all other nations should bond together and not allow themselves to be turned into enemies by the "big men of the world" (5).

That very phrase—"big men"—would probably have had strong connotations for the Marxists of McKay's day. It would have suggested plutocrats who profited both from the war itself and also from the way the war divided workers. Yet the war also threatened the power of the rich, at least in the "losing" nations, and Marxists in particular benefited from the collapse of the old Russian monarchy. That collapse allowed them to found the "Soviet Union" (which soon became oppressive in its own ways). Of course, even in the small white European nations supposedly freed by the war's conclusion, real freedom was not achieved. Rich exploiters remained in control everywhere. Yet the black poor remained, perhaps of all the poor, the most exploited, and so a Marxist would probably be highly attracted to McKay's poem.

MULTICULTURAL critics, especially those interested in African American studies and Critical Race theory, would obviously be intrigued by McKay's poem. As an American, McKay was a citizen of the world's leading emerging power. The United States was growing daily in might and wealth and had largely escaped the physical and financial devastations of World War I. Few other nations were better-positioned, in 1919, to offer their citizens opportunities for wealth and freedom, yet the United States was, of course, notorious for its racial discrimination. Ironically, American blacks serving in the military had fought, ostensibly, for the freedom of various "little nations" in Europe without enjoying full freedom in their own lives at home. Just as ironically, recent white immigrants to America from the "little nations" of Europe usually had greater opportunities in the United States than did blacks whose families had lived in America for well over a century. In this sense, the phrase "weak and white" (2) is an oxymoron, since white Europeans newly arrived in the United States had, by virtue of their white skins, tickets to opportunities long denied to American blacks. In fact, much of the poem's phrasing seems similarly ironic. Thus, a metaphorical "veil of night" (4) could be lifted from white Europeans, but the dark skins of black Americans, and the oppression associated with it, seemed very tightly tied together. A "veil" is relatively easy to remove; skin color is permanent. Similarly resonant is the phrase "big men," which in an American context could only refer to "big" white men. Such people were more than willing to take away power and assets from defeated Germans and Austrians, but they were far less willing to sacrifice any of their own privileges to black people back in the United States. And, as a further irony, many white "little" people of the United States opposed greater opportunities for poor blacks, who in some ways should have been their natural allies. When McKay's poem is examined from a racial perspective, its phrasing is illuminated in numerous ways. Thus, the claim that blacks are "less than the trampled dust" (9) might seem merely hyperbolic until we realize that dust, by definition, could not feel the kind of physical, mental, and emotional pain suffered by blacks. Dust thus had an advantage over them. Similarly, the reference to the "ancient gods of greed and lust" (11) seems especially ironic when we recall that most of the persecutors of blacks were professed Christians. The idea of being "offered up in sacrifice" might seem merely an overstatement until we recall that lynchings and burnings of American blacks were especially prominent in the first decades of the twentieth century, while the word "dare" in line 13 subtly implies that blacks should somehow (perhaps even violently?) resist oppression by whites.

A MULTICULTURAL critic interested in POSTCOLONIALISM would also be intrigued by McKay's sonnet. Postcolonialist critics examine (and promote) the breakdown of colonial power, especially the power of white nations over much of the rest of the world. This domination began in the 1500s and then began to recede by the mid-1900s. World War I undercut the power of many colonial empires, just as it also inspired many colonized peoples (especially in India, Ireland, and China) to resist colonial oppression. The "little peoples" mentioned in line 2 of McKay's poem were Europeans suffering under the yoke of imperialism imposed by the strongest European countries, but most victims of nineteenth- and twentieth-century imperialism were persons of color. Claude McKay, a black man born in Jamaica, had at first lived under the thumb of the British empire; then, after emigrating to the United States, he found himself subjected by an empire that liked to think of itself as non- or even anti-imperial.

A postcolonial critic might approach McKay's poem in various ways. Such a critic might note, for instance, that McKay writes a Shakespearean sonnet in standard English (even though he had earned early fame for poems using Jamaican dialect). His use here of a traditional form and of "correct" English might be read as a capitulation to colonialism, or it might instead display McKay's ability to turn the resources of an imperial culture against the empire's interests. The poem's conventional form and phrasing can be read as a kind of "mimicry" that is both a concession to the facts of power and a way of trying to undermine colonial domination. Just as McKay uses "white" form and phrasing to challenge white racism, so he uses the contradictory logic of white politicians against them: if decolonization and freedom are good for small white nations, why are they not also good for blacks? The poem exemplifies what postcolonial critics call "hybridity" or "syncretism"—a blending of cultural traditions so as to reveal and challenge cultural injustice.

From a postcolonial perspective, the details of McKay's poem are especially interesting. The first line, for instance, might seem at first to refer to *all* the "little peoples of the troubled earth," but the second line immediately restricts its concern only to the "little nations that are weak and white." Ironically, of course, most of the largest nations in the world, at least in terms of population (such as China and India) were *non*white, as was most of Africa. Colonial nations such as Britain, France, Belgium, and Portugal were tiny in comparison, both geographically and in numbers of people. Caucasians, in this sense, were the *real* inhabitants of "little nations." They were, at least potentially, both "weak and white," if only nonwhites could throw off their colonial yokes. True, deep, and widespread freedom could not result from any "decree" from the powerful (6) but only from the oppressed themselves, if they were willing to "dare" (13) to build and assert their own power. Otherwise they would (in an ironic, subversive echo of a famous phrase from Rudyard Kipling) "The white world's burden . . . forever bear" (14).

MULTICULTURAL critics interested in Queer theory might note that although the poem calls attention to the political and economic power of "big men" (2), even those men, in McKay's era, could not have been powerful if they had tried to be openly gay. Even the most powerful persons of McKay's time had to keep any homosexuality hidden or risk dire consequences, including, in some cases, arrest, imprisonment, and even death. McKay himself was apparently gay or at least bisexual, but he could not afford to make his sexual orientation clear. He could write openly as a black man and as a leftist but not as a "queer." Ironically, one view that tended to unite almost all people of McKay's time—both rich and poor, both "big" and "little")—was a strong, shared contempt for homosexuals, who were usually classified as "deviants" and "perverts." McKay himself was involved for a time with a man named Michael, a hustler who apparently made money by blackmailing men with whom he had had secret sex. Michael's power was rooted in the fear these men felt of being condemned as "queers" (Cooper, pp. 86–7). The very existence of homosexuals was seen as a threat by most men of McKay's time, and so gays were often persecuted for being sick, criminal, or, at the very least, effeminate. Most men of McKay's era, including the powerful "big men" the poem mentions, had no problem with effeminate behavior as long as it was the behavior of women. But they were often violently contemptuous of effeminate men. Even among gays who seemed stereotypically "masculine," expressing an interest in sex with other men could result in being beaten, imprisoned, or killed. McKay could openly identify himself as a proud black man, but neither he nor the many other gay participants in the "Harlem Renaissance" could afford to proclaim themselves homosexuals or advocate the rights of "queers." If blacks were considered "less than the trampled dust" (9), gays were even lower in society's eyes. Various "little peoples" around the world might realistically look forward to eventual freedom, but not until the very late twentieth century could gays hope for any such widespread liberation. Gays—whether white, black, yellow, or red—were indeed often "offered up as sacrifice[s]" in a world still widely full of disgust at their very existence.

8

Isaac Rosenberg (1890–1918): "Break of day in the trenches"; "Louse hunting"; "Returning, we hear the larks"

BREAK OF DAY IN THE TRENCHES

The darkness crumbles away.
It is the same old druid Time as ever,
Only a live thing leaps my hand,
A queer sardonic rat,
As I pull the parapet's poppy   [5]
To stick behind my ear.
Droll rat, they would shoot you if they knew
Your cosmopolitan sympathies.
Now you have touched this English hand
You will do the same to a German   [10]
Soon, no doubt, if it be your pleasure
To cross the sleeping green between.
It seems you inwardly grin as you pass
Strong eyes, fine limbs, haughty athletes,
Less chanced than you for life,   [15]
Bonds to the whims of murder,
Sprawled in the bowels of the earth,

The torn fields of France.
What do you see in our eyes
At the shrieking iron and flame   [20]
Hurled through still heavens?
What quaver—what heart aghast?
Poppies whose roots are in men's veins
Drop, and are ever dropping;
But mine in my ear is safe,   [25]
Just a little white with the dust.

ARISTOTLE might admire this poem because he valued phrasing that was clear but not common. Excessively simple phrasing lacked distinction; excessively complex phrasing was confusing. The best style, then, should carefully be between the plain and the unusual. Unusual words added interest but should not be overused (p. 33). Rosenberg's poem might therefore please Aristotle for combining usually simple phrasing with words distinctive enough to be striking without seeming pretentious. Words such as "druid," "sardonic," "parapet," "droll," "cosmopolitan," "haughty," "chanced," and "quaver" are not mundane, but neither are they extremely unfamiliar. Rosenberg's style, then, displays the moderation Aristotle prized (p. 34). The poem also sometimes uses striking metaphors, a talent Aristotle considered the mark of true poetic genius (p. 35). The use of "crumbles" and "druid," for instance, exemplifies Rosenberg's gift for metaphor, as do "sleeping green," "whims of murder," and "shrieking iron." These unusual touches make his phrasing uncommon but not incomprehensible. Aristotle would probably admire both his inventiveness and his restraint.

FORMALIST critics, interested in the detailed "close reading" of texts and in their complex unity, would explore the potential richness and resonance of Rosenberg's poem. They might begin by noting, for instance, that even its paradoxical title foreshadows many other paradoxes that follow. The title immediately links a new, revivifying beginning with an old, deadly routine, just as it also juxtaposes light with darkness and the sky with the earth. The word "crumbles" (1) makes the darkness seem almost palpable, and while change from darkness to light is often considered positive, line 2 immediately cancels or qualifies that impression: time in the trenches is often monotonous (although also often not). But no sooner is monotony emphasized than a sudden surprise appears: a "live thing" (phrasing that creates momentary suspense) "leaps" onto the speaker's hand, moving with energy and speed (unlike the slowly crumbling darkness). A rat (often considered a mere, inferior pest) seems to view humans in a "sardonic" way, with the contempt and superiority people often feel for rodents. In the trenches, tables are turned: rats are far more likely to prosper there than people.

No sooner, however, does the speaker mention the rat (a conventional symbol of filth and ugliness) than he also mentions that he "pull[s] the parapet's poppy" (5), suggesting both an appreciation of beauty and beauty's death. Formalists are not reluctant to debate the success or flaws in a literary text's precise phrasing, and it is easy to imagine some formalists wondering if the heavy repetition of "p" sounds here is excessive. Other formalists might defend such alliteration if it contributed somehow to the work's effectiveness. In any case, most formalists would probably note that there seems only one poppy on the parapet to pluck, implying the relative absence of beauty in and around the trenches and perhaps also symbolizing how easily life can be destroyed during war. The speaker's desire to stick the poppy behind his ear suggests his desire for beauty in an ugly landscape, and certainly his physical contact with the poppy contrasts greatly with his unwanted contact with the rat.

Formalists would continue to move carefully through the poem, line by line, word by word, syllable by syllable, trying to explain how the poem does or does not succeed as a carefully crafted and effective work of art.

ARCHETYPAL critics, interested in shared human responses to the same stimuli, would look for anything in Rosenberg's poem that might provoke widely shared reactions. Certainly the poem begins with an experience—the transition from night to daylight—almost all people experience (except, perhaps, the blind). Most humans have also experienced time as occasionally humdrum and monotonous, and most people, throughout history, have probably perceived untamed rats as at least mildly threatening, especially if they crawl on humans. Rats have often been perceived as pests, partly because they sometimes consume food set aside for human consumption, and partly also because they sometimes bite and sometimes infest human habitations, creating filth and spreading disease. In many ways, then, they contrast with small, beautiful, nonthreatening poppies. Simply in the first few lines, therefore, Rosenberg's speaker already draws on deep-seated fears and desires, especially the fear of pain and the desire for comfort and beauty.

Those lines also draw on other common archetypal reactions, such as dread of isolation, fear of death, fear of enemies, and yearning for pleasure. The speaker continually uses archetypal imagery and exploits reactions that are common if not entirely universal. Thus the reference to "Strong eyes, fine limbs, [and] haughty athletes" (14) suggests the vitality of humans at their physical and psychological peaks, but these archetypes are then undercut or complicated by the ensuing description of these "athletes" as "Bonds to the whims of murder" (16). Almost all humans fear death, especially murder. Rosenberg thus roots his poem in reactions that are almost literally instinctive.

A MULTICULTURAL critic responding to Rosenberg's poem might discuss all the various cultures the poem mentions or implies. Obviously it alludes to conflict between Germany and England (two Christian countries with Protestant majorities and Catholic minorities)—nations that were, ironically, nominally ruled by closely related royal families. Germans took pride in a self-proclaimed "Kultur" they considered superior to England's, and the English of course considered their culture better than Germany's. In both nations, however, Jews such as Rosenberg were a distinct, often persecuted minority. Ironically, they were sometimes compared, at least by virulent anti-Semites, to rats who had to be controlled. One way, in fact, to read this poem is to see it as expressing Rosenberg's desire to present himself as a loyal Briton, although his continued affiliation with the Jewish community certainly gave him the kind of "cosmopolitan sympathies" (8) that are here, ironically, attributed to the rat. Yet Rosenberg was not simply a Jew fighting for one Christian nation against another; he was also notoriously small, weak, and inept. Thus his references to the "Strong eyes" and "fine limbs" of "haughty athletes" (14) seem particularly intriguing. Ultimately, however, even powerful bodies could not prevent soldiers from being "Sprawled in the bowels of the earth" (14), and so the physical traits that distinguished them from men like Rosenberg were finally less important than the common soldierly culture they shared.

An ECOCRITIC might highlight how Rosenberg's poem shows humans interacting with nature. The opening allusion to Druids, for instance, might remind us of their legendary close ties to nature and even their worship of it—an attitude strongly contrasting with the widespread, horrific destruction of nature during World War I. Even the speaker, after all, feels moved to pick the poppy rather than simply admiring it. Ironically, then, our love for natural beauty often leads us to destroy it. Yet the poppy plant will, presumably, survive and produce more flowers, thereby suggesting nature's resilience—a resilience that humans should, however, never take for granted. Paradoxically, the rat even better symbolizes nature's endurance; the rat has adapted itself to life in or near "No Man's Land"—a particularly resonant phrase for an ecocritic. The pockmarked, muddy, treeless, grassless battlefields, with their lines of ugly gaping trenches, symbolize the ways humans often deface and destroy nature. By contrast, the rat (usually considered an obnoxious pest) has made his peace with his environment; he only wants to survive. He and his fellow rats do not unite to kill other rats. Which species, then—rats or humans—is morally "superior"? In any case, the poem's speaker does not seem especially hostile to the rat, and in some ways he even seems to admire it and its "cosmopolitan sympathies" (8). His respect for this other form of life, along with his apparent love of beauty, might make war less likely if such attitudes were more widely shared. Rosenberg's poem, with its imagery of "torn fields" (18) and other stunning damage, reminds us that when humans go to war, they destroy much more than themselves. They abuse nature at least as much as they abuse each other. But Rosenberg uses a lowly rat and simple poppy to remind us that nature in its own domain and, even in the face of wholesale decimation, is more resilient than any human being.

LOUSE HUNTING

Nudes—stark and glistening,
Yelling in lurid glee. Grinning faces
And raging limbs
Whirl over the floor one fire.
For a shirt verminously busy   [5]
Yon soldier tore from his throat, with oaths
Godhead might shrink at, but not the lice.
And soon the shirt was aflare
Over the candle he'd lit while we lay.

Then we all sprang up and stript   [10]
To hunt the verminous brood.
Soon like a demons' pantomime
The place was raging.
See the silhouettes agape,
See the gibbering shadows   [15]
Mixed with the battled arms on the wall.
See gargantuan hooked fingers
Pluck in supreme flesh
To smutch supreme littleness.
See the merry limbs in hot Highland fling   [20]
Because some wizard vermin
Charmed from the quiet this revel
When our ears were half lulled
By the dark music
Blown from Sleep's trumpet.   [25]

HORACE, interested in writers needing to satisfy readers, might feel ambivalent about this poem. On the one hand, its language is relatively clear and its "plot" is uncomplicated. The fact that it is often anthologized suggests its wide appeal. The speaker preserves decorum by not repeating the soldiers' apparently shocking curses (6–7); thus, no reader can be offended. Horace might wonder, however, whether the poem's sometimes lofty language—such as "Yon" (6), "aflare" (8), "verminously" (5), "Godhead" (7), "verminous brood" (11), "supreme flesh" (18), "hot Highland fling" (20), and "Sleep's trumpet" (25)—sounds inappropriately pretentious. Perhaps, however, the lofty language is *meant* to sound humorously out of place and is therefore funny and ironic rather than incongruous. Any feature that seemed appropriate and that contributed to the poem's actual effectiveness would please Horace.

FORMALIST critics, with their interest in the potential artistic success and complex unity of literary works, would examine "Louse Hunting" closely, looking for its detailed artistic effectiveness (or lack thereof). A formalist might begin, for instance, by noting how the title surprises us and immediately creates interest. Its opening word—"Nudes"—is also provocative and would certainly have interested Rosenberg's first readers. The whole opening line might sound intriguingly erotic, and in fact not until a few lines later does the poem's actual "plot" become clear. Meanwhile, the opening lines tantalize by suggesting nudity, license, and wild abandonment. Merely through sound effects the poem provokes interest, as in the strong metrical emphasis, in the first lines, on all the key syllables; the alliteration of such words as "Yelling in lurid glee" (2); the triple alliteration of "Whirl over the floor one fire" (3); and so on. Sound effects are crucial to a formalist's evaluation of any poem: a poet displays his artistic skill partly by carefully crafting sounds, along with imagery, syntax, line lengths, stanzaic structure, and the connections between all of a poem's various components. A formalist might note, for instance, the way lines 14, 15, and 17 all begin with the word "See"—a technique known as "anaphora." Here it contributes to the work's rhythm, structure, and unity and also makes readers feel almost present as actual witnesses of the actions the poem describes. Formalist analyses of literary works are almost inevitably *much* longer than the works they analyze, because even the tiniest details interest "close readers."

READER-RESPONSE critics, interested in the ways different readers or kinds of readers might react to the same work, could argue that soldiers would be especially able to "relate" to this poem. Obviously, anyone who has ever had lice would also probably feel an especially personal response. In contrast, people who have never had such problems would be less likely to respond viscerally to this poem and might even consider it merely crude. Meanwhile, anyone who has ever had to battle pests of any sort (such as fleas, ants, or other insects) might especially sympathize with the soldiers here. Yet those who have never had to combat pests might find the idea of lice infestation especially odious, whereas people who have lived with pests for most of their lives (such as poor people in extremely underprivileged places) might consider Rosenberg's soldiers weak or comic. In short, one can imagine almost as many different possible responses to this poem as there are possible different readers. For reader-response critics, the text ultimately cannot dictate responses (even though it may try to do so); each reader, ultimately, determines what a text "means" to him or her.

Readers influenced by ECOCRITICISM, which focuses on ways humans relate to nature, would clearly be interested in this work. An "ecocritic" might consider it significant that the poem is set inside a building, in an environment designed to protect humans. If it were set in the trenches or in a forest or field, the presence of lice would be easier to understand. Precisely because they have invaded a supposedly "safe" environment, their invasion seems all the more repulsive. This poem is deliberately un- or even anti-Romantic: rather than emphasizing harmony between happy humans and a pleasant, satisfying environment, it instead undercuts sentimental views of nature. Indeed, nature here seems active rather than passive; it is disturbingly present rather than part of the mere background or scenery. The poem suggests what can happen when "nature" escapes human control. Urban dwellers, in particular, often forget what it is like to live in close contact with nature as it is, rather than as they might wish it to be. The poem reminds us that humans are far more vulnerable to natural forces (especially parasites) than we often like to believe. Yet works such as this poem have perhaps encouraged humans to control nature through such measures as pesticides, which ironically have often caused more damage than they have prevented. In any case, the poem reminds us quite graphically that we can never forget that we inevitably live in constant, close contact with natural powers we can never entirely control.

DARWINIAN critics would also be interested in how this poem presents relations between humans and nature. They might note, for instance, that lice seem to have existed far longer than humans have and infest other mammals to degrees we can only imagine. The soldiers' frantic attempts to escape the lice remind us that Darwin considered all life a constant struggle for survival. The lice are not malign: by sucking blood, they are merely obeying instincts to survive and reproduce. They symbolize, in a way, the blind processes of evolution. Unlike humans, they aspire to nothing "higher" than mere existence. Of course, World War I was supposedly (and ironically) fought to promote and defend such "higher" goals, whether "liberty" or "kultur." Soldiers had much more to fear from enemy combatants, motivated by supposedly lofty human ideals, than from lice. Yet lice infestations were unpleasant facts both sides faced. Ironically, lice infestations symbolized the opposing armies' shared humanity. The need to combat parasites should, perhaps, remind all humans that they are involved in a far larger struggle for survival than the struggles symbolized by particular wars. It was, in fact, ultimately an influenza epidemic in 1918 that caused far more deaths—of soldiers and civilians alike—than even the war produced.

RETURNING, WE HEAR THE LARKS

Sombre the night is:
And though we have our lives, we know
What sinister threat lies there.

Dragging these anguished limbs, we only know
This poison-blasted track opens on our camp—   [5]
On a little safe sleep.

But hark! Joy—joy—strange joy.
Lo! Heights of night ringing with unseen larks:
Music showering our upturned listening faces.

Death could drop from the dark   [10]
As easily as song—
But song only dropped,
Like a blind man's dreams on the sand
By dangerous tides;
Like a girl's dark hair, for she dreams no ruin lies there,   [15]
Or her kisses where a serpent hides.

A reader influenced by PLATO might argue that this poem reflects
that philosopher's opinion that music can be a powerful force, either
for good or for ill. In this case, the influence of the lark's song is
mainly positive. It does not discourage the soldiers or distract them
from doing their duties (outcomes Plato would censure). Instead,
it provides relief, consolation, and renewed strength. Music (Plato
believed) could find its way into the soul's inward places (Preminger
et al., p. 63), and proper music could "correct any discord which
may have arisen in the courses of the soul, and . . . be our ally
in bringing her to harmony and agreement with herself" (*Timaeus*
47a–e). For Plato, the beauty described by the poem imperfectly
imitates the idea and ideal of Beauty itself. Music heard with the ears
is imperfect because it is mutable and fades, but Rosenberg's poem
tries to give it a kind of permanence that, of course, is inevitably
incomplete. Yet the poem reminds us of the ideal of Beauty, an ideal
we should strive to achieve as much as we can.

Plato might be bothered by anything suggesting fear (such as
lines 3, 14, and 16), and he might also object to the hint of eroticism

in the final line. In general, however, he would probably approve of this poem not only because it celebrates beauty but also because its overall tone is generally strong and stoic. Birdsong reminds the soldiers of a beauty greater than themselves and more enduring than their present pain. In these senses, the poem is Romantic in ways that Plato would probably applaud.

A TRADITIONAL HISTORICAL critic, interested in literature's relations with its historical contexts, might begin to interpret this poem in light of Rosenberg's own life. Rosenberg grew up in poverty, lived in London's slums, and had to leave school at fourteen to work and help support his family. He was largely self-educated, and this poem can be seen as a product of his own desire for learning, self-improvement, and accomplishment in the "higher arts," including serious poetry and serious painting (another of his strong interests). It seems significant, for instance, that he does not use this poem to celebrate a more "common" kind of music, such as music from a harmonica. Instead, he celebrates the song of the lark, a bird often extolled by canonical Romantic poets. In fact, even some of the poem's phrasing (especially in lines 7–9) sounds conventionally Romantic, and it is Rosenberg's juxtaposition of lofty Romantic diction with the grim details of modern warfare that gives the poem part of its impact. Given his hard life in the slums and the discrimination he faced as a Jew and as a somewhat physically inept soldier, Rosenberg could easily have been embittered. Instead, this poem suggests that experiencing war only intensified his love of beauty and his ability to appreciate it wherever and whenever it presented itself.

A THEMATIC critic, interested in the ideas literary works express and the ways authors often explore the same ideas repeatedly, might see Rosenberg's poem as suggesting the common idea that beauty gives life meaning and can make it seem worth living. This idea seems especially relevant in wartime, and so the poem both celebrates external beauty and creates a beauty of its own. The lark sings spontaneously and without conscious thought; conversely, the poet is inspired by the lark's song to fashion a thing of beauty in a far more deliberate and skillful way. Soldiers in battle may especially need beauty's consolations, but people in general—whose common fate is death—can also appreciate beauty's power to make existence seem not only endurable but also sometimes joyful. Rosenberg's poem does not suggest any afterlife in heaven following death (a common Christian idea), and this absence of any hint of eternal joy therefore makes the possibility of even temporary earthly joy seem all the more important and precious. The poem's very last line, which mentions "kisses where a serpent lies" (16) encapsulates such key themes of this poem as the contrast between pleasure and pain and the contrast between beauty and ugliness.

ARCHETYPAL critics, interested in the ways literary works tap into the depths of a common human psychology, would clearly be interested in Rosenberg's poem. Obviously it plays on the strong tendency to think of night symbolically, either as a symbol of peace and rest or as a symbol of danger and even death. The fact that night can suggest such contrasting connotations illustrates an important point: the meanings of archetypal symbols are dictated by context. Thus, fire can have positive connotations in one context (as, say, a campfire) and negative connotations in another (as, say, a forest fire). In this poem, the connotations of night are mainly ominous; nearly all people know the experience of feeling tired and/ or vulnerable in the dark, and nearly all can relate to the beauty of birdsong, especially in an otherwise unpleasant environment. Thus the poem taps into widely shared and deeply rooted psychological responses in ways that have very little to do with a reader's gender, race, wealth, language, ethnicity, or other distinguishing factors. Music is a nearly (if not in fact actually) universal aspect of human cultures, and although kinds of music may differ from culture to culture, the instinct to want, make, and be pleased by music seems very basic, as if hardwired into the human mind.

Not only does this poem appeal, however, to very broad "instincts"; it also implies archetypal reactions in much specific phrasing. Thus, most humans can relate to the idea of a "camp" as a place of only temporary rest, and nearly all humans fear "poison" (5). Most people can imagine how vulnerable a blind person must feel; most would share fears of "dangerous tides"; and fear of serpents is very widespread (14–16), which is one reason snake-charmers and snake-handlers often provoke awe and incredulity. In short, Rosenberg's poem draws on many different archetypal reactions—reactions that give it much emotional and psychological power.

DIALOGICAL critics are interested in multiple forms of real or metaphorical dialogue. These may involve characters within a text, the text and its readers, or dialogue with other texts. Such critics would almost certainly be interested in Rosenberg's poem. It clearly involves a kind of dialogue with the Romantic tradition in poetry, which often celebrated birds and birdsong as symbols of natural beauty and freedom. Shelley's "To a Skylark" is a typical Romantic text, but the Romantic tradition, in turn, was itself involved in a kind of dialogue with the religious poetry that often preceded it. In religious poetry, God, not nature, would have been the chief source of consolation for isolated individuals. The Romantics, of course, make far fewer references to God than religious poets had made, and Rosenberg obviously makes no such reference here. This poem does not, for instance, resemble "The Windhover," by the latter-day religious poet Gerard Manley Hopkins. In Hopkins' poem, the sight of a bird inspires worshipful thoughts of God. Nor does Rosenberg's lyric resemble a poem like "The Lark Ascending," by the Victorian poet George Meredith. Instead, any latent Romanticism in Rosenberg's text is tempered by his poem's emphasis on death and suffering. Like all literary works, this one implies a kind of "intertextual" dialogue with preceding works. Even *within* this poem, romantic impulses are in dialogue with impulses that are non- or even anti-Romantic. Rosenberg's poem also exists in a kind of dialogue with other war poems of its time and with other kinds of poetry of its era. It is an implied riposte to naïve, jingoistic war poetry, and it is an implied retort to traditional, conventional poems of all sorts, with their heavy emphasis on predictable rhymes, rhythms, stanzas, and meters. By emphasizing the ways individual works are in dialogue with other individual works and with whole literary traditions, dialogical criticism helps highlight the special, distinctive features of any particular piece of literature. In that sense, dialogical criticism has much in common with formalism.

Leon Gellert (1892–1977): "A night attack"; "Anzac Cove"

A NIGHT ATTACK

Be still. The bleeding night is in suspense
Of watchful agony and coloured thought,
And every beating vein and trembling sense,
Long-tired with time, is pitched and overwrought.
And for the eye, the darkness holds strange forms.   [5]
Soft movements in the leaves, and wicked glows
That wait and peer. The whole black landscape swarms
With shapes of white and grey that no one knows;

And for the ear, a sound, a pause, a breath,
A distant hurried footstep moving fast.   [10]
The hand has touched the slimy face of death.
The mind is raking at the ragged past.
. . . A sound of rifles rattles from the south,
And startled orders move from mouth to mouth.

Any reader influenced by ARISTOTLE would probably greatly admire Gellert's poem. Aristotle (like latter-day formalists) believed that literary works should be both complex and unified. He believed that every part of a work should, as much as possible, lead up to and look back toward every other part. Gellert achieves such unity by building enormous suspense. Even the title suggests suspense, as do the first two words, with their stunning abruptness. As each new part of the poem falls smoothly into place, the work more and more displays the harmony and wholeness Aristotle highly valued. Each part follows every other part "by causal necessity" (p. 24), and the work would probably also please Aristotle because it seems just the right size, being neither too long nor too short to deal effectively with its "plot" (another unifying factor). Partly the poem is unified simply because it adheres to a standard form (the Shakespearean sonnet); even more important for Aristotle, however, would be the organic unity it achieves. One unifying factor is its growing suspense; another is the way the poem progresses from emphasizing seeing (5) to emphasizing hearing (9), touching (11), and thinking (12). The poem would also otherwise please Aristotle. Thus, it uses phrasing appropriate to its subject (pp. 29–30); it reveals no inconsistencies (p. 30); and its style is clear but not common (p. 33). And, because Aristotle considered effective metaphors the greatest indication of poetic talent, he would probably admire such striking metaphors as "Bleeding night" (1) and "coloured thought" (2). Finally, he would probably appreciate the ways Gellert manages to avoid five specific poetic errors: any elements that seem (1) "impossible," (2) "irrational," (3) "morally hurtful," (4) "contradictory," or (5) "contrary to artistic correctness" (p. 38).

STRUCTURALIST critics also look for ways human creations are unified. They especially stress the importance of interrelated "binary opposites." Taken together, these paired contrasts (such as black/white) reinforce one another and thus contribute to the underlying structure of a work in ways not immediately obvious. Thus, the fact that Gellert's poem is structured as a Shakespearean sonnet is instantly recognizable (at least to what structuralists sometimes call "competent readers"). Less overt, but no less important, are the underlying paired opposites that help structure the text. In the following list of such opposites, each term mentioned first tends to have positive connotations, while each term mentioned second tends to imply something negative (opposites implied, rather than openly stated, are in square brackets): stillness/[sound]; [health]/bleeding; [day]/night; [calm]/suspense; [peace]/agony; [plain thought]/colored thought; [calm pulse]/beating vein; [calm sense]/trembling sense; [feeling rested]/feeling tired; [feeling balanced]/feeling overwrought; [stillness]/movement; [goodness]/wickedness; [bright light]/faint light; [brightness]/blackness; [stillness]/swarming movement; [clarity]/imprecision; [knowledge]/lack of knowledge; and so on. In this listing, most terms mentioned first are merely implied, while most mentioned second are open and obvious. For a structuralist, however, the list of explicit terms only makes sense in relation to the list of implied terms, since the meaning of anything is defined by its relationship to its opposite. The two lists, taken together, help define both the overt and the underlying structure of the poem.

The sonnet form, meanwhile, is merely the work's *most* obvious structure; far more important is the structure lying beneath and within that form. Yet structuralists would not ignore the poem's sonnet pattern. They would, in fact, argue that a truly competent reader would know this aspect of the poem's structure, and they would also be interested in that form's evolution over time (its so-called diachronic development) as well as the way this sonnet resembles and/or differs from other sonnets written during the same era (the poem's so-called synchronic dimension). The Shakespearean sonnet structure is one "code" of sonnet-writing in English, and a structuralist critic would be greatly interested in any and all codes that might affect a work's structure.

A reader influenced by DECONSTRUCTION would show how the neat binary opposites that interest structuralists are rarely if ever neat, tidy, and simple. Thus Gellert's poem seems to present stillness positively, but of course complete stillness would mean death. Similarly, the poem apparently values daytime over nighttime, although it was actually during daytime that most deaths in World War I occurred. Likewise, the poem apparently presents calmness as more appealing than suspense, but suspense (and the alertness it required) was often the best way to preserve calmness, peace, and quiet. In short, rarely—for a deconstructor—are apparent opposites really and clearly distinct. Attempts to keep them neatly separate almost always fail.

Consider, for instance, the poem's opening phrase: "Be still" (1). It suggests that there are reasons *not* to be still. The very use of such phrasing stimulates mental activity and, in that sense at least, the opposite of stillness. Likewise, although the poem seems highly suspenseful and unpredictable, it *is* a sonnet, an especially predictable poetic form. The poem continually alludes to potential chaos, but it does so in a very tightly controlled structure. The speaker seems to prefer peace to war, yet this war was supposedly fought to create peace. He seems to favor safety over conflict, yet this conflict was justified as a way to create safety. The poem celebrates calmness but functions by reporting (and creating) great suspense. In short, for a deconstructor practically any use of language is full of contradictions; the "binary opposites" of structuralists collapse or bleed into one another. Supposedly clear concepts seem opaque and unstable, and nothing is ever as simple as it might at first appear.

DIALOGICAL critics, interested in various kinds of dialogue a literary work can manifest, might focus on ways the poem's speaker seems to be in dialogue with himself and his readers and on ways the poem participates in a kind of dialogue with the English sonnet tradition. Thus the opening two words—"Be still"—might at first seem addressed either to readers or to other persons within the text, although ultimately the speaker seems to be addressing himself. It is as if his rational mind is speaking to, and trying to calm, the parts of his mind now feeling fear, danger, and possible panic. Because the poem begins by jumping into the midst of things (*in medias res*), it surprises us, leaving us unsure, at first, precisely *whom* it addresses. It opens with dialogue that is in one sense merely internal or imagined, but it closes by describing dialogue that is quite literal and actual. The opening dialogue asserts the need for stillness and calm; the closing dialogue signals that frenzied, hectic action is about to begin. Yet ultimately even the final dialogue is only imaginary, only a part of the poem's invented (if realistic) "story." The poem's real and most important dialogue is with readers. To succeed, it must finally intrigue and interest *them*. It must successfully communicate to *them* the experiences of frontline soldiers, so that the speaker speaks not only for himself but for others facing similar circumstances. The poem ends by focusing on communication between and among soldiers, and other soldiers would obviously be among the best readers of (the best participants in any dialogue with) a poem like this. But the best war poems also help civilians experience life on the battlefield, and in fashioning this poem Gellert obviously had to imagine possible readers and write in ways they could appreciate (in various senses of that verb).

DARWINIAN critics, interested in ways evolution has helped shape the minds and emotions of all human beings (including writers and readers), might note how variously this poem alludes to reactions that seem hardwired into the human psyche. The need to keep calm and quiet in the face of danger, for instance, results from the fact that the humans and prehumans living over many eons who were capable of such self-control were far more likely to survive and pass on their genes than those who were more nervous and impulsive. Likewise, the poem's references to "every beating vein and trembling sense" (3) reminds us that humans (and many other animals) usually react to fear in common, instinctive ways: with rapid heartbeats, with surges of adrenalin, and with the "fight or flight" impulses that dominate life on most battlefields. The abilities to keep calm, think strategically, and work cooperatively with comrades would all have had real survival value for humans and prehumans over millions of years. Thus it is not surprising that those abilities are described and emphasized in this poem. Nor is it surprising that even people who have never been in battle can "relate" to the reactions to danger this poem describes. Most people, for instance, are especially afraid of danger in darkness, because darkness robs us of an enormous evolutionary asset: clear sight. The dangers this poem describes, and the reactions they provoke, are almost primal. Nearly everyone knows (or soon learns) how it feels to be under threat, and so nearly all readers can imagine quite vividly how Gellert's speaker feels and also what he is thinking.

ANZAC COVE

There's a lonely stretch of hillocks:
There's a beach asleep and drear:
There's a battered broken fort beside the sea.
There are sunken trampled graves:
And a little rotting pier: [5]
And winding paths that wind unceasingly.
There's a torn and silent valley:
There's a tiny rivulet
With some blood upon the stones beside its mouth.
There are lines of buried bones: [10]
There's an unpaid waiting debt:
There's a sound of gentle sobbing in the South.

LONGINUS, like many other early theorists (especially Aristotle and Horace), was much more concerned with the *literary* aspects of literary texts than is often true of various recent critics. In other words, he was often at least as concerned with how works were phrased and structured as he was with what they said or "meant." Thus in his treatise *On the Sublime*, he discusses the effective use of various rhetorical devices that definitely appear in Gellert's poem. These include anaphora (Preminger et al., pp. 208–9); realistic images (Preminger et al., p. 205); the combination of anaphora and vivid description (Preminger et al., p. 208); and the use of variation, so that order becomes disorderly and disorder becomes orderly (Preminger et al., p. 209). In Gellert's poem, for instance, patterning of words and lines definitely exists, but it never becomes entirely predictable and monotonous. Longinus might also admire how Gellert uses visualization to bring urgency and passion into his words (Preminger et al., p. 205) and also how he uses figures of speech to lend his phrasing realism and vigor (Preminger et al., p. 208). Emotion (Longinus says) can carry us away when it seems generated by a moving occasion, as it is in "Anzac Cove," and Longinus also praises other stylistic traits present in Gellert's text, including accumulation, variation, climax, and a vivid use of the present tense (Preminger et al., pp. 210–11). There are many reasons, then, to think Longinus would admire "Anzac Cove," particularly for its rhetorical effectiveness.

A TRADITIONAL HISTORICAL critic would almost certainly begin by explaining the poem's title. "Anzac" abbreviates "Australia and New Zealand Army Corps," and Anzac Cove was the site of one of the most famous, most bloody battles of the war—the "Battle of Gallipoli." For eight months in 1915, Allied forces attempted to overcome the resistance of German-allied Turkish forces on Turkey's Gallipoli peninsula. Casualties among Anzac forces, in particular, were extremely heavy, and ultimately the attempt was abandoned. Allied troops managed to withdraw so secretly to waiting ships that the Turks were taken by surprise. Thus Anzac Cove was associated by many of Gellert's readers with a lost battle in which many soldiers had been killed or wounded but also in which troops from Australia and New Zealand had nevertheless distinguished themselves.

Historical research shows that the evacuation was in many ways a tactical triumph. The poem captures quite effectively the appearance of the place and the mood the evacuation provoked—a mood of disappointment, defeat, and mourning for fallen comrades. But historical details cast the poem in a slightly different light: the Allies pulled off a major coup, one requiring plenty of intelligent preparation and very careful execution. In some ways it was a major victory, with astonishingly few casualties. Eventually the Turks found just a barren, useless beach full of material that had been disabled or destroyed. If nothing else, such historical knowledge helps us see the poem as more complex (less entirely bleak and dreary) than it might seem if read without such knowledge. The closing reference to "gentle sobbing" (12) may minimize Allied grief, suggesting stoic fortitude rather than anger, bitterness, or extreme sorrow. Meanwhile, the reference to an "unpaid waiting debt" (11) may suggest either the metaphorical debt the Turks and Germans will eventually pay to the Allies, or perhaps the debt Britain owes to its supporters in Australia and New Zealand.

A NEW HISTORICIST, interested in the sheer complexity of history and of attempts to "represent" history in writing, might note the many various ways the Gallipoli campaign can be (and has been) depicted. The Turks considered the battle a great victory; it hugely promoted the growth of Turkish nationalism. Success at Gallipoli helped propel new Turkish leaders into political power. The battle is also a central event in the history of Australia and New Zealand, many of whose residents think their men were treated shabbily by the British. Thus the experiences at Anzac Cove also helped fuel nationalism in Australia and New Zealand. However, in the splendid 1981 film titled *Gallipoli*, the sacrifices of Australians are emphasized, while New Zealanders are neglected, and in many histories the contributions of French, Nepalese, and Indian troops receive little attention. As these examples suggest, history is often told from varied perspectives, and the ways it is told often depends not only on who happens to be telling it but also on the kinds and amounts of power the tellers possess. Moreover, historical accounts often change over time, even when the tellers are from the same countries or ethnic groups as previous historians. New historicists emphasize that historical accounts, almost by definition, cannot be completely accurate or objective. Even historians who want and try to be disinterested almost inevitably cannot completely succeed. Their accounts are almost inevitably biased in one way or another. New historicists are usually more interested in *how* history is told than in whether it is "objective" or "true," since objectivity and truth are almost impossible to achieve.

The title "Anzac Cove" already suggests the poem's implied point of view, while the closing reference to "gentle sobbing in the South" again implies the speaker's sympathies with (and for) readers from Australia and New Zealand. It is also easy to imagine how this poem might have been (and still could be) appropriated by pacifists as an antiwar text, even though Gellert himself seems not to have been a pacifist. In short, New Historicists would be interested in the ways any historical event, and any historical account, could be variously used, for various reasons, by various persons or groups. For a New Historicist, there is no single historical perspective; there are only perspectives (plural), which often clash and conflict.

MULTICULTURAL critics, especially those interested in postcolonialism, would almost certainly be intrigued by Gellert's poem. The ANZAC forces, after all, consisted of men from two major British colonies, and one original reason for the war was Germany's envy of Britain's status as the world's major colonial empire. Yet ironically, of course, the white citizens of Australia and New Zealand could themselves be perceived as colonialists who had imposed their rule on their islands' nonwhite native populations. Gellert, interestingly enough, was himself the son of a Hungarian immigrant to Australia, yet he immersed himself in British culture and voluntarily enlisted to support Britain during the war. Meanwhile, the British desired an even greater colonial presence in the Middle East than they already possessed, and indeed the war in that region could be seen as a conflict between the British and the Ottoman empires. By encouraging Arab nationalism, the English sought to undermine the power of the Ottomans, while Turks themselves acted as colonialists in some ways, especially in their infamously bloody treatment of Armenians. And, to complicate matters even further, the Germans often saw themselves as superior to, and in control of, their Turkish allies. Thus, in all these ways, the entire conflict—especially the fighting at Gallipoli—can definitely be viewed in terms of colonialism, anticolonialism, and postcolonialism.

The forces fighting at Anzac Cove also included men representing other British colonial populations, including soldiers from India, Ceylon (although these were whites only), and also Jewish volunteers in the Zion Mule Corps. Given the heavy presence of colonialist fighters and colonialist motives in this battle, it seems significant that Gellert's poem focuses so heavily on the acquisition and loss of territory. Territorial ambitions, after all, were at the heart of most colonialist enterprises. Most efforts at colonization initially begin with acquisition of relatively small pieces of land, and British leaders felt that by acquiring control of Gallipoli they might hamper Germany's imperial ambitions. For all these reasons, "Anzac Cove" in some ways epitomizes (1) the territorial ambitions of empires, (2) the resistance those ambitions sometimes meet, and (3) the failure those ambitions often produce.

Readers interested in ECOCRITICISM, which emphasizes relations between humans and nature, might find Gellert's poem variously symbolic. After all, it describes how humans fight over pieces of nature, often destroying the environment in the process. The "torn and silent valley" of Anzac Cove (7)—briefly infested with humans and then abandoned—typifies how people often show little concern or respect for their natural surroundings. The fort and pier, once symbols of human power, are now mere wrecks and thus symbolize how ephemeral human mastery of the earth can be. The landscape, which now resembles a lifeless moonscape, will eventually renew itself, but the dead men in "trampled graves" (4) are dead forever. Human lives are temporary; only nature (an ecocritic might say) really endures—or at least that might have been true in Gellert's day. Present-day armies have access to weapons far more potentially destructive than anything Gellert and his contemporaries knew. The landscape in Gellert's poem may sound horrid, but today we are far more capable than during World War I of permanently obliterating not only each other but also the earth as well. Fortunately (an ecocritic might say), we are perhaps also more conscious and wary of our destructive powers. Thus, readers imbued with the environmental consciousness ecocritics seek to instill are probably far more likely than readers in Gellert's day to read this poem as also lamenting the rape of nature rather than simply the loss of human life.

9

Marian Allen (1892–1953): "The wind on the downs"

THE WIND ON THE DOWNS

I like to think of you as brown and tall,
As strong and living as you used to be,
In khaki tunic, Sam Brown belt and all,
And standing there and laughing down at me.
Because they tell me, dear, that you are dead,   [5]
Because I can no longer see your face,
You have not died, it is not true, instead
You seek adventure in some other place.
That you are round about me, I believe;
I hear you laughing as you used to do,   [10]
Yet loving all the things I think of you;
And knowing you are happy, should I grieve?
You follow and are watchful where I go;
How should you leave me, having loved me so?

We walked along the towpath, you and I,   [15]
Beside the sluggish-moving, still canal;
It seemed impossible that you should die;
I think of you the same and always shall.
We thought of many things and spoke of few,
And life lay all uncertainly before,   [20]
And now I walk alone and think of you,
And wonder what new kingdoms you explore.
Over the railway line, across the grass,

While up above the golden wings are spread,
Flying, ever flying overhead,   [25]
Here still I see your khaki figure pass,
And when I leave the meadow, almost wait,
That you should open first the wooden gate.

PLATO, or a reader influenced by him, would almost certainly
admire this poem's emphasis on immortality—on an immortal
soul and also on a love that transcends death. The poem implicitly
celebrates what Plato called the "glorious fame of immortal virtue"
(Preminger et al., p. 28), and it also implicitly teaches us how to
respond nobly to loss and grief, partly by displaying temperance
and moderate emotion (Preminger et al., pp. 28–9). The speaker's
appreciation of her dead lover's beauty (both of spirit and of body)
helps lead her to appreciate beauty in an even higher, more general
sense (Preminger et al., p. 29). "The beauty of soul," according to
Plato, "is more precious than the beauty of the outward form"
(Preminger et al., p. 29). Spiritual beauty (which the poem both
celebrates and displays) is "absolute, separate, simple, and
everlasting" (Preminger et al., p. 30). The poem implies the existence
of an appealing afterlife and suggests that death—for the dead—is
not terrible (Preminger et al., pp. 49–50). Meanwhile, the speaker
herself displays the courage of spirit and control of emotions that
Plato valued. She certainly neither provokes weeping nor gives way
to it herself (Preminger et al., pp. 89–90).

PSYCHOANALYTIC critics, who often emphasize the impact of
sexual feelings on literature, might note that lines 1–2 of Allen's
opening sonnet sound almost erotic. It is as if the speaker is still
attracted, at least in memory, to the dead man's handsomeness and
masculinity—traits enhanced by his military uniform. The opening
lines, then, seem to express the speaker's id, the seat of desires and
fears. These lines imply the sexual yearning she seems to have felt
(and may still feel) for the dead man, and perhaps the lines also imply
a sexual relationship between them. Yet the speaker's expression of
these emotions is not extreme. She does not seem irrational, nor
does she seem to be dwelling excessively on the past. Her emotional
id seems controlled by her rational ego and moral superego; she
seems to have made emotional peace with the fact that her lover is
dead, and in fact she imagines him in a higher, better place. She is
neither paralyzed by grief nor bitter and angry. Her reaction to his

death seems healthy and mature, implying a healthy, balanced ego. She even momentarily seems to regard the dead soldier almost as a father-figure, especially in lines 4 and 13. In the former line she recalls the man standing taller than her and laughing down at her as a father would chuckle at his amusing daughter. For the most part, however, their relationship seems to have been a relationship of equals (especially in line 15), a mature and healthy blending of masculine and feminine. She copes with his death as society might hope and expect her to do, and her memories of him seem sources of strength rather than causes of psychic stagnation.

FEMINIST critics would almost certainly applaud the fact that Allen and other women poets writing about World War I are now receiving attention after decades of relative neglect. Feminists might be troubled, however, by the actual and symbolic subordination the speaker sometimes seems to assume when she discusses her dead male loved one, especially in line 4, where he literally looks down on her and laughs in ways that might be considered patronizing in the full meaning of that word. The lover, in some ways, embodies male patriarchal power, not simply because he *is* a male but also because is a member of the military, which mostly excluded women. But other lines imply a genuinely mutual relationship rooted in real affection. It is as if these lovers were equals who complemented one another and felt reciprocal respect. The dead man does not seem to have been someone the woman was expected merely to revere and obey; she does not seem to have felt oppressed. Apparently he greatly pleased her, and although the poem can be read as reflecting stereotypically feminine emotion and sentimentality, it is far less sentimental than it might have been. The speaker displays a courage often associated with men but just as much a female trait in any women who are raised to feel and show it.

A feminist less sympathetic to this poem might argue that it reinforces stereotypes of women as less willing than men to confront reality and more prone than men to fantasize. A feminist critical of the poem might argue that the speaker presents herself as mainly passive, even as she imagines the male, though dead, as the more active and assertive of the two. In her fantasy, he is off seeking "adventure in some other place" (8) and is exploring new "*king*doms" (22; emphasis added). At the very end of the work, she remains passive, almost waiting for *him* to open the gate for her, as apparently he used to do. She likes to imagine that he is still thinking of her and watching out for her (13), but in fact all we can know for sure is that he is still—at least for the moment—the central focus of her existence. Perhaps this implies her stereotypically feminine dependency, or perhaps, from a more positive perspective, it illustrates the stereotypical tendency of women to take relationships very seriously and to truly commit themselves to others.

POSTMODERNIST readers, skeptical of "grand narratives" offering comprehensive explanations of an immensely complicated or even chaotic reality, might argue that this poem merely takes for granted the truth of an especially influential narrative: the idea of life after death. This is a narrative for which there are no (or, at the very least, few) supporting data. Yet it is also a narrative that almost by definition cannot be proven false. Thus it survives from one generation to the next, and this poem not only draws on it but helps perpetuate it. The poem exemplifies the human need to impose order on a reality that often seems painfully disorderly and incomprehensible. This poem, then, is *not* a postmodern work, but postmodernism can help expose its distinctive traits. Even in its imitative use of traditional forms (it consists of two sonnets), the poem is conventional and predictable. Both in thought and in structure it would probably strike a postmodernist as stale and even trite. Nothing about the poem seems especially original, inventive, or experimental. Instead it reflects and promotes (from a postmodernist viewpoint) dull, conservative thinking. Yet the poem is full of instabilities and internal contradictions if one only stops to think about them (as the speaker does not). Thus the speaker presents herself as still passive in her relationship with her now-dead lover, who still somehow seems active and full of vitality even though dead. She, however, is actually the truly active one—the one who actively creates a poem to try to make sense of her loss, yet the one whose poem can never really accomplish that objective. This poem, precisely because it *is* so conventional and traditional, might seem to some readers especially vulnerable to deconstruction and to postmodern skepticism of all sorts. Its effort to impose a "grand narrative" succeeds only (such readers would say) in suggesting that narrative's shortcomings.

A DARWINIAN critic, interested in how literature relates to biological evolution, might begin by noting the speaker's reference to her dead loved one as "brown," "tall," and "strong" (1–2)—adjectives that suggest his health and sexual attractiveness and thus his fitness as a mate and a potential father. Partly because of his physical appearance and partly for other reasons, he is precisely the kind of man most women (according to Darwinian theory) would find attractive. The speaker considered him virile, vital, courageous, and self-confident. She thought him strong but not self-centered—stereotypically "masculine" but also capable of laughter, love, and devotion to a mate. It seems especially tragic, then, that this kind of man has died before (apparently) being able to pass on his genes. After all, the poem never mentions children. But in a sense the poem itself serves to celebrate, make attractive, and in that sense pass on his traits to other men. The poem implicitly encourages other men to behave like this man—to embrace the same traits he displayed, if only because those traits are obviously attractive to women. At the same time, the poem also functions (from a Darwinian perspective) as an advertisement for the speaker (who presumably speaks for the poem's author). Anyone capable of writing such a poem would presumably make a good mate, since she implicitly presents herself as intelligent, loyal, selfless, vital, and interested in erotic pleasure while also being capable of love and commitment. The love the speaker displays for the man who has died implies her ability to love another man just as intently and loyally. Nothing suggests that she is so distraught with grief, so obsessed with the past, that she will be unable to adjust to a vital future with another mate. The speaker does not seem self-centered. Instead, she seems capable of appreciating a good man, and she also seems capable of getting on with life—honoring the dead but loving the living. The poem also displays how myths of immortality help give survivors strength, helping them live even after their dearest loved ones have died. The poem reminds us of all the many millions of soldiers (who were in some ways the best specimens of manhood) who perished in the war before being able to ensure the truest, least debatable kind of immortality by producing physical heirs.

Vera Brittain (1893–1970): "To my brother (*In memory of July 1st, 1916*)"

TO MY BROTHER (*IN MEMORY OF JULY 1ST, 1916*)

Your battle-wounds are scars upon my heart,
    Received when in that grand and tragic "show"
You played your part,
    Two years ago,

And silver in the summer morning sun   [5]
    I see the symbol of your courage glow—
That Cross you won
    Two years ago.

Though now again you watch the shrapnel fly,
    And hear the guns that daily louder grow,   [10]
As in July
    Two years ago,

May you endure to lead the Last Advance
    And with your men pursue the flying foe
As once in France   [15]
    Two years ago.

A reader influenced by HORACE might admire this poem for various reasons. After all, Horace emphasizes the poet's need to describe a character in terms of age-appropriate traits (p. 54), and certainly this poem's emphasis on a young soldier's heroism fulfills that requirement. Horace also advises depicting people who do their duties to their nation, friends, parents, and siblings (p. 56)—advice obviously relevant here. An effective writer, says Horace, should inspire courageous warlike deeds (p. 57), and again Brittain's poem satisfies this criterion. In addition, the poem's phrasing is lucid; its structure is clear; it departs only moderately from conventional ways of writing (particularly in its stanza structure); and it displays satisfying unity, particularly in its use of repetition. All these features might lead Horace to genuinely admire this poem.

A MARXIST, concerned primarily with socioeconomic justice and equality, might begin by noting that both Vera Brittain and her brother Edward came from a financially comfortable background. Their father was a businessman (not a landed aristocrat). He owned mills, employed workers, and thus made his own money (a Marxist would say) from others' labor. Vera Brittain's brother volunteered for military service and, due to his social status, immediately became an officer. Even Vera was able to volunteer as a nurse rather than having to work, for instance, in a grimy, unhealthy factory producing war munitions. For a Marxist, it might seem ironically appropriate that Edward was awarded a military "Cross" (7) for leading others to their deaths, especially since the established Church wholly supported the war rather than protesting against it or trying to promote peace. Even this poem itself, a Marxist might say, helped promote the war. It focuses on one man's courage rather than on the unnecessary slaughter of millions.

A Marxist might argue that the war's true heroes were the pacifists and conscientious objectors who opposed the conflict, often at great peril. War resisters were often imprisoned, and although many were put to work on the home front, many others were forced to join the army. Any among the latter who disobeyed orders were imprisoned. Opponents of the war were often denounced as cowards or even traitors. Yet a Marxist might argue that if enough people in all the countries involved had followed the conscientious objectors' lead, the war would have been impossible to begin or sustain. If international workers had united to demand what was rightfully theirs, poems such as this one would have been unnecessary.

FEMINIST critics might begin discussing this poem by noting that Vera Brittain's wealthy industrialist father did not want her to attend college. He believed that women should instead prepare themselves for marriage. Vera, however, did go to college, and she even also regretted that women could not be more active in the war: "whether [the war] is noble or barbarous I am quite sure that had I been a boy I should have gone off to take part in it long ago; indeed I have wasted many moments regretting that I am a girl. Women get all the dreariness of war and none of its exhilaration" (*Testament of Youth*, p. 104). Yet her participation in the war effort, particularly as a nurse, opened her life to many more varied, serious, and enlightening experiences than she might otherwise have had, even as a female college graduate.

Her tone in this poem seems stereotypically feminine. It is hard to imagine a male—even a male relative—writing to another man this way. She celebrates her brother for fulfilling his conventionally masculine role. She hopes that he and his "men" will "pursue the flying foe" (14). Vera herself would never have had the chance to lead or command men unless they were (for instance) lowly hospital orderlies, and as a nurse she would have taken orders from male doctors. As a woman—even as a woman from a wealthy background—she was condemned to play a relatively modest role in the "grand and tragic 'show'" of World War I (2).

NEW HISTORICIST critics, interested in the ways literary works reflect and contribute to negotiations of power in a broad cultural system, might begin discussing Brittain's poem by noting that when the work was written there were two basic, competing "discourses" about the war. One was prowar, while the other (growing in influence) was antiwar. External evidence (such as the sentences quoted above, in the section on feminism) suggests that Brittain's own attitudes were ambivalent from the start. Supporters of the war argued that the conflict had to lead to final victory; others favored immediate negotiations. Some people were frustrated with the British government for not making clear its ultimate objectives; often they feared that those objectives were imperialistic. Some felt that only profiteers benefited from the conflict. A reader lacking awareness of such debates might assume that Brittain's own attitudes were simpler than they were and reflected widespread British support for the war. But when the poem is read with knowledge of contemporary letters written by Vera and Edward, far more complex responses to the text become possible. Thus, a few months before composing this poem (which she wrote, ironically, shortly before her brother's death in battle), Vera had written this to her mother:

> We have heaps of gassed cases at present who came in a day or two ago; there are ten in this ward alone. I wish those people who write so glibly about this being a holy war and the orators who talk so much about going on no matter how long the war lasts and what it may mean, could see a case—to say nothing of

ten cases—of mustard gas in its early stages—could see the poor things burnt and blistered all over with great mustard coloured suppurating blisters, with blinded eyes—sometimes temporarily, sometimes permanently—all sticky and stuck together, and always fighting for breath, with voices a mere whisper, saying that their throats are closing and they know they will choke. The only thing one can say is that such severe cases don't last long; either they die soon or else improve—usually the former; they certainly don't reach England in the state we have them here, and yet people persist in saying that God made War, when there are such inventions of the Devil about. (*Testament of Youth*, p. 395)

Read in light of such evidence, Brittain's poem seems open to varied, sometimes contradictory, interpretations. It can be seen as participating in various contemporary "discourses." Although it might initially be read as prowar, it can also be read as advocating the quickest possible end to the conflict (through military triumph) and thus the quickest end to the killing. Or the poem can be read mainly as personal encouragement of Brittain's brother, who had little choice but to continue fighting. Or the poem can be read as encouragement to other troops. Or perhaps it can be read in all these ways at once. The poem, in other words, can be seen as both reflecting and contributing to various political, social, personal, and familial "discourses," with all those discourses themselves being inflected with issues of power and conflicts among various kinds of powerful special interests. In some ways, the poem is interesting partly for what it leaves *un*said. It is patriotic but not rabidly jingoist, nor is God openly invoked. The more fully the poem can read in light of many competing discourses of its day, the more its full resonances and participation in the cultures of the time can be discerned.

A MULTICULTURAL critic with an interest in Queer theory might be intrigued by the fact that Vera Brittain, despite greatly loving her brother and having a close relationship with him, apparently had no idea he was sexually attracted to other men and seems to have acted on those desires. Years after he died in battle, Vera was told by his commanding officer that incriminating letters had been discovered shortly before Edward's death and that Edward learned that he would probably be court-martialed (Bostridge and

Berry, pp. 130–1). Thus his death, not actually witnessed by others, may have been a suicide (a bullet hole was found in his head), or he may have made himself an easy target for an enemy sniper. In any case, Vera believed for years that he had died a conventional "hero's death."

For a "queer theorist," Edward might still easily be seen as heroic—indeed, perhaps as especially heroic. After all, he fought and died for a culture that despised homosexuals. That culture had forced him to hide some of his deepest desires, not only from his parents but also from his beloved sister and, probably, from most of his friends (including, apparently, his very best friend, Vera's fiancé). Edward commanded men who generally would have loathed him if they had known he was "gay" (a term not yet widely used, and an identity openly acknowledged by almost no one). His natural fear of physical injury in battle was probably, in some ways, less intense than his fear of being exposed and disgraced, and of disgracing his family. He would have feared the severe punishments the military could impose on homosexual conduct (imprisonment for two years for "gross indecency"; imprisonment for ten years for sodomy; and added punishment for any officer sexually involved with subordinates, as may have been the case with Edward). And Edward might also have feared the judgment he would have suffered from members of contemporary religious groups. Thus Vera's celebration of his military cross seems doubly ironic.

A queer theorist might argue that if Edward had simply been free to live as he wished, he might have helped dispel, through his undeniable bravery, the common stereotype of gay men as "sissies." But Vera would almost certainly have been unable to publish a poem extolling an openly gay man, and she may not even have wanted to try. She was apparently appalled when she learned her brother's secret. When she asked their mother if the secret might be true, her mother informed her that Edward had been in trouble for homosexual behavior when he had been at school—another fact that he and others apparently kept from Vera. And, for the rest of her life, Vera kept such secrets from the reading public who had greatly admired her very popular memoir about the war, *Testament of Youth*, written before she knew the full story of her brother's life and death.

Margaret Postgate Cole
(1893–1980): "The veteran"

THE VETERAN

We came upon him sitting in the sun
Blinded by war, and left. And past the fence
There came young soldiers from the Hand and Flower,
Asking advice of his experience.

And he said this, and that, and told them tales,   [5]
And all the nightmares of each empty head
Blew into air; then, hearing us beside,

"Poor chaps, how'd they know what it's like?" he said.
And we stood there, and watched him as he sat,
Turning his sockets where they went away,   [10]
Until it came to one of us to ask "And you're—how old?"
"Nineteen, the third of May."

A reader influenced by ARISTOTLE might argue that this poem, especially in its final line, combines reversal and recognition—a sudden change that also involves a sudden realization. Aristotle valued this combination as a sure sign of a well-structured tragedy (p. 26), and so he may also have valued its appearance here. The reversal involves our assumption that the word "veteran" implies an older man; the recognition involves our realization that this particular veteran is far younger than we probably assumed. Thus the final line combines shock and clarification, just as it also complexly unifies the poem. At the same time, the final line also reminds us, with shocking clarity, that very young men were indeed fighting, dying, and being seriously maimed and that the war was in some ways even more tragic for those who survived with profound injuries than for those who died. Aristotle would probably also admire the fact that nothing here makes the combined reversal and recognition seem implausible. The final twist follows naturally from everything previously mentioned, but it could not have been easily anticipated or foreseen. The poem thus displays the unity and careful craftsmanship Aristotle prized. And the poem is also tragic in other recognizably Aristotelian ways. It involves misfortune befalling a good person; it results in a single outcome; and, most of all, it inspires readers' pity and fear (pp. 27–8). The one exception to Aristotle's criteria for tragedy is that the veteran here does not really seem personally responsible for his fate. He seems guilty of no pride, error, or character flaw. Perhaps, though, he is a victim of the pride, errors, and flawed characters of those who started and sustained the war.

A TRADITIONAL HISTORICAL critic, interested in relating literature to history, might discuss this poem in light of attitudes toward the blind and handicapped when Cole wrote. Persons blinded in war, for instance, were more likely to receive public assistance than those born blind, and blind people in general—whose disability was hard to deny—were more likely to receive assistance than people less obviously disabled, such as the emotionally or psychologically scarred. Likewise, soldiers who had lost limbs in battle were eligible for public support, while those who had lost limbs in other ways were not. Paradoxically, then, a disabled veteran was often better-positioned, both socially and financially, than a disabled civilian. Disabled veterans whose injuries were undeniably severe (such as the blind) were more likely to receive assistance than those whose afflictions (such as internal diseases) were less readily apparent. There was, in fact, almost an incentive to prove one's injuries were severe: anyone able to work was expected to do so, to whatever degree possible. Even the blind were often encouraged not to *appear* overly dependent; use of seeing-eye dogs and even of white canes was often discouraged, lest the blind—especially blind soldiers—seem weak or unmasculine (see du Feu). Cole's veteran, then, fits a contemporary ideal that even severely disabled persons should seem strong, stoic, and uncomplaining.

The poem's reference to the "Hand and Flower" (3) may allude to a famous London pub, thus enhancing the text's authenticity. Certainly the reference alludes to *some* pub, thus implying the importance of pubs in British culture of this time. Pubs were places of communal gatherings, especially places where men gathered. The fact that the soldier seems to be sitting away from the pub rather than inside or immediately outside symbolizes his social isolation, and particularly his isolation from other young men. He seems to be sitting alone; literally and figuratively, he is cut off from others. Yet he speaks as an Englishman of his time would speak (especially when saying "chaps" [8]); he exemplifies the stoic English ideal of the "stiff upper lip"; and he reminds us that many young men fought, died, or were injured in World War I even though they had no real say in political affairs, since the voting age at the time was twenty-one. In all these ways, then, historical criticism sheds much light on Cole's poem.

THEMATIC critics are primarily interested in the themes or ideas literature implies or makes explicit. Often they are interested in how these ideas help unify literary works, which is why they are often concerned with "central themes" (key ideas stated or suggested repeatedly throughout a work). One theme suggested by Cole's poem, for instance, is the idea that true wisdom is rooted in genuine experience. Thus, mere assumptions about war are less important than actual, firsthand knowledge. Paradoxically, Cole uses a blind man to help us really "see" war's realities. Her poem allows us to profit from his experiences without having had to undergo such experiences ourselves. Ironically, however, the blind man in the poem apparently tells the inexperienced soldiers "tales" that help allay their fears (5). He may, in other words, tell them untruths to help calm their nerves—a nice example of how a thematic approach can illuminate potential complexities in literary works rather than making those works seem simplistic in their treatment of ideas. The young man in the poem, apparently, does not want to depress the other young men; thus he seems mature in more ways than one. Cole's poem, however, reveals painful truths (especially in its final line) and thus can seem, in a sense, more honest than the blind soldier. The young men who talk to *him* walk away relieved; readers of Cole's poem, on the other hand, are left feeling troubled, pained, but also admiring. These are just a few ways that a concern with the poem's "themes" can help us appreciate its intellectual, emotional, and artistic complexity.

FORMALIST critics would intently examine "the poem itself" (a procedure known as "close reading") to discover how it functions and succeeds as a *work of art*. They might note, for instance, that ultimately its title seems ironic, since this "veteran" is not old (as we may have expected) but a youth who is almost a boy. Formalists admire irony since by definition it exemplifies complex unity, a trait they almost always value. Turning from the title to the poem, formalists might immediately focus on the phrase "came upon," since it suggests that the speaker and her party did not seek out the young blind man but happened upon him by chance. Yet this chance encounter has moved her and opened her eyes, making her want to describe her experience. In a sense, she happens upon the soldier on the street much as we happen upon him in and through her poem, and both for her and for us the chance encounter is a revelation.

The speaker's reference to herself as part of a pairing or group (a "we") already helps emphasize the blind man's relative isolation. This isolation will be emphasized repeatedly and thus helps unify the poem as a work of art. The opening line displays an utterly regular iambic beat (in which odd syllables are unaccented and even syllables are accented): "We *came* upon him *sit*ting *in* the *sun*" (1). This meter, then, suggests nothing unusual or irregular. Yet the second line breaks this easy, predictable pattern by unexpectedly stressing the very first syllable, which is also an especially important syllable: "Blind." That word, in turn, immediately follows "sun," which appears at the end of line 1. This juxtaposition is effectively ironic, since "sun" suggests sight, vitality, and health, whereas "Blind" suggests darkness and disability. The syllable "Blind" is further stressed when line 2 resumes a regular iambic beat. This iambic rhythm appears throughout the rest of the first stanza except for the similarly important stressed syllable "Ask," which begins line 4. Meanwhile, in line 2 the phrase "and left" receives special emphasis by following a comma, while the pub's name seems effectively symbolic, suggesting the plucking of something fresh and beautiful, as the blind youth's own youthfulness has, in a sense, been taken from him. A formalist would proceed in this fashion, looking for any evidence of the poem's complex unity and beauty.

DIALOGICAL critics might be especially interested in Cole's poem, partly because it contains (and explicitly emphasizes) actual dialogue. In line 4, the young soldiers directly address the veteran; in line 5 he replies; in line 8 he addresses the speaker and another person or persons; in line 11 someone asks how old he is; and in the final line he replies. There are thus five exchanges in only twelve lines, so that the poem is "dialogical" in the strictest sense. Yet the poem is also dialogical in larger, broader ways. Thus the poem's speaker is a single individual, but in another sense she finally represents anyone shocked by the war's impact on the young. The poem can also be seen as instigating metaphorical dialogue with any readers who hold naively militaristic views. Cole's text "speaks" with and to militaristic poems and/or with and to government propaganda, implicitly challenging both. Perhaps the young veteran can even be seen as participating in a kind of dialogue with himself. Apparently he tells the inquisitive, inexperienced soldiers something less than the whole truth, so as not to feed their "nightmares" (6); then, in line 8, he may imply that he knows far more than he has said. Perhaps he regrets his own youthful naiveté. Perhaps, in calling them "poor chaps," he adopts the tone and voice of the stoic old wise man. He may want to sound more "grown up" than he actually is. Partly the poem lets the young veteran literally speak for himself. The speaker offers no explicit reaction to his comments and no evaluation of them. The tone of the poem itself—the tone it sounds in its own dialogue with the reader—is less deliberately moralizing, less openly propagandistic, than it easily might have been. And, partly for that reason, perhaps it is all the more effective; it does not try to badger readers into accepting any explicit, simplistic point of view. It allows them to reach their own conclusions, as effective interlocutors often do. In a poem about a blind man, it lets us come to our own individual insights.

10

Wilfred Owen (1893–1918): "Anthem for doomed youth"; "Arms and the boy"; "Disabled"; "Dulce et Decorum Est"; "Futility"; "Strange meeting"

ANTHEM FOR DOOMED YOUTH

What passing-bells for these who die as cattle?
     Only the monstrous anger of the guns.
     Only the stuttering rifles' rapid rattle
Can patter out their hasty orisons.
No mockeries now for them; no prayers nor bells,   [5]
     Nor any voice of mourning save the choirs,—
The shrill, demented choirs of wailing shells;
     And bugles calling for them from sad shires.

What candles may be held to speed them all?
     Not in the hands of boys, but in their eyes   [10]
Shall shine the holy glimmers of good-byes.
     The pallor of girls' brows shall be their pall;
Their flowers the tenderness of patient minds,
And each slow dusk a drawing-down of blinds.

PLATO believed that poets should support self-sacrifice in the interests of the greater good. He might therefore be troubled by this poem if he felt (a big "if") that it would subvert a worthy cause. Plato believed that a virtuous death, even of a son or brother, was not terrible and should not be lamented if the cause was just. A nation's defenders (he felt) should scorn fear of death (p. 50). They should obey their commanders and be courageous and endure (p. 53). Heroes should be depicted as better than ordinary people; they should not be shown suffering; they should face calamity with patience. Soldiers fighting for a good cause, Plato felt, should not pity themselves or make others sorrow (p. 74). A virtuous government was justified in lying if doing so promoted the public good (p. 51). For all these reasons, Plato might conceivably have wished that Owen's poem had never been written or published.

A TRADITIONAL HISTORICAL critic might be interested in the manuscripts of this poem. These suggest the stages of composition and thus throw light on the phrasing Owen ultimately chose. Particularly interesting are the various versions of line 5. In one manuscript, that line reads as follows: "Of choristers and holy music, none." In another version it reads "No wreaths for you, nor balms, nor mellow choirs." In yet another version it is "No chants for you, nor balms, nor wreaths, nor bells," and in another it is "No chants for them, nor wreaths, nor asphodels" (Stallworthy, pp. 217–20). Finally Owen seems to have chosen "No mockeries," although in at least one manuscript "No mockeries" *almost* looks as if it could read "No mock cries," which would fit better with the earlier drafts and would also make more sense in context (Stallworthy, p. 221). In any case, one key job of the traditional historical critic is to investigate a text's various manuscript versions (if they survive) and try to determine which is the best "final" text. Recently this impulse has been criticized, and, in the case of Shakespeare especially, there is a growing willingness to publish multiple versions and let readers decide which text they prefer. This willingness is far more typical of the so-called new historicism than of traditional historical criticism.

FORMALIST critics might also be interested in this poem's various drafts, but they would be much less concerned than traditional historical critics with establishing a "final" text reflecting Owen's ultimate intentions. Instead, they would be

interested in how the various versions help illuminate the phrasing
of whichever version a formalist might choose to analyze. For
example, one draft presents this version of line 1: "What minute
bells for these who die so fast?" A formalist might argue that the
phrase "die so fast" seems much less effective (because much less
vivid and suggestive) than "die as cattle," and that "minute bells" is
much less immediately clear than "passing-bells." The phrase "die
as cattle" implies humans being butchered as if they were "mere"
animals. Various other drafts of this line use the phrase "die in
herds," which is also arguably much less precise and vivid than
"die as cattle." One draft uses the words "dumb-dying cattle."
Various drafts, instead of using "these who die," use "you who
die," phrasing that implies much more immediacy and involvement
between the speaker and the soldiers he describes. A formalist,
concerned with the poem's beauty and artistic success, might even
argue that "you" would have been a better choice than "these,"
although a formalist would definitely be interested in hearing any
arguments in favor of the phrase Owen finally chose. Similarly, one
version of line 2 mentioned the "monstrous anger of our guns,"
but then Owen considered changing "monstrous" to "solemn."
Ultimately he reverted to "monstrous"—a much more effective
word (a formalist might contend) than "solemn" and also more
appropriate to the rest of the poem.

MARXIST critics might be interested in the phrase "die as cattle"
for significantly different reasons than formalists. They might argue
that the phrase symbolizes the ways most people, in capitalist
societies, are treated as animals and as expendable commodities.
Marxists might also suggest that this poem highlights the stark
contrasts between the empty formalities of meaningless religious
observances and the real brutalities of war. The poem suggests that
religion provides no real help in preventing or coping with war,
and thus it is not surprising that the speaker never appeals to God
for strength. The poem can in fact be read as an implied satire on
the hollowness of religious explanations and consolations. From
this perspective, the word "mockeries" (5) makes perfect sense. An
early draft used the phrase "priest words," suggesting empty clichés.
Perhaps Owen finally changed that phrasing to avoid seeming too
offensive, especially since the church was still a powerful force in
his society. Nevertheless, in line 11, the word "holy" may imply,
from a Marxist perspective, that loving relations between people,

rather than old tired rituals, are the true sources of genuine holiness if anything is. Owen's poem would ideally help break readers' addiction to the opiate of religion.

POSTMODERNIST critics, skeptical of grand explanations of practically anything, might argue that this poem's first line juxtaposes attempted meaning and lack of meaning, implied significance and genuine insignificance. The phrase "passing-bells" implies an attempt to impose some kind of religious significance on death, but the dead here die simply like cattle. Religion cannot make sense of deaths so senseless, and the poem can be read as an implied rejection of religion, which is perhaps the grandest of all grand narratives—the one that tries literally to explain *everything*. This poem displays the exhaustion, pessimism, and disillusionment that have sometimes been associated with postmodernism, as well as the skepticism about ideas of progress also often linked with that term (Ward, p. 10). This poem can also be seen as an example of a postmodern mixture and blending of literary genres: a realistic war poem undercuts or complicates a conventional elegy. Rather than merely reflecting "reality" (one function of literature according to some traditional theories), this poem instead helps influence and determine how "reality" is experienced. The common distinction between "real" and "imagined" thus becomes fluid and unstable, and the poem amounts to a small, modest, local narrative implicitly challenging or contradicting large, holistic explanations. The poem may imply absence of meaning; at the very least it seems to imply skepticism toward old ways of explaining life—ways that now seem exhausted and literally meaningless.

ARMS AND THE BOY

Let the boy try along this bayonet-blade
How cold steel is, and keen with hunger of blood;
Blue with all malice, like a madman's flash;
And thinly drawn with famishing for flesh.

Lend him to stroke these blind, blunt bullet-heads   [5]
Which long to nuzzle in the hearts of lads.
Or give him cartridges of fine zinc teeth,
Sharp with the sharpness of grief and death.

For his teeth seem for laughing round an apple.
There lurk no claws behind his fingers supple;   [10]
And God will grow no talons at his heels,
Nor antlers through the thickness of his curls.

HORACE might admire this poem for varied reasons, including its
unity and simplicity, its clear, plain language, the appropriateness of
its phrasing to its genre and subject matter, and the way (especially
in its use of near-rhymes) it follows a tradition (in this case the
tradition of rhyming) while displaying moderate innovation. "It is
hard," Horace wrote, "to treat a commonly known subject in an
original way" (p. 53), but Owen certainly does so here. Owen does
not simply imitate what others have done repeatedly (p. 53). Instead
he uses vivid imagery so that the reader's mind is stirred into almost
seeing what the poem describes (p. 54). The poem begins without
any elaborate introduction. Instead, in the best Horatian fashion,
it starts by jumping into the midst of things (*in medias res* [p. 53]).
In all these ways, Owen creates a poem that seems simple but that
would be difficult to imitate (p. 55).

A THEMATIC critic, interested in the ideas explored or expressed
in literature, might argue that this is a poem primarily concerned
with the theme of innocence versus experience and that this
"central motif" helps organize and unify the text. The "boy" (1), for
instance, can be seen as symbolizing innocence, while the weapons
can be seen as symbols of painful experience. The poem thus also
implies such related, complementary themes as life versus death
and also the processes of initiation and maturation. Any "boys"
who managed to survive this war would quickly have become men
and would have had their basic outlooks forever altered by their
wartime experiences. In juxtaposing boys and deadly weapons, the
poem also implies such themes as the natural versus the unnatural,
the human versus the inhuman, pleasure versus pain, and gentleness
versus violence. As these pairings suggest, thematic criticism often
resembles structuralism in its emphasis on "binary opposites," and
there is evidence that Owen himself interpreted the poem in explicitly
thematic terms—that is, in terms of the "message" he intended it to
convey. In a draft list of contents for a planned book, this poem was
placed under the heading "Protest—the unnaturalness of weapons"
(Cross, p. 85). Thus anyone who read the poem thematically would
simply be following Owen's own lead.

A FORMALIST critic, interested in a work's complex unity and in its success as a carefully crafted work of art, would find much to admire in this poem. A formalist might argue, for instance, that much of its effectiveness depends on traits of sound, meter, and imagery. Thus Owen skillfully uses alliteration in such phrases as "boy . . . bayonet-blade" (1); "cold"/"keen" (2); line 3 in general; "famishing for flesh" (4); "blind, blunt bullet-heads" (5); "Sharp . . . sharpness" (8); and "through the thickness" (12), to mention just a few examples. Assonance appears in such wording as "madman's flash" (3), "teeth . . . grief" (7–8), and "teeth seem" (9). Owen also shows his artistry in using meter not only by the unconventional rhythms of line 1, the special emphasis on both syllables of "cold steel" in line 2, and the unexpectedly accented "Blue" of line 3, but also (after all those variations from expectations) in the unexpected appearance of a completely regular line of iambic pentameter in line 4. In that line, as in lines 10–12, the predictable iambic beat helps highlight, by contrast, all the metrical experimentation elsewhere. A formalist, of course, would argue that successful sound effects must seem integral to the work rather than self-indulgent distractions, but strong arguments can be made that this is precisely the case in Owen's poem. Owen is alive to the sounds of words; his poems therefore often brim with intense, energetic, and highly memorable phrasing.

Yet a formalist might also admire much more about "Arms and the Boy" than its sound effects. The poem not only uses vivid personification but also combines that technique with paradox: steel, after all, cannot really "hunger" for "blood" (2), and bullets do not literally "long to nuzzle in the hearts of lads" (6). Only other humans—other persons—can make inert objects seem full of life and intention in this way. Yet the poem's imagery is also striking, particularly in the ways it evokes various senses, as in "cold steel" (2), "Blue . . . malice" (3), and "famishing for flesh" (4), just as it is also strangely sensual, as in the verbs "stroke" (5) and "nuzzle" (6) and in the closing reference to "the thickness of his curls" (12). Thus a poem about killing sometimes almost sounds erotic, and a poem about death possesses a kind of rich vitality and beauty. For a formalist, the poem would be interesting less for its message (a protest against the unnaturalness of weapons) than for the skillful, striking ways in which that message is phrased.

DIALOGICAL critics, interested in both literal and metaphorical dialogue both within and between texts, would surely be intrigued by Owen's poem, beginning with its title. It clearly—and somewhat ironically—alludes to the famous opening words of Virgil's *Aeneid* ("Arma virumque cano" [I sing of arms and of the man]), which describe a great military hero in an epic poem full of heroic battles. But Owen's title may also have reminded readers of George Bernard Shaw's comedy of 1894, *Arms and the Man*, whose own title alludes to Virgil's epic. Already, then, even before it properly begins, Owen's poem is engaged in a complicated dialogue with at least two previous works (and, through its echo of Virgil, with the whole epic tradition).

In Shaw's play, which satirizes naïve thinking about war, actual battle is distant from the main action and the work is ultimately a romance with a happy ending. In Owen's poem, by contrast, the archetypally named "Boy" is in the thick of combat. No attractive young women are featured (as in Shaw's comedy), and the tone of Owen's work is somber and ominous. Shaw's play mocks the creative writers who are often responsible for romantic, unrealistic ideas about war; Owen's poem clearly repudiates and undercuts any naïve romanticism. In some respects Owen's lyric more directly echoes Virgil's epic, especially since Virgil's depictions of war are often notoriously dark. The *Aeneid*'s very last lines, for instance, abruptly and chillingly describe how Aeneas kills his chief enemy, Turnus: "burning with rage, he buried his sword deep / in Turnus's breast: and then Turnus's limbs grew slack / with death, and his life fled, with a moan, angrily, to the Shades" (A. S. Kline translation). Nothing more is said; no attempt is made to glorify this death. A dialogical critic would say that Owen's poem participates in a meaningful—if metaphorical—conversation not only with Virgil's epic and Shaw's comedy but also with various other works, including (to mention just a few cited by Jon Stallworthy in his edition of Owen's poems [1: 151) poems by Shelley, A. E. Housman, Harold Monro, and even a poem by Bret Harte ("What the Bullet Sang"), whose first lines are these: "O joy of creation, / To be! / O rapture, to fly / And be free! / Be the battle lost or won, / Though its smoke shall hide the sun, I shall find my love—the one / Born for me!" All literature, for a dialogical critic, is engaged in dialogue of various kinds, including with other texts and also with living readers.

A MULTICULTURAL critic, especially one interested in Queer theory, might be intrigued by Owen's poem. Owen himself seems to have felt and acted on homoerotic yearnings. His poems, in any case, are full of homoerotic phrasing, and "Arms and the Boy" can be read as one such poem. Even the repeated word "Boy" suggests a young man, and reference to "lads" in line 6 reinforces the suggestion. The references to laughing teeth, supple fingers, and thick curls all, again, imply young soldiers, while erotic undertones seem clearly conveyed in the references to bayonets "famishing for flesh" (4) and bullets "Which long to nuzzle in the hearts of lads" (6). The entire final stanza is richly sensual, and in general the poem implies that war is particularly wasteful when it destroys the fine bodies of handsome young men in the prime of their physical lives.

DISABLED

He sat in a wheeled chair, waiting for dark,
And shivered in his ghastly suit of grey,
Legless, sewn short at elbow. Through the park
Voices of boys rang saddening like a hymn,
Voices of play and pleasure after day,   [5]
Till gathering sleep had mothered them from him.

*   *   *

About this time Town used to swing so gay
When glow-lamps budded in the light-blue trees
And girls glanced lovelier as the air grew dim,—
In the old times, before he threw away his knees.   [10]
Now he will never feel again how slim
Girls' waists are, or how warm their subtle hands.
All of them touch him like some queer disease.

*   *   *

There was an artist silly for his face,
For it was younger than his youth, last year.   [15]
Now he is old; his back will never brace;

He's lost his colour very far from here,
Poured it down shell-holes till the veins ran dry,
And half his lifetime lapsed in the hot race,
And leap of purple spurted from his thigh.   [20]

*   *   *

One time he liked a bloodsmear down his leg,
After the matches, carried shoulder-high.
It was after football, when he'd drunk a peg,
He thought he'd better join.—He wonders why.
Someone had said he'd look a god in kilts,   [25]
That's why; and maybe, too, to please his Meg,
Aye, that was it, to please the giddy jilts,
He asked to join. He didn't have to beg;
Smiling they wrote his lie: aged nineteen years.
Germans he scarcely thought of; all their guilt,   [30]
And Austria's, did not move him. And no fears
Of Fear came yet. He thought of jewelled hilts
For daggers in plaid socks; of smart salutes;
And care of arms; and leave; and pay arrears;
Esprit de corps; and hints for young recruits.   [35]
And soon, he was drafted out with drums and cheers.

*   *   *

Some cheered him home, but not as crowds cheer Goal.
Only a solemn man who brought him fruits
Thanked him; and then enquired about his soul.

*   *   *

Now, he will spend a few sick years in institutes,   [40]
And do what things the rules consider wise,
And take whatever pity they may dole.
Tonight he noticed how the women's eyes
Passed from him to the strong men that were whole.
How cold and late it is! Why don't they come   [45]
And put him into bed? Why don't they come?

PLATO would be bothered if this poem inspired fear in potential soldiers and regret or even bitterness in veterans. He might, conversely, admire it if it inspired communal commitment to disabled soldiers. His assessment would depend greatly on whether or not he believed the poem promoted the national welfare. He might dislike the poem's focus on private, physical, self-centered pleasures. The young recruit's concerns with women, personal glory, and erotic satisfaction might particularly trouble Plato. Plato, after all, believed that all citizens owed their first duty to the commonwealth, and so the merely personal, private motives of both the soldier and the citizens who ignore him might earn Plato's censure.

A PSYCHOANALYTIC critic might begin by noticing that the soldier in this poem, because of his physical disabilities, now feels (and is treated by others) as if he is not much more than a damaged body. Denied full use of his flesh, he is unable to act on the sensual impulses of his id, and neither his rational ego nor his moralistic superego can quite reconcile him to the sacrifices he has made. He joined the war effort not because his superego (seat of the conscience) prompted him (30–1); instead, he was motivated mainly by his pleasure-seeking id. At first we see him mainly externally, but eventually the poem takes us inside his psyche, giving us access to his deepest thoughts and emotions. His psychological suffering seems even greater than his physical pain, and since his id is now denied pleasure, it expresses itself in anger, frustration, and self-recrimination. His attitude toward women is especially interesting. At first he understandably regrets that they no longer find him physically appealing, but eventually he actually blames them for his decision to join the army and thus risk life and limb. He tries to displace his anger at himself by expressing anger at them. In a phrase that sounds as if it might be spoken by the soldier rather than by an objective narrator, we are told that he joined "to please the giddy jilts" (27). Indeed, an especially interesting aspect of this poem is the way it is written in the third person but continually moves into the soldier's own consciousness, a process especially true in the final lines. Throughout the poem we sense how closely the id and ego are intertwined, not only in this young man but in human beings in general. Denied the sensual pleasures associated with the id, he suffers even more, perhaps, from damaged self-esteem—from a pained ego. Nor can his superego console him: the only reference to his "soul" (39) sounds trite and even condescending. He has been disabled physically, but even worse damage has been done, in some ways, to his mind and emotions. Meanwhile, the poem stimulates readers' ids (especially their own fears of extreme physical vulnerability), although ideally it should also stimulate their superegos, their own consciences, and inspire them to try to help other victims of war.

A FEMINIST might argue that the poem's speaker has, in a sense, been turned into a stereotypical woman of his time and place. He seems helpless, needy, dependent on others, and lacking in power and self-respect. He is patronized and treated as less than fully human, even by those who claim to care for him. He is, in short, no longer a "real" man; he has been emasculated and feminized. Even the playing boys (4) are at least potential men, and although their mothers supervise them (6), such mothering will eventually diminish and end for them—but not for the soldier. He will need to be mothered for the rest of his days, and most of his caretakers are likely to be women. This will be true not only because women are stereotypically kinder and more caring than men, but also because caretakers were rarely paid enough to make caretaking financially attractive to men.

The soldier, however, also variously knows now how it feels to be a woman. Women, after all, have long been valued according to their physical attractiveness. Now women will treat him as superficially as men treat women. He resents being considered mainly a body, but women have long resented such treatment. He thinks of "his Meg" (26) as a possession, and he blames a desire to please "giddy jilts" (27) for luring him into the army. Before joining, he thought as women are stereotypically expected to think: of how good he would look in a certain outfit (a kilt, no less [25]) and of how jewels would enhance his appearance (32). He even liked the idea of showing off his legs and was concerned with fashion right down to his colorful socks (33). Now he completely depends on others, and, rather than taking women to bed (as he might earlier have done or hoped to do), he must now wait to be "put . . . into bed," almost certainly by women (46).

NEW HISTORICIST critics, interested in how power circulates in cultures and also interested in marginalized groups, might be especially intrigued by this poem. It focuses, after all, on the disabled, a particularly powerless, marginalized group in most societies. New historicists would argue that how a culture treats marginal groups tells us much about that culture's larger values, structure, and power relations. Yet they would also argue that social relations are rarely static, that cultures are always changing, and that changes in treating marginalized groups often indicate how the larger culture itself is being transformed. Owen's poem can be read both as reflecting on the plight of a particularly powerless group, partly to try to improve the group's power and status. Thus the poem does not merely reflect a static historical context (as traditional historical critics might argue) but is itself a social act, an assertion of social power. It attempts to influence its culture, not simply mirror an unchanging set of social relations.

As Owen's poem makes clear, the politics that often matter most to most people are *micro*politics rather than *macro*politics. In other words, the disabled soldier was (and still is) far less concerned with foreign relations than with relations with other individuals in his own small community. This is not a poem about ideological conflicts or about the ruling or working classes of competing empires. Those conflicts might especially interest traditional historical critics. Instead, this is a poem about how particular individuals live their everyday lives in particular social settings that nonetheless influence, and are influenced by, the culture as a whole.

MULTICULTURAL critics—especially those interested in the rapidly developing field of DISABILITY STUDIES—would also focus on how this poem depicts a young veteran facing severe physical and mental challenges. According to advocates of disability studies, people facing such challenges are often marginalized or ignored, both in life and in literature. Owen's poem helps combat ignorance (in various senses of the word). It emphasizes the thoughts, feelings, and experiences of a "disabled" person. It implicitly invites able-bodied readers to imagine this man's existence, especially since his disabilities need never have happened. They were preventable if only war had been avoided. Disabilities existing from birth or resulting from accidents are tragic enough, but disabilities resulting from bad decisions are awful in their own ways.

However, while the young soldier obviously suffers physically, his psychological anguish is in some ways even more painful. Enemy soldiers ruined his body, but his own people contribute to his mental pain. Their treatment of him reminds us how much we tend to judge others—and are judged ourselves—according to physical appearance and physical skills, including positive ones (such as athletic prowess). The soldier's earlier handsomeness and strength make him now feel especially weak and unattractive. Even his chair must be "wheeled" by someone else, and he is "waiting for dark" (l) both literally and figuratively. His situation is bad enough, but even worse, in some ways, are the predicaments of people severely disabled from birth. They have never experienced the pleasures he once enjoyed. The poem emphasizes disabled war veterans but implies the plight of disabled people in general.

DULCE ET DECORUM EST

Bent double, like old beggars under sacks,
Knock-kneed, coughing like hags, we cursed through sludge,
Till on the haunting flares we turned our backs,
And towards our distant rest began to trudge.
Men marched asleep. Many had lost their boots   [5]
But limped on, blood-shod. All went lame; all blind;
Drunk with fatigue; deaf even to the hoots
Of tired, outstripped Five-Nines that dropped behind.

Gas! GAS! Quick, boys!—An ecstasy of fumbling,
Fitting the clumsy helmets just in time;   [10]
But someone still was yelling out and stumbling,
And flound'ring like a man in fire or lime . . .
Dim, through the misty panes and thick green light,
As under a green sea, I saw him drowning.

In all my dreams, before my helpless sight,   [15]
He plunges at me, guttering, choking, drowning.

If in some smothering dreams, you too could pace
Behind the wagon that we flung him in,
And watch the white eyes writhing in his face,
His hanging face, like a devil's sick of sin;   [20]
If you could hear, at every jolt, the blood
Come gargling from the froth-corrupted lungs,
Obscene as cancer, bitter as the cud
Of vile, incurable sores on innocent tongues,—
My friend, you would not tell with such high zest   [25]
To children ardent for some desperate glory,
The old Lie: *Dulce et decorum est*
Pro patria mori.

Although most readers might immediately assume that this is a tragic poem (perhaps one of the most tragic in English), ARISTOTLE might disagree. He, after all, believed that a truly tragic figure had to be somehow responsible for his fate, either because of an erroneous choice or because of a deeper flaw in a generally virtuous personality. The suffering men Owen often depicts do not seem tragic in this very strict sense; instead, they seem virtuous victims whose pain is unmerited. Aristotle explicitly states that a true tragedy cannot show a good person "brought from prosperity to adversity," for this provokes "neither pity nor fear," the emotions he considered central to tragedy. Instead, he believed, the fall of a good person "merely shocks us" (p. 26). Partly for this reason the great poet W. B. Yeats controversially excluded Owen's works from his edition of the *Oxford Book of Modern Verse*. Yeats argued that "passive suffering is not a theme" for truly worthy poetry (see Schweizer, p. 107). Whether this poem does indeed fall short of being tragic in the Aristotelian sense, looking at it from an Aristotelian point of view helps highlight important issues, especially those connected with how we define literary genres and thus interpret individual literary works.

A TRADITIONAL HISTORICAL critic might note, very generally, that World War I was one of the first wars in which so many soldiers—both officers and enlisted men alike—were fairly well educated and thus able to produce so many literate, potentially publishable reactions to their service. The publishing industry had grown massively because more and more people could read. Radio (which was in its infancy) provided little competition, and television had not yet been invented. For various historical reasons, then, many soldiers wrote and many readers consumed what they produced. These productions included newspaper articles, extended memoirs, short stories, and novels, but they also included so many poems that eventually many publishers felt overwhelmed. Many magazines and newspapers actually began discouraging further submissions dealing with the war. Much printed war poetry was simplistic and jingoistic, and Owen's poetry is so historically important partly because it is neither. Setting his verses within historical and literary contexts of his time helps heighten our sense of his literary achievement.

A historical focus, however, can also help us appreciate the details of individual works, including "Dulce et Decorum Est." This poem's very title, of course, alludes to a famous line by Horace, often translated as "It is sweet and appropriate to die for one's country." By echoing this line, Owen also evokes an entire cultural ethos, of his era and earlier—an ethos which stressed such ideals as patriotism, selfless service, and self-sacrifice. Millions of soldiers and their families embraced these ideals. Far fewer people dissented from them than we often imagine. In penning poems like this one, Owen was thus writing against the historical grain of his era. He was staking out a decidedly minority position, and historical study can help us appreciate just how unusual his poem would have seemed to its first readers.

Yet historical study can also help illuminate much more about "Dulce et Decorum Est" than simply its title's significance. Practically every line seems more resonant when read with historical facts in mind. Thus the reference to "sludge" (2) seems especially meaningful to anyone familiar with wartime memoirs, which repeatedly mention heavy mud. The reference to "flares" in line 3 is intriguing when we realize that World War I was the first major conflict in which flare guns (invented in 1877) and other kinds of pyrotechnics (such as "star shells") were so widely and frequently employed. One historical source reports that the "British alone used 10 million position light flares per month" (*Military Explosives* pp. 2–11), and the common use of flares obviously increased dangers for soldiers who could no longer count on darkness for protection. The reference to "Five-Nines" in line 7 is to explosives from a "German 5.9 inch (15 cm) heavy howitzer, with a hundred-pound shell and [a] maximum range of five and a half miles" (Benstead, p. xxv). One historian calls this weapon the one "most feared by the Allied forces" (Smith, n.p.). References like these help establish the poem's authenticity and also help emphasize that success in this war often depended as much, if not more, on technology as on courage and strength. Thus the poem's heavy emphasis on gas alludes to an especially notorious and disturbing technological development of this war. Only historical knowledge can help us appreciate how shocking a gas attack would have seemed to people of Owen's time.

FORMALIST critics, interested in the success or failure of literary works as works of art, might try to account for the widespread admiration this poem usually provokes, not only from professional literary critics but from everyday readers, especially students. A formalist might point, for instance, to the effective use and combinations of alliteration in lines 1–2 (and throughout the work), and a formalist might also notice how well Owen there also uses assonance (as in "sacks"/"hags" or "bent"/"beg-"), a striking simile, vivid imagery, and emphatic metrical effects, as in the first syllable of both lines 1 and 2. There is even a hint of onomatopoeia in the word "coughing," and in general the first two lines overwhelm us with varied sensual effects that combine to produce poetry of a sort that seemed—and still seems—highly original and overwhelming. For a formalist, what matters most is not so much *what* the speaker says as *how*—and how memorably—he says it, and it is hard to imagine lines more memorable than these. Yet this, of course, is a poem that proves to be full of such lines, and the lines all seem to work together, reinforcing one another to create an exceptionally powerful text illustrating the "organic unity" so prized by formalists.

Formalists would move carefully through the poem, noting not only particular details but also how they interact. Thus, after the highly unpredictable rhythms of the first two lines, lines 3 and 4 are pure examples of regular iambic pentameter—a shift that seems appropriate in lines describing men trudging forward. Lines 1–4 constitute one long, exhausting sentence, while the first half of line 5 is surprisingly abrupt. The phrase "blood-shod" in line 6 recalls the earlier phrase "Knock-kneed" in line 2, and both phrases have the kind of concentrated rhythmic force one expects to find in poems by (for instance) Gerard Manley Hopkins. In line 6, the brevity of the phrases in the second half ("All went lame; all blind") is made even more emphatic by the repeated word "all," while the metaphor that opens line 7 is all the more striking for being so paradoxical and ironic (since we often think of being drunk as a pleasurable sensation). Meanwhile, the phrasing in line 8 is so specific, so apparently rooted in actual experience, that it gives a powerful impression of authenticity even while it brims with assonance, which makes it memorable in sound as well as in imagery.

Everything about this poem seems, in retrospect, carefully designed, yet every aspect of its phrasing also seems inevitable and appropriate. Thus the sudden shift in line 9 to a new paragraph, with its outburst of exclamations and its shift from narration to excited speech, catches readers by surprise, much as a gas attack surprised its targets. The use of a fragment in the second half of line 9 seems appropriate to a situation in which normal rules and orderly procedures suddenly seem unimportant, while the hint of disaster averted, implied in line 10, is immediately and effectively undercut in the shift to line 11. The word "someone" is effectively vague, implying the speaker's lack of clear perception as well as the relative unimportance of the victim's precise identity. The imagery of lines 12–13 seems appropriately surreal, while the word "drowning" in line 14 seems sickeningly fitting yet paradoxical (how can someone drown above water?), while the sudden shift to explicit first person brings home to us that this incident not only had a huge impact on the victim's body but also on the speaker's psyche. Meanwhile, the fact that eight lines followed by six lines constitute the common structure of a sonnet (a kind of poetry often used to deal with love, not hate and death) adds one further element of irony.

To say all this, however, is merely to scratch the poem's surface, at least from a formalist's point of view. Formalists consider the best works of literature to be so rich, so resonant, so complex in all the best senses of that term that no analysis, no matter how detailed, can do full justice to those works as *works of art*.

A MARXIST critic might begin by arguing that the poem's opening comparison of soldiers to "old beggars" (1) is highly appropriate. Beggars, after all, are at the economic mercy of people wealthier than they, and soldiers are in precisely that situation. In one way or another—whether through war or through everyday economic exploitation—capitalism (according to Marxists) oppresses people and uses them destructively. Many soldiers served because they needed money (the poet Isaac Rosenberg was one). Others were eventually drafted unwillingly. Even persons who volunteered did so partly because they were conditioned to do so by the dominant ideology, which served the interests of the wealthy. The only persons who benefited from the war were war profiteers, and therefore it is not surprising that this war led to the rise of the first Marxist government in history (in the Soviet Union).

Women, too, suffered during the war, even if they were far from the front lines. Thus the poem's description of soldiers "coughing like hags" (2) might remind us not only of poor, elderly women of the slums of polluted cities but also of women who labored in the often dangerous conditions of wartime factories. Indeed, the conditions described in lines 1–4 recall, in various ways, the conditions faced by the working class, whether in urban factories or in rural coal mines. Poor soldiers off at war fought to defend a system that exploited them, and in fact the war helped distract their attention from the kinds of economic conflicts and tensions that might otherwise have existed at home. Meanwhile, the poem's references to howitzers, shells, and gas remind us that this was an *industrial* war on an unprecedented scale. Much industrial might, and much working-class labor on both sides, was poured into a war effort in which poor people were the main victims, both at home and on the battlefield. Indeed, the governments themselves did not typically manufacture the weapons and other supplies their armies used; instead, those weapons and supplies were mainly made and sold (at a handsome profit) by private companies. As this poem vividly reminds us—especially with its depiction of a body being "flung" into a "wagon" (18)—the war reduced human beings to the status of things, to be used and then tossed away, like pieces of discarded factory waste. Ultimately the poem satirizes the kind of jingoistic ideology or false consciousness that prompted workers to think of themselves as German or English or French rather than as members of an international proletariat with common interests and common enemies. Yet the war also sometimes gave Owen and some other relatively privileged people like him some ability to identify and sympathize with the suffering masses, whom they might previously have regarded as mere inferiors.

DIALOGICAL critics, intrigued by interactions within and between texts and also between texts and readers, might be especially interested in the ways this poem participates in a kind of dialogue with a particular poem by Horace (*Odes* 3.2) as well as with the whole poetic tradition that exalted heroism and warfare. Horace's poem (in the translation by Anthony S. Kline), opens as follows:

> Let the boy toughened by military service
> learn how to make bitterest hardship his friend,
> and as a horseman, with fearful lance,
> go to vex the insolent Parthians . . .

Its most famous passage, however—the passage from which Owen borrows his poem's title—is its fourth stanza:

> It's sweet and fitting to die for one's country.
> Yet death chases after the soldier who runs,
> and it won't spare the cowardly back

or the limbs of peace-loving young men.

Horace wrote when warfare typically involved hand-to-hand combat (as his poem makes abundantly clear). Owen, in contrast, wrote when soldiers were often blown to bits by shells fired from miles away, or were mowed down by machine guns hundreds of yards distant, or, as in this poem, suffocated without warning by clouds of poisoned gas. It may be, then, that Owen's poem does not reject patriotism or personal heroism but instead rejects muddleheaded jingoism that ignores the practical conditions of actual modern warfare. The warfare Horace describes is almost literally epic: a queen and princess watch from atop a tower as an enemy hero, resembling a raging lion, prepares to slaughter the princess's inexperienced fiancée. Owen's soldiers do not rely on spears and swords, and there are no beautiful women around to witness any brave deeds. Anyone familiar with Horace's poem (as Owen and many of his readers would have been) would have found "Dulce et Decorum Est" in an extremely ironic dialogue with Horace's ode. Indeed, Owen's poem itself has become so famous and so widely and deeply admired that it is hard, any longer, to read Horace's text without thinking of Owen's response. The dialogue between the two poems has thus become a dialogue indeed; it is not simply a matter of Horace's poem having influenced Owen's, but also of Owen's poem changing the way we now read Horace's ode. Yet Owen's poem is dialogical in yet another sense: its final lines explicitly, and somewhat sarcastically, address any "friend" (25) who tells children "the old Lie" once taken as a simple truth (27). These so-called friends may include teachers, politicians, priests, or any other kind of authority figures, including even parents. The work's final lines implicate many sorts of people, including many of the poem's potential readers.

FUTILITY

Move him into the sun—
Gently its touch awoke him once,
At home, whispering of fields half-sown.
Always it woke him, even in France,
Until this morning and this snow.   [5]

If anything might rouse him now
The kind old sun will know.

Think how it wakes the seeds—
Woke once the clays of a cold star.
Are limbs, so dear-achieved, are sides   [10]
Full-nerved, still warm, too hard to stir?
Was it for this the clay grew tall?
—O what made fatuous sunbeams toil
To break earth's sleep at all?

HORACE, who emphasized simplicity, unity, and appropriate and consistent phrasing, might greatly admire this poem. Its language, after all, is extremely lucid and accessible, and its imagery is highly coherent, especially in the way both stanzas emphasize the basic idea of the sun promoting life. The mere fact that the two stanzas are the same length also contributes to the work's unity, as does the repetition of such ideas as sleep, awakening, growth, and the seasons. Yet the second stanza offers a more cosmic perspective than the first and thus is not merely repetitive. It explicitly raises questions and provokes thought, while the first stanza had been almost fanciful in its focus on practical behavior. "For me," Horace wrote, "the ideal of poetic style is to mould familiar material with such skill that anyone might hope to achieve the same feat. And yet so firmly would the material be ordered and interconnected (and such is the beauty that one may draw out in that way from the familiar) that he would work and sweat in vain to rival it" (p. 55). Surely Horace would admire the seemingly simple but actually difficult achievement of this brief but splendid poem.

ARCHETYPAL critics, who stress the thoughts and feelings most humans share, might note how this poem both reflects and appeals to deep-seated human desires for life, love, and gentleness, as well as for work that is not onerous and for a close, nurturing relationship with the environment. The young man's early tasks involved close cooperation with nature: he tilled fields and thus promoted the kind of life and growth that have now, for him, suddenly ended. No reference appears to any hunting or killing on his part, but now he has, in a sense, been himself hunted down and killed. In a sense, he lived, in his youth, the kind of existence many people yearn for—the kind enshrined in the myth of the

Garden of Eden, where people supposedly flourished in harmony
with nature, working but not really painfully laboring, growing
but not really growing old in all the worst senses. In his youth,
the young man lived an ideal, idyllic, pastoral life, and the sun
was associated with warmth, light, and life. Its "touch" and
"whispering" (2–3) seemed gentle and tender, almost as the tone
of the speaker here is also gentle and tender. The sun was almost
the youth's parent or grandparent: it was both old and kind.
Indeed, myth critics are especially interested in any tendency to
treat matter as if it were alive and human, as the sun is treated
here. The animistic, anthropomorphic impulses—the impulses to
perceive everything as if it were alive and full of personality—are
two of the most ancient of all instincts, and both instincts seem
relevant here. When the youth was young(er), he lived the kind
of life nearly any human would enjoy. The poem thus appeals to
some of our deepest archetypal yearnings, even as it arouses some
of our deepest archetypal fears. These include, most obviously, the
fear not of death but of death that seems sudden and premature.
And they also include the fear that life may have no meaning,
that the universe may have no purpose, and that any pleasure we
experience may only be temporary and ultimately futile.

STRUCTURALIST critics, who look for the ways humans
impose meaning on existence by interpreting it in terms of
binary opposites, might point out that this poem brims with such
contrasts. It emphasizes such ideas and imagery as sun, warmth,
light, spring, fields, crops, youth, growth, awakening, *being* awake,
morning, home, a pleasant past, seeds, creation, meaningful work,
movement, and activity, and all these items are associated with
such ideals as life, gentleness, love, and certainty. But all these traits
are meaningful mainly through their contrasts with a whole list of
opposites, including darkness, cold, snow, inanimate clay, distance
from home, sleep, lack of movement, and passivity, which are all
associated with death, indifference, and uncertainty. Each pattern of
ideas and images is part of a larger structure of opposed ideas and
images, and it is this overall structure that makes the poem coherent
and meaningful. The poem exemplifies the innate human tendency
to see nearly everything in terms of opposites that help define and
clarify one another.

DECONSTRUCTIVE critics are interested in the ways all kinds
of writing—including literary works—are almost inevitably full of

irresolvable paradoxes and contradictions that undermine the neat, coherent structures that structuralist critics look for (and usually find). In this poem, for instance, a youth is dead (itself a paradoxical situation in some respects), but the dead youth was also a trained killer. He seems a victim of war because he has died young, but he was inevitably also, as a soldier, a victimizer who would readily have killed enemy soldiers just as young as he. Yet both he and those enemy soldiers can themselves be seen as victims of the political and military systems that sent them into battle against each other. In all these ways, then, and in typical deconstructive fashion, what might have seemed neat, clear opposites collapse into messy, irreducible complexities. Any attempt to impose coherent order or find simple meanings is itself a kind of futility.

Another example of this kind of complexity (a complexity that will seem frustrating only to those looking for easy explanations) involves the poem's tone. On the one hand this work can be seen as realistic and anti-Romantic: its second stanza, in particular, undercuts sentimental ideas about particular human lives and about human life in general. In a sense, then, the poem is "always already" deconstructed (to use a favorite deconstructive term and idea): its final lines imply that it is pointless to look for meaning in a meaningless universe, yet the poem does just that, and part of its meaning is precisely its final suggestion that no meanings exist. In its tone and imagery the poem is both Romantic and anti-Romantic, both idealistic and realistic, both gently nostalgic and deeply skeptical.

ECOCRITICS, with their focus on relations between humans and nature, would clearly be interested in this poem, in which such relations play such an obviously central role. The opening lines (especially 2–4) emphasize a close, symbiotic relationship between the youth and his environment. Farming often symbolizes cooperation between humans and the earth, and when the youth was younger and helped raise crops, he was (in almost every sense of the word) at "home." His relations with nature caused no pain or suffering but in fact just the opposite: significantly, he is presented as someone who helped plant crops rather than as someone who shot game, butchered cattle, or slaughtered pigs. His relations with nature were peaceful; only his relations with other humans were violent. The "kind old sun" (7) seems a nurturing, benevolent influence, not only on the now-dead youth but also on the entire planet. Indeed, the poem ultimately implies that life has existed for eons and that the natural system grew up and endured long before humans appeared. No God is mentioned or even implied; instead, the poem suggests a naturalistic (rather than supernatural) explanation of life on earth. No otherworldly heaven is imagined as an answer or alternative to death: nature and people, it would seem, are all that exist. Humans may long for close, almost affectionate links with nature, and nature, imagined in fancifully anthropomorphic terms, may sometimes seem to answer that longing. But humans often destroy each other, and nature, as beautiful and beneficent as it often appears, may have no larger purpose or meaning at all. In some ways, in fact, the poem can be read as profoundly androcentric: it is as if (the final lines seem to suggest) life on earth might just as well never have happened if humans die and if human life makes no ultimate sense. For an ecocritic, such a suggestion would seem profoundly egotistical and therefore typically human.

STRANGE MEETING

It seemed that out of the battle I escaped
Down some profound dull tunnel, long since scooped
Through granites which Titanic wars had groined.

Yet also there encumbered sleepers groaned,
Too fast in thought or death to be bestirred.   [5]
Then, as I probed them, one sprang up, and stared
With piteous recognition in fixed eyes,
Lifting distressful hands as if to bless.
And by his smile, I knew that sullen hall—
By his dead smile I knew we stood in Hell.   [10]

With a thousand pains that vision's face was grained;
Yet no blood reached there from the upper ground,
And no guns thumped, or down the flues made moan.
"Strange friend," I said, "Here is no cause to mourn."
"None," said that other, "save the undone years,   [15]
The hopelessness. Whatever hope is yours,
Was my life also; I went hunting wild
After the wildest beauty in the world,
Which lies not calm in eyes, or braided hair,

But mocks the steady running of the hour,   [20]
And if it grieves, grieves richlier than here.
For by my glee might many men have laughed,
And of my weeping something had been left,
Which must die now. I mean the truth untold,
The pity of war, the pity war distilled.   [25]
Now men will go content with what we spoiled,
Or, discontent, boil bloody, and be spilled.
They will be swift with swiftness of the tigress,
None will break ranks, though nations trek from progress.
Courage was mine, and I had mystery;   [30]
Wisdom was mine, and I had mastery:
To miss the march of this retreating world
Into vain citadels that are not walled.
Then, when much blood had clogged their chariot-wheels
I would go up and wash them from sweet wells,   [35]
Even with truths that lie too deep for taint.
I would have poured my spirit without stint
But not through wounds; not on the cess of war.
Foreheads of men have bled where no wounds were.

I am the enemy you killed, my friend.   [40]
I knew you in this dark; for so you frowned
Yesterday through me as you jabbed and killed.
I parried; but my hands were loath and cold.
Let us sleep now . . ."

A reader influenced by ARISTOTLE's ideas about literature might variously admire this poem. Although Aristotle focused most attention on tragic drama, his comments on that genre imply the traits he would value in literature in general. These traits (also prized by latter-day formalists) would involve complex unity. Thus, a particular kind of story-line or "plot" would dictate the use of characters appropriate to that plot, thought appropriate to those characters, and phrasing appropriate to that kind of thought. All a work's elements, in other words, would unite to produce an appropriate effect. The ideal work would have a beginning, middle, and end (all clearly connected) and would seem appropriate in length to the plot (seeming neither too long nor too short).

Owen's "Strange Meeting" satisfies all these general Aristotelian criteria, but it also exemplifies some of the philosopher's specific ideas about tragedies. Thus, the poem's characters seem to be basically good men; the plot is serious and complete; and the emotions the poem arouses include pity and fear—pity for the soldiers described and fear that their suffering is not peculiar only to them. When the slain soldier suddenly realizes that he is addressing the man who slew him, the poem also combines reversal and recognition. This kind of combination, Aristotle felt, was not only appropriate to tragedy but also epitomized the kind of careful union of design and surprise typical of a work of carefully crafted art. What seems at first unexpected should, in retrospect, have been well prepared. Yet Owen's poem also seems "tragic" in several other senses, particularly since it presents a basically good man who seems to have done something bad through a mistake or flaw. A horrific deed has been done in a kind of ignorance. Aristotle *does* say that if "an enemy kills an enemy, there is nothing to excite pity either in the act or in the intention,—except so far as the suffering itself is pitiful" (p. 27). Yet in Owen's poem the killing does seem tragic because we sense that these two men had much in common and could easily have been close comrades under other circumstances. As the German soldier puts it, "I am the enemy you killed, my friend" (40). Surely Aristotle would regard that line as particularly tragic.

READER-RESPONSE critics could easily imagine a wide variety of possible reactions to this poem. Soldiers, for example, especially members of the infantry, would obviously be ideal readers of this work. They might "relate" to it in ways that many civilians might not, but some civilians might also be ideal readers, especially if they were curious about experiences distant from their own. Anyone who had ever been in a tragic situation would probably find this poem moving, and anyone familiar with being underground (such as a miner) would also probably respond to this work in distinctive ways. In short, the poem might provoke distinctive reactions by almost any imaginable reader or groups of readers. For a reader-response critic, the experience of reading the work would differ according to the readers involved, producing, in a sense, a different work for any and all persons who happened to read it, including the same person at different times and under different circumstances. Yet some reader-response critics might contend that the poem implies various kinds of "ideal" readers (readers especially well equipped to perceive and appreciate this text's special features). Thus readers familiar with the "Inferno" section of Dante's *Divine Comedy* would probably be ideal readers of "Strange Meeting," partly because both works describe troubling encounters in hell. Similarly, readers who remembered other literary works that Owen echoes might also be ideally positioned to recognize his poem's methods and achievement. Readers who valued creative writing as much as Owen and the two characters in his poem would be ideal readers of this work, and perhaps ultimately the truly ideal reader of this work or any other might be the work's own author. Thus "Strange Meeting" might imply an ideal reader capable of appreciating unusual sound effects, and also a reader tolerant of romanticism but also distrustful of anything too unrealistic. Finally, an ideal reader of this poem would almost certainly be a reader who could imagine how an "enemy" might also be a friend.

STRUCTURALIST critics are interested in the structures people impose on reality. These structures, which help us make sense of experience, typically consist of interconnected contrasts—contrasts that help reinforce one another to produce an overarching structure. This structure may or may not exist in reality, but it definitely exists in the mind of the person using it to perceive reality. Thus, in the following list derived from a reading of "Strange Meeting," each term on the left of the slash mark contrasts with each term on the right of the slash mark, and all the terms on the left reinforce one another, just as all the terms on the right do the same: peace/war; escape/imprisonment; rest/battle; safety/danger; underground/aboveground; being asleep/being awake; knowledge/mystery; earth/hell; comfort/pain; friend/stranger; silence/noise; satisfaction/mourning; hope/hopelessness; life/death; beauty/ugliness; happiness/grief; beauty that is eternal/beauty that changes or decays; eternity/time; laughter/weeping; truth/lies; truth told/truth untold; pity/hatred of war; contentment/discontent; friendliness/anger; human/animal; individuality/regimentation; progress/regression; courage/weakness; wisdom/foolishness; being clean/being covered with blood; water/blood; being pure/being tainted; cleanliness/filth or pollution; friend/enemy; giving life/killing.

Some of these oppositions are obvious; some are only implied; and, in some cases, one term in an opposition is obvious while the contrasting term is implied. Taken all together, however, they help constitute the poem's underlying structure and the way the poem structures the experiences it describes. This is how human minds make sense of reality: by structuring it in terms of oppositions and by matching those oppositions to produce a larger, comprehensive pattern of linked contrasts.

DECONSTRUCTIVE critics would look for ways the tidy patterns found (or projected) by structuralists and other kinds of critics begin to unravel as soon as they are examined closely. The opening lines of "Strange Meeting," for instance, can already be read in deconstructive fashion. Thus the word "seemed" ("It seemed that out of battle I escaped") already implies that there may indeed be no escape from battle—that the escape with which the poem begins is only a false escape. Indeed, the word "seems" in a sense deconstructs the entire poem: how, after all, can this poem in any sense be "real" if its apparently living speaker turns out to be dead? Is the poem then simply the report of a dream? Dreams are almost by definition deconstructive because almost nothing is stable, dependable, or predictable in a dream. Does this mean, however, that dreams are nothing *but* figments of the imagination and are therefore untrustworthy and lacking in truth? Or are dreams in fact (as various psychologists have suggested) in some ways more truthful, more revealing, more valuable than consciously formed (and often consciously censured) ideas? Almost from its first word, then, "Strange Meeting" can appear ambiguous, ambivalent, and indecipherable. The poem is, of course, open to interpretation, but any interpretation is also open to interpretation, and any interpretation of any interpretation is similarly open to interpretation, and so on. There is (in a variation of a famous phrase by Jacques Derrida) nothing outside interpretation.

For deconstructive critics, clear distinctions collapse under the slightest bit of interpretive pressure. In "Strange Meeting," for instance, war and peace are hard to keep separate, as are life and death, friend and enemy, safety and danger, earth and hell, and the speaker and the man he meets. In this poem, physical descent results in a kind of moral and spiritual ascent, and escape from pain results in pain of a different sort. The poem in some ways seems clearly a piece of fiction, but in other ways it may be more truthful and valuable than what seems a piece of truthful narration, such as a newspaper report about the battle the poem seems to describe. The newspaper report may convey objective "facts" (numbers of men wounded, numbers of men killed, amount of territory taken or lost), but in some ways an inventive poem such as this may convey truths of a different sort, although even their status as "truth" in any simple, stable sense is open to question. For deconstructive critics, everything is finally open to question; there is no end of questions and questionings.

DIALOGICAL critics listen for different kinds of voices within literary works, including voices both literal (such as characters' voices) and figurative (as in allusions, sources, and tones, including overtones and undertones). "Strange Meeting" is dialogical in a very obvious sense, since one character speaks to another and the second character responds at length. Yet, because both characters are clearly fictional, this poem in another way merely dramatizes a kind of dialogue going on inside the poet's own mind. But the poem also tries to engage its readers in a dialogue: it tries to elicit our responses and may even provoke dialogues between and among readers, as in classroom discussion, on the internet, or in the pages of scholarly journals. Even in simply writing the poem, Owen was engaged in a kind of dialogue with his own mind: various manuscripts by Owen similar to this poem exist, in different versions, with various alterations, so that the very creation of this work, like the creation of most works, involved a kind of back-and-forth between the writer and himself.

"Strange Meeting" is, however, dialogical in other ways as well. As the notes in Jon Stallworthy's edition of Owen's poems demonstrate, this work is a tissue of allusions to other writings, including texts by Percy Shelley, Harold Munro, John Keats, Oscar Wilde, Henri Barbusse, Owen himself, and the translation of Dante's *Inferno* by Henry Cary, which may also have influenced the passage from Keats echoed by Owen. Stallworthy even hears an echo in line 28 of the Bible's reference to Saul and Jonathan as "swifter than eagles" (p. 127). Whether this proposed allusion is convincing will be up to each reader to decide, and in fact a formalist might argue that allusions are mainly important insofar as they help call attention, through comparison and contrast, to what the poet actually got on paper. Yet critics of many types are likely to concede that allusions to the Bible are often especially important since the Bible was, for centuries, the one text most readers could be expected to know, so that biblical echoes were the ones most likely to be heard and recognized. Owen's first readers may or may not have recognized allusions to relatively unknown writers such as Harold Munro, but allusions to the Bible and other canonical texts were much more likely to have been perceived as part of a "dialogue" in which Owen's poem participated.

11

E. E. Cummings (1894–1962): "I sing of Olaf"; "My sweet old etcetera"

I SING OF OLAF

i sing of Olaf glad and big
whose warmest heart recoiled at war:
a conscientious object-or

his wellbelovèd colonel(trig
westpointer most succinctly bred)   [5]
took erring Olaf soon in hand;
but—though an host of overjoyed
noncoms(first knocking on the head
him)do through icy waters roll
that helplessness which others stroke   [10]
with brushes recently employed
anent this muddy toiletbowl,
while kindred intellects evoke
allegiance per blunt instruments—
Olaf(being to all intents   [15]
a corpse and wanting any rag
upon what God unto him gave)
responds, without getting annoyed
"I will not kiss your f.ing flag"

straightway the silver bird looked grave   [20]
(departing hurriedly to shave)

but—though all kinds of officers
(a yearning nation's blueeyed pride)
their passive prey did kick and curse
until for wear their clarion   [25]
voices and boots were much the worse,
and egged the firstclassprivates on
his rectum wickedly to tease
by means of skilfully applied
bayonets roasted hot with heat—   [30]
Olaf(upon what were once knees)
does almost ceaselessly repeat
"there is some s. I will not eat"

our president,being of which
assertions duly notified   [35]
threw the yellowsonofabitch
into a dungeon,where he died

Christ(of His mercy infinite)
i pray to see;and Olaf,too

preponderatingly because   [40]
unless statistics lie he was
more brave than me:more blond than you.

Readers influenced by the ideas of PLATO might be disturbed by Cummings' poem, particularly if they assumed that America was fighting for a just and noble cause in World War I. If that were the case, then Plato would support the war and would expect each citizen to do his or her duty. In particular, Plato believed that the "guardians" of a virtuous state should respect their leaders (p. 52), value heroes (p. 54), and imitate courageous, temperate, holy, and ethical persons (pp. 57, 61). Of course, one could argue that the officers this poem depicts lack such traits and that Olaf is in fact the most courageous and virtuous character. The main debate about this poem, then, from a Platonic perspective, would be whether the American cause was virtuous. If it was, then Olaf should have served willingly and enthusiastically. If the cause was unjust, he might have had good reason to be a conscientious objector. Can a good cause be corrupted by unworthy leaders? Should Olaf reject military service because his officers are not good men? Or should the cause matter more than the men charged with overseeing it? These are the kinds of questions—ultimately moral questions—that Cummings' poem might raise for Plato and for Platonic critics.

PSYCHOANALYTIC critics might argue that the officers and men who brutalize Olaf have given in completely to their irrational ids; they exhibit none of the restraint and self-control associated with the ego and superego. They violate the moral dictates associated with conscience and morality. Although they nominally serve higher values, such as patriotism and unselfish duty, these men actually resemble perverse sadists, especially in their symbolic rape of Olaf with their bayonets. It is Olaf who seems most truly devoted to the ideals associated with the superego; it is he who willingly suffers for a righteous cause. His tormentors knock him on the head (8), the symbolic seat of rationality; they try to silence him and thus prevent him from sharing his thoughts and reasons; and the reference to their own "intellects" (13) is quite clearly ironic. They employ brute strength against Olaf, but he seems strongest in every way: physically, rationally, and morally. Thus their display of raw power ironically implies their own ethical, psychological, and intellectual weakness. The officers and soldiers in this poem (except for Olaf) are psychopaths, perhaps serving a psychopathic system.

A MARXIST might see Olaf as symbolizing all war resisters, many of whom were socialists. In the United States, harsh laws were passed to penalize overt resistance to the war, and many who suffered from these laws were Marxists. Olaf's "big" size (1) makes him sound like a member of the working class, while his Scandinavian name suggests that he is not a member of the traditional white Anglo-Saxon Protestant power structure that essentially ruled the United States until well into the twentieth century. Whether he "recoiled at war" (2) for religious reasons (unlike Marxists) or for political reasons (like Marxists) is not made clear, although his later use of profanity favors the latter possibility. Certainly Marxists would sympathize with Olaf and his plight. He rejects indoctrination, resists the military hierarchy, and, by implication, repudiates the oppressive political system that tries to control both the minds and the bodies of the people, especially the working class. The figures who abuse Olaf treat him not as a person but as a thing, and in that sense they typify the way capitalism and capitalists tend to treat human beings. The powerful pit the less powerful against each other: the officers egg "the firstclassprivates on" (27) as the latter torture Olaf in particularly disgusting ways. They are "firstclass" in rank only, not in any true sense of the word.

The reference to "our president" (34) seems especially significant from a Marxist viewpoint. The men who abuse Olaf are not disobedient renegades; instead, they symbolize the larger power structure. In fact, it is ultimately the president who seems responsible for Olaf's death. Although President Woodrow Wilson was (and still is) often seen as a "progressive" leader, to Marxists then and since he was little more than a stooge of the ruling classes. He did nothing to fundamentally benefit the workers or to transform politics or the economy, and his support for the war led to an especially bad episode of political oppression—an episode in which Marxists and their causes suffered most.

A NEW HISTORICIST critic might be interested in this poem's focus on a relatively neglected "marginal" group: conscientious objectors. World War I *soldiers* have often been studied, but conscientious objectors have been relatively neglected. The fact that such people existed reminds us that the war (especially America's involvement) was highly controversial. Millions of Americans initially opposed participation, and even after that participation began, some people continued to resist. The way such people have been "written out" of most histories of the period would exemplify, to a new historicist, the fact that history is politicized and that writing history is a political act and a site of contention and negotiation.

World War I was the first war in which American conscientious objectors (CO's) were actually exempted from combat duty (Moore, p. 169). They were supposed to be treated with courtesy, although this was not always how they were actually dealt with (Moore, p. 169). Persons who objected to service for religious reasons were often better received than those who objected for different reasons, but all CO's were placed under military jurisdiction, all were expected at least to prepare for combat duty, and all were encouraged to change their minds (Moore, p. 170). David W. Moore notes that "Shaming, taunting, physical abuse, threatening court-martial, and a variety of other tactics were used to convince the objector of his 'patriotic duty'" and that "Roughly 16,000 succumbed to the pressure and abuse and agreed to accept combat roles." Another 1,300 agreed to accept noncombat roles (p. 170). Such facts make Olaf's defiance all the more unusual and impressive. Many CO's (according to Moore) were taunted, beaten, dunked in water, bayoneted, handcuffed while standing in solitary confinement, and/or put on a bread-and-water diet. In some camps, abuse aimed at breaking CO's was permissible. Five hundred and forty CO's refused to cooperate in any way and were found guilty in courts-martial; one trial lasted 18 minutes. Seventeen CO's received death sentences; 142 received life imprisonment; 345 were punished with sentences averaging 16.5 years. No death penalties were actually carried out; some sentences were reduced; but it was not until 1933 that the last World War I CO was released from prison. At least 17 men died as prisoners. Psychological abuse led to at least one suicide. CO's were often considered cowards, slackers, and generally unpatriotic traitors. Even their own families, friends, and religious communities often criticized them. CO's who were sullen and defiant (like Olaf) were supposed to be court-martialed (Moore, p. 170). All this historical information makes the abuse of Olaf seem less the result of individual psychopathy than of government policy. Yet this poem was not simply influenced *by* history but was an attempt by Cummings trying to *in*fluence history. In this respect as in the others already mentioned, his poem would attract the intense interest of new historicist critics.

POSTMODERNIST critics might suggest that Olaf appeals to no kind of "grand narrative" to justify his behavior. He does not openly identify himself with any political or religious group. Instead, all that the poem reveals is that his "warmest heart recoiled at war" (2). Ironically, if he had been affiliated with a group—especially a religious group—he might have received better treatment. Instead, he seems simply an independent freethinker who trusts his own instincts. He is an individualist and is therefore the kind of person most in line with postmodernist assumptions. He thinks and acts as he wishes, feeling no need to justify or defend himself. He refuses to conform to conventional expectations. His use of curse words implies not only the vehemence of his feelings but also his freedom of thought and speech. He violates standard decorum of the time, and so does this poem by quoting him. By using profanity, the poem rejects polite conventions while touching base with the popular culture of its era.

Postmodernists would especially appreciate the formal experimentation this poem exhibits—its unusual spelling, punctuation, grammar, sentence structure, and mere appearance on the page. The military is a rigidly organized hierarchical system. Olaf rejects such rigidity, and so does the poem. The poem's apparent disorder defies those who value order and conformity. Olaf thought for himself, spoke freely, and could not be intimidated, and in a sense Cummings does the same thing.

MY SWEET OLD ETCETERA

my sweet old etcetera
aunt lucy during the recent

war could and what
is more did tell you just
what everybody was fighting   [5]

for,
my sister

isabel created hundreds
(and
hundreds)of socks not to   [10]
mention shirts fleaproof earwarmers

etcetera wristers etcetera, my
mother hoped that

i would die etcetera
bravely of course my father used   [15]
to become hoarse talking about how it was
a privilege and if only he
could meanwhile my

self etcetera lay quietly
in the deep mud et   [20]

cetera
(dreaming,
et
cetera, of
Your smile   [25]
eyes knees and of your Etcetera)

PLATO might censure this poem. He embraced, after all, various
values that this work seems to mock, such as the importance of
honoring God and one's parents (Preminger et al., pp. 49, 84),
the need for poets to write in noble ways (Preminger et al., p. 50),
the idea that serious, public-spirited people should avoid laughter
(Preminger et al., p. 51), and the importance of temperance,
especially in sexual matters (Preminger et al., p. 52). Plato disliked
stories about disobeying one's parents and about sexual matters
in general (Preminger et al., p. 53), and he thought that literature
should not encourage vice (Preminger et al., pp. 57–8), self-
indulgence (Preminger et al., p. 60), irrationality (Preminger et al.,
p. 75), and coarse humor (Preminger et al., p. 76). Soldiers, in
particular, should only be exposed to literature of a severe style,
designed to encourage virtue (Preminger et al., p. 60). For all these
reasons, Plato might dislike Cummings' poem, in which the speaker
seem to mock his parents and other members of his family, and in
which he seems, at the very end, to indulge in the kind of suggestive
sexual humor that Plato would probably not find very funny.

A PSYCHOANALYTIC critic might note that the poem's first
two lines seem to reflect the influence of the superego: they imply
respect for "aunt lucy" (2) in particular and for elders in general.
They thus appear to exhibit the deference to superiors and to social
expectations associated with the responsible, conscientious, obedient
part of the mind. As the poem evolves, however, the independent,
self-focused id increasingly asserts itself, especially in the final lines,
when sexual meanings are strongly suggested. Yet a psychoanalytic
critic might also be interested in how the poem implies not only
the speaker's distinctive personality but also the personalities of
other "characters" as well. In fact, by the middle of the poem our
interest is particularly provoked by the seemingly strange attitudes
of the speaker's parents, especially since the speaker cleverly delays
the crucial adverb "bravely" when he reports that his "mother
hoped that / i would die etcetera / bravely of course" (13–15).

Meanwhile, the father, perhaps lamenting the loss of his own youth and virility, seems less interested in his son than in fantasizing about his own imagined involvement in the war (17–18). Both parents, plus the sister, present themselves as representatives of the socially responsible superego. Meanwhile, our reactions to all the personalities the poem presents will inevitably say much about our own personalities as well. Yet however we respond, the entire poem suggests the importance of one's immediate family to any person's life and self-perceptions—an idea with which most psychoanalysts would concur. Psychoanalytic critics would also note that the poem implies the importance of "dreaming" (22).

An ARCHETYPAL critic, interested in the deep-seated traits nearly all humans share, might note that this poem implies the universal importance of both family relationships and sexual desire. Although most people desire positive relations with their parents, such relations may not be fully present in this poem. Thus part of the shock of the initial reference to the mother here is that her frank willingness to contemplate her son's death can seem so peculiar, unexpected, and even "unnatural." Indeed, one might argue that all the characters *except* the mother behave in archetypal ways. This seems surprising, since we often think of mothers as having an especially innate concern for the welfare of their children. The mother's comment can initially seem both shocking and funny precisely *because* it violates our expectations about mothers' archetypal thoughts and feelings. The poem certainly appeals to our deep-seated desire to be amused, and its reference to lying in mud (19–20) probably arouses unpleasant feelings in practically everyone. Furthermore, dreaming seems a universal trait (22), as does the desire for beauty and pleasure. The final hints of sexual desire seem exactly what one might expect from an archetypally healthy young male.

A FEMINIST might find this poem somewhat patronizing in its view of women, who make up most of its characters. Aunt Lucy exemplifies the sexist stereotype of the know-it-all woman; the sister seems stereotypically naïve; the mother is stereotypically concerned with her own social image; and the woman implied at the end of the poem is a mere stereotypical sex-object. None of the women seems to have any realistic or sympathetic view of the true nature of war, and women are the butts of most of the poem's implied sarcasm. Even the characterization of the aunt as "sweet" (1) might strike some feminists as condescending, and surely the poem mocks her unfounded claims to expertise. Yet the poem fails to acknowledge that the reason women had little actual experience of war was because they were prohibited from fighting, and even the mother's willingness to see her son die as long as he dies "bravely" (15) can be read as reflecting her submission to the values and propaganda of a male-dominated society. The father also submits to gender stereotypes, as does everyone else in the poem, including the speaker in his stereotypical view of women (especially at the end). The sister provides for the physical needs and desires of men in one way; the woman the poem addresses does so (or at least the speaker hopes she will do so) in others. The poem stereotypically contrasts the relative comfort and safety of the women with the actual discomfort of the male speaker. The father also conforms to the social expectations of a patriarchal society: he does not want to seem weak and womanly. He wants to assert his masculinity and virility. The speaker himself also implicitly exhibits those traits, not only by expressing sexual desire at the end of the poem but also by calling subtle attention to his stoic bravery as he lies in the mud in a distant battlefield (19–20). One way to read the poem is as a typically sexist product of a typically sexist era.

A READER-RESPONSE critic might argue that Cummings' poem excellently demonstrates the value of "affective stylistics," a term coined by the prominent theorist Stanley Fish. According to Fish, a work of literature is not so much an object as a *process*: we move through it one word at a time, never knowing quite what to expect but often making assumptions about what will or will not come next. Sometimes the work surprises us. Certainly Cummings' poem seems surprising, for instance, in line 11 (the word "earwarmers" is probably not what most people would have expected to come after "fleaproof"). And the text seems especially surprising in lines 13–15: "mother hoped that // i would die etcetera / bravely," where "bravely" is very cleverly postponed. Yet, as Fish himself later admitted, "affective stylistics" has much in common with formalism, since a work's structure does greatly dictate reader responses, as in the delayed appearance of "bravely." By organizing the poem as he does, Cummings makes us slow down as we read; he forces us to pause and to pay attention to particular word choices.

In addition, by repeatedly using the phrase "et cetera," the speaker positively invites us to fill in various blanks and interpret the same phrase in potentially different ways and with potentially different tones. Each reader will have his or her own particular response to the final (and the only capitalized) "Etcetera" (26), both in the way its meaning is interpreted and in the way one responds to that meaning. Most readers will probably assume that something erotic is implied, and some may even imagine a specific part of the female anatomy. Some readers may find the final line amusing; some may find it stimulating; some (especially at the time the poem was written) could even find it offensive. Part of the wit of the ending, in fact, is that the speaker deliberately leaves interpretation of the final word up to each reader, thus achieving plausible deniability: if a reader finds the line too crude, that is only because the reader chooses to interpret the final word in a crude way.

David Jones (1895–1974): *In Parenthesis* (excerpt from Section VII)

IN PARENTHESIS (EXCERPT FROM SECTION VII)

Across upon this undulated board of verdure chequered bright
when you look to left and right
small, drab, bundled pawns severally make effort
moved in tenuous line
and if you looked behind—the next wave came slowly,
   as successive surfs creep in to dissipate on flat shore;   [5]
and to your front, stretched long laterally,
and receded deeply,
the dark wood.

Although ARISTOTLE is remembered mainly for his ideas about the origins and effects of tragedy as a genre, he was also intensely interested in the intricacies of literary style. He believed, for instance, that the best style was clear but not undistinguished (pp. 32–3). An absolutely clear style would use only very common words, but such a style would seem pedestrian. Unusual words should therefore be added to the mix, but only in moderation. Jones arguably achieves this kind of balance in the quoted passage: most of its words are very simple, accessible, and of Anglo-Saxon origin. But Jones also adds distinction to his style by using such Latinate words as "undulated," "verdure," "tenuous," "dissipate," and "laterally." Using too many such words (as he arguably does in much of the rest of *In Parenthesis*) would strike Aristotle as a serious stylistic flaw.

A MARXIST critic might be interested in the way this passage compares soldiers to "pawns" (3), thereby suggesting that they are manipulated by the powerful and that their primary purpose is to be sacrificed to protect the powerful. Soldiers treated as pawns have no choice in how they are moved or controlled. In fact, the "pawns" here are "small, drab, [and] bundled" (3), suggesting their lack of financial and therefore social status. They must do as they are told, but they actually "make effort" to do so (3), thus resembling workers who genuinely labor in ways that contradict their own interests. The excerpt compares these men to "wave[s]" and "surfs," but waves and surfs are not destroyed, as these men are, nor do waves and surfs suffer fear and pain. Waves and surfs are also inexhaustible (in several senses), but this, of course, is far from true of vulnerable human beings. Marxists would highlight the differences between metaphorical waves, surfs, and pawns (on the one hand) and (on the other hand) the real human beings who fought, bled, and died on the battlefields of Europe.

A STRUCTURALIST might argue that even an excerpt as short as this reveals certain underlying structural patterns consisting of similar groups of binary oppositions, such as artificial/real; game/war; appealing/unappealing; light/darkness; ordered chessboard/disorderly ocean; and so on. Yet this passage also suggests, perhaps, how difficult it sometimes is to see any real pattern or structure in the opposites a text contains. In some texts, the binary opposites can seem to line up perfectly in neat rows. In this text, however, the opposites can sometimes feel imposed and artificial. How, for instance, do such contrasts as water/land, or ocean/forest, or past/present fit the pattern already mentioned above? A deconstructor might argue that all patterns are merely imposed and inherently unstable; a formalist might argue that any patterns the poem reveals are distinctive and appropriate only to that particular poem, and that the patterns need not contribute to any rigidly consistent structure.

As mentioned, DECONSTRUCTIVE critics might argue that any attempt to find rigid, meaningful patterns in this passage will simply involve *imposing* such patterns. The patterns do not inhere *in* the passage; they are forced *onto* the passage by critics (whether structuralists or formalists or almost any other kind of critic) eager to find order where no real order exists. Thus the "verdure chequered bright" (1) might seem to symbolize life, in contrast to "the dark wood" (8), which might seem to symbolize death. Yet most of the killing and dying would have taken place on the bright green field, while relatively safety would have been present in the "dark wood." Similarly, the "small, drab, bundled pawns" (3) may seem powerless from one point of view, but on them, of course, depends the power of the military and political leaders who send them into battle. Where structuralists see neat, tidy order and coherent meanings, deconstructors instead see the inevitability of endless interpretation.

Jones's *In Parenthesis* is a good example of how difficult it can be to define or explain the term "POSTMODERNISM," since in many ways this poem seems to have been postmodernist well in advance of that term's invention. Jones's work also illustrates how hard it sometimes is to distinguish modernism from postmodernism. Yet however one chooses to categorize this poem, postmodernists would surely value the way it disrupts conventional expectations about genre, style, structure, and so on. Some critics, for instance, consider *In Parenthesis* a novel; others see it as a poem; while others see it as a hybrid work or something uniquely *sui generis* (of its own kind). The excerpt given is one of the work's most immediately accessible portions; it most clearly resembles a traditional "poem." For that reason, it is one of the least "postmodern" portions of *In Parenthesis*. It seems far more immediately accessible and comprehensible than much of the rest of the work.

12

The kinds of questions different critics ask

Christina M. Garner

The following lists of questions are derived from Robert C. Evans's book *Close Readings* and are designed to give students and other readers a practical series of questions to ask of any literary work as they try to make sense of its phrasing, structures, and meanings.

Plato

How does the work

- reflect enduring reality?
- appeal to the reader either mainly logically (which is good) or mainly emotionally (which is bad)?
- attempt (successfully or unsuccessfully) to influence society?
- ask and/or answer philosophical questions?
- stress subject matter and content as opposed to form and craftsmanship?
- utilize logic or reason rather than emotional or sensory stimuli to explore truth?
- convey ideas about absolute truth and beauty?

- help readers discover philosophical truths?
- inform or instruct rather than simply entertain?
- seem objective, rational, and systematic?
- attempt to make reason and virtue attractive?
- endorse or undermine truth?

Aristotle

How does the work

- suggest or reveal enduring truth?
- demonstrate conscious, deliberate craftsmanship?
- reflect the writer's skill in using a particular genre (or kind) of writing?
- reflect any general insight into human nature, thoughts, and actions?
- combine unity and complexity, especially in relations between its various parts?
- imply natural, inevitable, consistent connections between different parts of the work?
- reflect some natural, necessary way of ordering or understanding experience (such as tragic experience or comic experience)?
- help satisfy an innate, inevitable human desire for knowledge?
- reveal how individual experience reflects larger truths?
- reflect the existence of a general human nature?
- provoke general, typical human responses rather than idiosyncratic ones?
- provoke responses to both its form and its content, which are inseparable?
- reveal the dynamic forms, patterns, or processes inherent in reality?
- reveal the way a thing can change while still remaining the same thing?

- help us discover truths about reality, both external and internal?
- help us understand meaningful patterns of human behavior?
- lend itself to objective, rational, and systematic examination?
- seem valuable as an imitation of reality?

Horace

How does the work

- reflect or respond to the preferences of its intended audience?
- adhere to or depart from the requirements of a particular genre?
- reflect literary traditions or customs?
- make each character look or act in ways that are appropriate or expected for that character? (For example, how does an old, male character look or act like a stereotypical old man?)
- connect events in the text in ways that seem natural or expected?
- balance simplicity and complexity and seem consistent?
- utilize or fail to utilize language which is familiar to the reader?
- reflect real life, especially by presenting characters who seem realistic or credible?
- reflect the deliberate craftsmanship of the writer?
- instruct and/or entertain the reader?
- appeal to a broad audience?
- meet or violate the reader's expectations?
- imply the values, customs, and conventions of its intended audience?
- reflect any general insight into human nature?
- reflect the ways that conventions and audiences change over time?

Longinus

How does the work

- demonstrate the writer's conscious, deliberate craftsmanship?
- reflect the character of the writer?
- display the writer's genius or inspiration?
- convey sublime spiritual, moral, and/or intellectual power?
- inspire artistic or ethical achievement in others?
- reflect the fact that humanity is capable of producing great, powerful works?
- display noble ideas or elevated language?
- achieve unity and harmony?
- reveal the author reflecting or building upon the skill of his/her predecessors?
- emphasize spiritual and ethical greatness as opposed to triviality or materialism?
- reveal the shared human nature and fundamental desires that people possess?
- use rhetorical devices (such as metaphor, simile, etc.)?
- encourage noble aspirations?
- transcend the boundaries of class, gender, race, nation, and time to appeal to a wide variety of readers?

Traditional historical criticism

How does the work

- reflect the writer's values?
- reflect the values of a particular historical era?
- reflect the author's individual experiences?
- become more comprehensible the more we know about the era in which it was written?
- give us insights into the period in which it was written?
- reveal the influence of previous texts?

- become more comprehensible the more we understand the language of its era?
- seem open to different interpretations in different historical eras?
- seem affected by the society in which it was produced?
- influence the society in which it was produced?

Thematic criticism

How does the work

- intentionally or unintentionally incorporate abstract ideas?
- use abstract ideas or concepts to convey meaning?
- imply the beliefs and values of its author?
- repeat or reflect ideas emphasized in other works by its author?
- imply that ideas are important aspects of reality?
- reflect any general insight into human nature?
- reflect any larger truths about existence or the nature of the world?
- repeatedly emphasize one central theme or motif?
- provoke thoughts about abstract ideas?
- focus on ideas rather than on details of phrasing or structure?
- use one or more ideas to convey the overall message or meaning of the text?
- use general ideas to make sense of particular details of the work?
- rely on the human desire or need to understand experiences in terms of large, meaningful patterns or ideas?
- emphasize broad, familiar ideas (good vs evil; right vs wrong; the purpose of living; the nature of happiness; fate vs free will; war and peace; crime and punishment; the nature of love, or of justice, or of duty, or of truth, etc.)?
- convey lessons about and/or insights into the ideas it explores?

Formalism

How does the work

- attempt to reveal truth?
- reflect the writer's skill in the use of a particular genre (or kind) of writing?
- demonstrate conscious, deliberate craftsmanship?
- exhibit complex unity, so that every part of the work is necessary to the work as a whole?
- reveal connections between different parts of the work that seem natural and inevitable?
- reflect, through its own complexity, the complexity of reality?
- provoke responses both to its form and to its content (which are inseparable)?
- suggest the dynamic forms, patterns, or processes inherent in reality?
- help us understand meaningful patterns of human behavior?

Psychoanalytic criticism

How does the work

- suggest the unconscious drives or motives of the writer, the reader, and/or the works' characters?
- reveal the influences of the writer's unconscious mind?
- suggest the interaction of the *id* (the subconscious, instinctual, pleasure-seeking mind), the *ego* (the conscious, rational mind), and the *superego* (the conscience), either in the writer, the reader, and/or the work's characters?
- imply repression (especially sexual repression) of the *id*, either in the writer, the reader, and/or the work's characters?
- suggest or reveal larger truths about various stages of human development?

- imply or express ideas about psychosexual or gender roles?
- imply or present a writer and/or characters who express highly individual or personal psychological realities?
- imply the collective psychology of society during the writer's lifetime?

Archetypal criticism

How does the work

- appeal to thoughts and feelings that almost all readers share?
- provoke general, typical human responses rather than idiosyncratic reactions?
- reveal multiple levels of complexity and psychological significance?
- reveal both a surface meaning and an underlying level of meaning which is, in many cases, more important than the surface meaning?
- use patterns of imagery or themes that provoke the same responses in most people?
- imply the existence of a general human nature?
- use general human associations to imply deeper meanings (e.g. by using darkness to suggest danger or springtime to symbolize life or rebirth)?
- explore the relationships between humans and nature?
- disclose underlying patterns that contribute to the text's deeper unity or coherence?
- use symbols that can have multiple meanings depending on their contexts?
- appeal to readers' most basic desires and needs?
- appeal to readers emotionally or psychologically rather than intellectually?
- transcend barriers of age, race, language, gender, and so on to appeal to a more universal human nature?

- resemble many other texts in its underlying meanings and impact?
- employ patterns or symbols also found in popular literature?
- imply universal feelings or responses that are typically very important or powerful and, therefore, very difficult to put into words?
- use symbols, themes, or ideas appropriate to the text's genre?
- manipulate characters, symbols, or themes to uphold or undermine the reader's expectations?

Marxist criticism

How does the work

- reflect the writer's socioeconomic circumstances?
- reflect its own social or historical contexts?
- depict or deal with the social structure that helped produce it? (For instance, does the work describe, distort, falsify, criticize, or endorse the social structure, or does it do some combination of these things?)
- reveal the distribution of power within the social structure?
- strengthen or weaken the interests of a particular economic class?
- reveal anything about power struggles or injustices within or between social classes?
- reveal how the dominant class uses "spiritual" or "natural" practices to maintain dominance?
- deal with values or systems of belief that stifle or weaken progress for the majority?
- reveal the social and/or political agenda(s) the characters and/or writer support?
- support or oppose the dominant ideology of its time?

- provoke different potential reactions in readers of different economic classes?
- challenge individual readers or society as a whole?

Feminist criticism

How does the work

- reflect the assumptions the writer or his/her culture makes about sexuality and gender?
- accept and/or reject prevailing assumptions about sexuality and gender?
- reflect the impact of the writer's gender or sexual identity?
- reflect and/or reject the sexual or gender stereotypes of the writer's culture?
- influence the sexual or gender stereotypes of the writer's culture?
- challenge and/or affirm the sexual or gender identities of audience members?
- show characters within the text behaving in terms of their gender identities?
- show characters upholding or challenging society's assumptions about gender and/or sexuality?
- promote or stifle social progress or individual freedoms, especially freedoms relevant to sexuality and/or gender?

Structuralist criticism

How does the work

- use particular codes or structured languages?
- reveal anything about the codes or structures that people use to understand the world around them?
- suggest that codes change in different cultures or time periods?

- use opposites (such as good vs evil, light vs dark, young vs old, etc.) to reveal meaning within the text?
- adhere to or depart from the rules or codes of its genre (or kind) of writing?
- use specific words or ideas that reveal or imply the codes that govern the text?
- present characters who abide by or oppose the codes within the text?
- seem consistent or inconsistent in its use of codes or structures?
- use codes or structures that allow a reader to understand the meaning of the text more deeply or completely?
- use overlapping codes or structures?

Deconstructionism

How does the work

- employ particular codes or structured languages?
- reveal that the codes or structures that govern the text are full of contradictions, inconsistencies, or even paradoxes?
- lack unity or patterns of consistent meaning?
- suggest that it is *readers* who impose structures on the text in order to find meaning within the text?
- imply anything about the codes or structures that people use to understand the world around them, especially the inconsistencies of those codes?
- reflect but also violate the rules of a particular genre?
- reveal parts that seem inconsistent with the text as a whole?
- seem consistent and/or especially *inconsistent* in its use of codes or structures?
- seem unsuccessful in depicting an objective reality?
- undermine readers' expectations or assumptions about reality?

Reader-response criticism

How does the work

- seem subject to the reader's control rather than controlling the reader?
- seem open to different interpretation by different readers or different kinds of readers?
- reveal that the author's control over the text is limited?
- suggest anything about different readers' differing perceptions of reality?

Dialogical criticism

How does the work

- show the effects of having been written for an intended audience, so that the text is in a kind of dialogue with its potential readers?
- seem focused on affecting its intended audience, so that the text seems shaped with this audience in mind?
- present literal or figurative dialogue within the text, as when characters speak to each other, or different styles seem to interact, or different worldviews interact?
- present individual voices in the text (whether those of the writer or those of the characters) that represent the interests, beliefs, or thoughts of multiple points of view?
- communicate, or seem engaged in a dialogue, with other texts?
- allude to or quote another text? How does any such reference affect the text's meaning or the ways readers interpret the text?
- use first-, second-, and/or third-person narration throughout the text?
- use different kinds of narrative points of view, such as omniscient or limited perspectives?

- use points of view that communicate with or represent various points of view in society?
- imply meaningful relationships between what the text says and what it leaves unsaid?

New historicism

How does the work

- suggest that it and/or its author are affected by multiple, even contradictory, influences?
- reveal highly complex historical contexts (plural)?
- seem affected by contemporary social forces while also trying to affect society?
- seem an active historical force rather than a passive product of historical influence?
- seem especially meaningful when read in light of other texts from its historical period, even (or especially) texts that do not seem immediately or obviously relevant?
- seem affected by diverse, conflicting, or unstable ideologies rather than a single, unified ideology?
- provoke complicated, conflicting, or unstable reactions from readers?
- suggest that the popular view of a historical event (such as the view presented in a history textbook) is not the only view or even the most accurate view?
- suggest that an individual's experience of reality is influenced by multiple forces?
- suggest that one individual's experience of reality may contradict another individual's experience of reality?
- suggest the numerous, often conflicting interests of individuals in a society?
- suggest relations of power and how those power relations change?
- explore historical figures or events in new or unusual ways?

Multiculturalism

How does the work

- reflect the fact that the writer is a member of multiple, often overlapping cultural groups? (Cultural groups can center on a nearly infinite number of values or characteristics. Some examples are race, sexual identity, nationality, age, gender, height, hair color, education level, religious affiliation, political affiliation.)

- reflect the influence of the groups to which the writer belongs?

- reveal anything about the writer's experiences as a member of a group or groups?

- appeal to readers as members of multiple, often overlapping cultural groups?

- seem open to different interpretations by members of different groups?

- present characters who seem to be members of multiple, often overlapping cultural groups?

- present characters who seem affected by their memberships in particular groups?

- suggest that a truly neutral or objective interpretation of the text may be impossible?

- suggest that each person experiences reality differently from every other person, partly because each person belongs to particular groups?

- suggest that a general "human nature" does not exist?

- explore—or attempt to ignore—human differences?

- either affirm and/or undermine the values or social powers of a cultural group or groups?

- reflect relations (often tense relations) between a dominant culture and a less powerful culture?

- reflect relations between a colonial power and a culture that is (or was once) colonized?

Postmodernism

How does the work

- explore multiple positions, roles, attitudes, or stances (for the writer, reader, and/or characters) within the work?
- seem complex, ambiguous, or even contradictory?
- suggest that incoherencies or chaos in the text represent a degree of freedom?
- interact with and appropriate popular culture?
- suggest that popular culture is in a constant state of change?
- blur the lines between "high" and "low" art?
- reveal internal gaps, inconsistencies, or randomness?
- mix, juxtapose, and/or combine varying genres?
- adhere to and/or depart from the traditional rules of traditional genre(s)?
- implicitly or explicitly reject the existence of a coherent, unified reality?
- seem to undermine or subvert systems of belief, ideologies, worldviews, logic, or reason?
- seem playful or ironic?
- implicitly or explicitly challenge ideologies (such as Marxism, structuralism, Christianity, Freudianism, etc.) that try to make sense of or impose order on the text or the world?
- emphasize surface meaning over the existence of some deep, underlying meaning?
- use elements that seem ornamental, decorative, or illusory?
- seem open to multiple, often contradictory interpretations?
- seem to lack any absolute, stable significance?

Ecocriticism

How does the work

- emphasize relationships between humans and nature, especially relations with other animals as well as plants, but also including the physical environment?
- reveal the ways that humans often misuse or exploit the rest of "nature" (in all the various senses of that term)?
- implicitly (and ideally) oppose human misuse of nature, especially other living things?
- appeal to a deeply rooted human love of nature and/or appeal to humans' sense of self-interest in being good stewards of nature?

Darwinian criticism

How does the work

- imply the existence of a general human nature resulting from millions of years of evolution?
- reflect and appeal to general psychological traits that have evolved over millions of years?
- suggest a general human artistic desire to make things "special" (or make "special things")?
- reflect the fact that the author is a human speaking to other humans in ways they will enjoy or comprehend because both author and audience share the same evolutionary past?
- reflect a basic human tendency to tell the same basic stories repeatedly and to find those basic stories continually relevant or interesting?
- imply relations between humans and nature that reflect millions of years of evolution?
- reflect or promote patterns of thinking and/or behavior that promote evolutionary "fitness," including the passing on of genes from one generation to the next?

Table 12.1 *An "Abrams scheme" of various literary theories*

	Writer	Text	Audience	Reality	Critic
Plato	imitates mere appearances; has no real knowledge	inaccurately reflects reality; thus typically offers false views of reality	likely to be emotional, irrational and thus easily deceived	can (and must) be known objectively through use of reason and logic	should use reason to make judgments and should act as monitor
Aristotle	skilled craftsman capable of true knowledge	complexly unified work of art that can communicate truth	capable of appreciating craft; eager to learn	reality is complex and can be grasped in various ways	a specialist who knows the details of poetic craft
Horace	seeks to satisfy a diverse audience	should follow custom and moderation	teaching and/or pleasing a broad audience is crucial	is understood in traditional or conventional terms	a fatherly advisor who helps poet avoid mistakes
Longinus	lofty, noble, inspired genius	expresses power of the author's soul	seeks elevation, ecstasy, nobility	human nature seeks elevation	spiritual advisor to poet, audience
Traditional historical criticism	is embedded in a particular historical era	reflects the ideas and circumstances of its time	respond in ways typical of their historical period	social realities differ during different periods	must possess thorough historical knowledge
Thematic criticism	expresses (often-recurring) ideas	interesting largely for its ideas	interested in ideas that texts express	ideas help shape social reality	studies ideas embedded in texts
Formalist criticism	highly skilled craftsman	richly complex unity	interested in subtle artistry	reality itself tends to be complex	closely analyzes text's complex unity and subtlety

Psychoanalytic criticism	torn between id, ego, superego	reflects conflicts in minds of writer and audience	respond according to individual "identity themes"	individual mental (especially unconscious) reality is crucial	must know human psychological complexities
Archetypal criticism	deeply affected by basic human fears, desires, and experiences	skillfully plays on basic human fears, desires, stories, symbols	compulsively respond to basic desires, fears, stories, symbols	all people share certain basic desires and fears (i.e. a basic human nature)	should study the impact of basic emotions, stories, images, events
Marxist criticism	inevitably affected by economic class conflicts, whether consciously or not	reflects, reinforces, and/or undermines interests of the dominant class	divided by economic class interests, whether they are aware of these or not	dominant ideas of society reflect economic divisions and conflicts in society	should study the complex relations between literature and society to promote progress
Structuralist criticism	must rely on codes commonly used within the culture to create and convey meaning	inevitably reflects the structures and (binary) codes of its society; e.g. red light vs green light	use cultural codes and structures—especially language—to interpret anything	humans make sense of reality by imposing structures or codes (e.g. words) on it	must be deeply familiar with the actual codes and structures specific texts reflect
Feminist criticism	is inevitably affected by society's gender categories, especially the category of "male" vs "female"	either reflects, reaffirms, and/or undermines society's gender categories; ideally questions them	experience reality in terms of gender categories, which often repress women	experience is structured by gender categories, especially the categories of "male" vs "female"	should know society's assumptions about gender and challenge them if they are repressive
Deconstructive criticism	can never impose complete or perfect control over any text	is inevitably full of irresolvable contradictions and paradoxes	can never escape the contradictions texts embody; should therefore accept them	"reality" can only be experienced through codes that are full of gaps and contradictions	searches out the contradictory, paradoxical aspects of texts that prevent unity

Continued

Table 12.1 *Continued*

	Writer	Text	Audience	Reality	Critic
Reader-response criticism	cannot really control how any audience responds to his/her text	each text will provoke a unique response in each audience	different audiences or persons respond differently to the same texts	each reader or group of readers will perceive reality in a distinctive way	must take into account the actual responses of varied audiences
Dialogical criticism	must be aware of, and capable of using, different voices and thereby engage in dialogue with audience and other texts	the best texts reflect more than one voice, tone, or point of view; these are often in dialogue, and the text is often in dialogue with its audience and with other texts	the complex nature of the audience will be reflected in divergent tones and voices within the text	can (and will) be perceived from different points of view; the richest texts reflect these differences	the sensitive critic must be alert to the multitude of voices or tones a text expresses or implies and the different kinds of dialogues in which a text participates
New historicist criticism	is embedded in a highly complex culture and cannot help reflecting the tensions inherent therein	the text will reflect, and take part in, the constant negotiation, exchange, and struggle for power	is composed of individuals and groups whose status is complex and constantly in flux	our experience of reality is inevitably social and reflects the struggle for power; any culture is a site of conflict	must be aware of the ways historical circumstances affected past texts and how they affect her own
Multicultural criticism	inevitably is a member of a group or groups and cannot escape this fact	will provoke different kinds of responses from different groups	inevitably belong to a group or groups and respond accordingly	numerous group differences shape and divide social reality	must be aware of the impact of group differences on the writing and reading of texts

Postmodernist criticism	can never impose order or control on the text and therefore should be open to all kinds of influences	the best texts are the ones that revel in their contradictions, complexities, and randomness	"reality" is so complex and chaotic that no explanation of it can ever be final or perfect	should give up their old-fashioned yearning for order and coherence and enjoy the fluidity of texts	should doubt any "grand explanations" and celebrate the instabilities inherent in any text
Ecocriticism	should write in ways that reveal human abuse of nature and should promote responsible attitudes toward the environment and other living things	will reflect in various ways the relationship between humans and nature, especially any human misuse or abuse of nature	is primarily physical and material; the health of the natural environment and ecosystem is crucial to healthy human existence	should be interested in, or be willing to be interested in, responsible human behavior toward nature	should examine works to see the ways they depict nature (including other creatures) and whether those depictions promote ecological responsibility
Darwinian criticism	will tend to write in ways that reflect the shared psychological traits of humans—traits that have evolved over millions of years	will reflect (in such matters as imagery, plot, themes, and characterization) the interests, fears, desires, and other traits that humans share as a result of millions of years of evolution	is primarily physical, material, and biological and particularly involves human interaction with the environment in a quest to survive and physically reproduce	consists of people whose similarities—especially in ways of thinking, feeling, perceiving, and reacting—have evolved over the course of millions of years. These basic biological and psychological similarities are far more important than individual or cultural differences	should be alert to the ways basic biological impulses (such as the impulses to survive, reproduce, and gain and maintain status) affect the writing and reading of literature and the ways literature presents characters and appeals to people

WORKS CITED

Abrams, Meyer Howard. *The Mirror and the Lamp: Romantic Theory and the Critical Tradition*. Oxford: Oxford University Press, 1953.

Alberge, Dalya. "Draft Siegfried Sassoon poem reveals controversial lines cut from Atrocities." *Guardian* February 2, 2013. www.theguardian.com/books/2013/feb/03/siegfried-sassoon-poem-atrocities. Accessed September 9, 2013.

Aristotle. "Poetics." Trans. S. H. Butcher. In Bate 19–39.

Bate, Walter Jackson. *Criticism: The Major Texts*. Enlarged edn. New York: Harcourt Brace Jovanovich, 1970.

Benstead, Charles R. *Retreat: A Story of 1918*. London: Methuen, 1930.

Bostridge, Mark and Paul Berry. *Vera Brittain: A Life*. London: Chatto and Windus, 1995.

Brittain, Vera. *Testament of Youth: An Autobiographical Study of the Years 1900–1925*. Originally published 1933. London: Penguin, 1989.

Brooks, Cleanth. "In Search of the New Criticism." *Community, Religion, and Literature: Essays*. Columbia: University of Missouri Press, 1995. 1–15.

Colley, Linda. "The Aesthetics of Dominance: The Cultural Reconstruction of the British Elite in an Age of Revolutions." *Main Trends in Cultural History: Ten Essays*. Ed. Willem Melcing and Wyger Velema. Amsterdam: Rodopi, 1994. 182–203.

Collins, John, et al. *Encyclopedia of Traditional British Rural Sports*. New York: Routledge, 2005.

Cooper, Wayne F. *Claude McKay: Rebel Sojourner in the Harlem Renaissance: A Biography*. Baton Rouge: Louisiana State University Press, 1987.

Cross, Helen, ed. *Wilfred Owen: Selected Poems and Letters*. Oxford: Oxford University Press, 2009.

du Feu, Jenny. "Factors Influencing Rehabilitation of British Soldiers after World War I." *Historia Medicinae* 2.1 (December 21, 2009): 1–5. www.medicinae.org/e10

Goddard, Nicholas and John Martin. "Fox-Hunting." In Collins et al. 122–4.

Horace. "Art of Poetry." Trans. Walter Jackson Bate. In Bate 51–8.

Janda, Lance. "Casualties, Combatant and Noncombatant." *World War I: A Student Encyclopedia*. Ed. Spencer C. Tucker and Priscilla Mary Roberts. 5 vols. New York: ABC-CLIO, 2006. 444–6.

Jobes, Gertrude. *Dictionary of Mythology, Folklore, and Symbols*. 2 vols. New York: Scarecrow, 1962.

Khan, Nosheen. *Women's Poetry of the First World War*. Lexington: University Press of Kentucky, 1988.

Kline, A. S., trans. *The Aeneid* by Virgil. www.poetryintranslation.com/PITBR/Latin/Virgilhome.htm

—, trans. *Odes* by Horace. www.poetryintranslation.com/PITBR/Latin/HoraceOdesBkIII.htm

Longinus. Excerpts from "On the Sublime." Trans. W. Rhys Roberts. In Bate 62–75.

—. "On Sublimity." Trans. D. A. Russell. In Preminger et al. 192–225.

Longley, Edna, ed. *The Annotated Collected Poems* by Edward Thomas. Tarset: Bloodaxe, 2008.

Military Explosives. Department of the Army Technical Manual TM 9-1300-214. Washington, DC: Headquarters, Department of the Army, 1984.

Moore, David W. "Conscientious Objectors." *The United States in the First World War: An Encyclopedia*. Ed. Anne Cipriano Venzon. New York: Garland, 1995. 169–71.

Owen, Wilfred. *The Complete Poems and Fragments*. Ed. Jon Stallworthy. 2 vols. New York: W. W. Norton, 1984.

Plato. Excerpts from *Ion* and *The Republic*. Trans. Benjamin Jowett. In Bate 43–9.

—. Excerpts from *The Symposium, Phaedrus, Gorgias, Ion*, Books III of *The Republic*, Book X of *The Republic*, and Book VII of *Laws*. In Preminger et al. 25–96.

Preminger, Alex, O. B. Hardison, and Kevin Kerrane. *Classical and Medieval Literary Criticism: Translations and Interpretations*. New York: Unger, 1974.

Schweizer, Harold. *Suffering and the Remedy of Art*. Albany: State University of New York Press, 1996.

Smith, Alan. *Do Unto Others: Counter Bombardment in Australia's Military Campaigns*. Newport, NSW: Big Sky, 2011.

Stallworthy, Jon. *Wilfred Owen*. Oxford: Oxford University Press, 1974.

Thomas, Edward. *The Icknield Way*. London: Constable, 1913.

Underhill, George Frederick. *A Century of English Fox-Hunting*. London: R. A. Everett, 1900.

Vamplew, Wray. "Fox-Hunting: An Alternative History." In Collins et al. 124–5.

Ward, Glenn. *Postmodernism*. Chicago: McGraw-Hill, 2004.

FURTHER READING

The present book, which is mainly concerned with applying literary theories to various texts, is an outgrowth of several previous studies that explore and explain literary theories in some detail while also offering many specific applications of them. Those studies include the following:

Evans, Robert C. *Ambrose Bierce's "An Occurrence at Owl Creek Bridge": An Annotated Critical Edition.* West Cornwall: Locust Hill, 2003.

—. *Close Readings: Analyses of Short Fiction from Multiple Perspectives.* 3rd edn. Montgomery: NewSouth, 2010.

—. *Frank O'Connor's "Ghosts": A Pluralist Approach.* Montgomery: Court Street, 2003.

—. *Kate Chopin's Short Fiction: A Critical Companion.* West Cornwall: Locust Hill, 2001.

The studies listed below offer full, accessible explanations of the theories discussed in the present book.

Bressler, Charles E. *Literary Criticism: An Introduction to Theory and Practice.* 5th edn. Boston: Longman, 2011.

Dobie, Ann B. *Theory Into Practice: An Introduction to Literary Criticism.* 3rd edn. Boston: Wadsworth, 2012.

Guerin, Wilfred L., Earle Labor, Lee Morgan, Jeanne C. Reesman, and John R. Willingham. *A Handbook of Critical Approaches to Literature.* 6th edn. Oxford: Oxford University Press, 2011.

Parker, Robert Dale. *How to Interpret Literature: Critical Theory for Literary and Cultural Studies.* 2nd edn. Oxford: Oxford University Press, 2011.

Tyson, Lois. *Critical Theory Today: A User-Friendly Guide.* 2nd edn. New York: Routledge, 2006.

PERMISSIONS

INDEX OF THEORIES
AND APPLICATIONS